AMANDA LAUGESEN is a historian, writer and lexicographer. She is Director of the Australian National Dictionary Centre at the Australian National Uuniversity, and Chief Editor of the Australian National Dictionary. She has written a number of books on Australian and US history, including several books on aspects of the history of the Australian lexicon.

'If you've ever wondered why to use bad language in Australia is to "swear like a bullocky", Amanda Laugesen's *Rooted* will give you the answer. Taking us on a colourful tour of more than two centuries of bad language that extends from the mildly offensive to the completely filthy, Laugesen tells the story of Australia through those words and phrases that have often been seen as unfit to print. This is an engrossing social history – a bloody beauty – from one of our leading experts on Australian English.'

– Frank Bongiorno, Professor of History, The Australian National University

'This important book shows that Australian "bad language" is inventive, rebellious, and subversive at the same time as it is offensive, abusive and racist. Laugesen's history of "bad language" in Australia, from convicts to bushmen to First World War diggers and through to contemporary Aboriginal hip-hop artists, provides a new and instructive gateway to understanding Australian culture and identity.'

– Bruce Moore, author of *Speaking Our Language: The Story of Australian English*

'Australia is built on blood, sweat and swears. Digging up the dirt, Amanda Laugesen finds out why, with flair, ferocity and other f-words.'

– David Astle, author of *Puzzled: Secrets and Clues from a Life Lost in Words*

'Its first dictionary was one of criminal slang; it's best-known adjective was "bloody". And Australia is still a primary contributor to the "in-yer-face" vocabulary of the anything but respectable. In *Rooted*, her appositely titled, exhaustive history of the national use of the obscene, the offensive and the ever-creative slangy, Amanda Laugesen proves that so-called "bad language" makes for some of the most inventive, descriptive and even character-defining in the world.'

– Jonathon Green, author of *Green's Dictionary of Slang*

AN AUSTRALIAN HISTORY OF BAD LANGUAGE
AMANDA LAUGESEN

NEWSOUTH

A NewSouth book

Published by
NewSouth Publishing
University of New South Wales Press Ltd
University of New South Wales
Sydney NSW 2052
AUSTRALIA
newsouthpublishing.com

© Amanda Laugesen 2020
First published 2020

10 9 8 7 6 5 4 3 2 1

A catalogue record for this
book is available from the
National Library of Australia

ISBN: 9781742236636
ebook: 9781742245089
ePDF: 9781742249605

Design Josephine Pajor-Markus
Cover design Peter Long
Cover image Alamy Stock Photo / H. Armstrong Roberts

CONTENTS

INTRODUCTION:
AUSTRALIANS AND THEIR BAD LANGUAGE

Is there a quintessentially Australian swear word? In the 19th century, visitor to the Antipodean colonies Alexander Marjoribanks in his book *Travels in New South Wales* (1847) claimed that the word *bloody* was ubiquitous in Australia – in fact, it was, he declared, 'the Great Australian Adjective'. While travelling through the colonies he observed with disdain that '[o]ne man will tell you that he married a bloody young wife, another, a bloody old one; and a bushranger will call out, "Stop, or I'll blow your bloody brains out."' He calculated that the average Australian bullock-driver – a notorious figure in the history of Australian bad language – would, in a lifetime, say this 'disgusting word' no less than 18 200 000 times.[1]

Sidney Baker in his classic study of Australian English, *The Australian Language* (1945), identifies *bloody* as one of what he calls 'the four Bs', sitting alongside *bugger*, *bastard* and *bullshit*. None of these words are exclusively Australian, of course, but each of them would likely evoke particularly Australian associations for many of us, and have been well used through our history. We might remember when Bob Hawke was caught out calling a member of the public a 'silly old bugger', Don Chipp's founding of the Australian Democrats with the slogan 'Keep the bastards honest', and Malcolm Turnbull labelling Tony Abbott's climate change policy 'bullshit', presaging an ongoing feud between the two that would help to bring down both their prime ministerships. Our politicians have rarely shied away from using strong language.

I

Do Australians have a special relationship with swearing? In his discussion of the 'four Bs', Baker was careful to state that few Australian slang expressions were vulgarisms. While Australians were fond of 'the Bs', they used them so repetitively, he argued, that it had robbed these words 'of their taint of indecency'. Australians were just as likely to say an offensive word with affection as aggression. Baker argued that this 'lack of insult in Australian profanity' was an expression of the 'personality' of Australians.[2] A recent linguistic study of Australian English notes that much has been made of this Australian affinity for swearing.[3]

To agree to the idea that Australians have a special relationship with bad language would be to extend a national mythology – which many Australians like to live up to – that we are more relaxed in our speech than other speakers of English. We are certainly renowned for our creativity with words and idioms, and this extends into the realm of the offensive. The online news site *Buzzfeed* compiled a list of the 'one hundred rudest things Australians say' in 2016. The list reveals some wonderfully creative obscenities and insults: *cunning as a shithouse rat, (to have) hair like a bushpig's arse, dickflop* and *not here to fuck spiders* are just a few of them.[4] While it is probably hard to argue that we swear *more* than others, we do our best – and we try to be inventive in the process.

But Australia also has a long history of repression, censorship, and control when it comes to bad language. Punishing bad language has long been a means of suppressing the power and voices of certain groups. Offensive language crimes remain on the books, often disproportionately targeting Indigenous Australians. People complain on a regular basis about swearing in advertisements and television shows, echoing a longer history of attempts to silence bad language. Racist and sexist language continues to be used in a variety of contexts, revealing deeper social anxieties and fissures, and attempts to eliminate such language frequently raise the ire of those who advocate the right to say whatever they like. Language has long been a battleground, and bad language has often been the frontline.

This book tells the story of how bad language has been used, experienced and understood in Australia from the beginnings of European settlement to the present. I argue that this story is fundamentally about power, and how that power (*of* bad language, and *over* bad language) has shaped lives, identities and experiences across our history. For example, think of the way convicts were flogged for insolence if they called their overseers *bloody buggers*, or the way university students called for revolutionary change in the 1970s through shocking the establishment with words such as *fuck* and *cunt* in their magazines, on their protest signs and in their public speech. On the flip side, attempts to punish bad language have frequently been a way of targeting and stigmatising particular groups in society, and the use of derogatory language to abuse people has also often been an exercise in power. Bad language can liberate and challenge, but it can also oppress and injure.

Profanity, obscenity and bad language are never absolutes – what a society considers offensive at one time may be quite different at another. While the general trajectory has been towards greater acceptance of swear words in our public discourse and popular culture, there are still plenty of words we find offensive as a society, with greater levels of tolerance for using these words depending on who you are, your cultural and religious sensibilities and background, and the social and other groups that you identify with and belong to.

In this book, I am interested in considering the words or phrases that may have offended in the past. But I also look at *why* these words and/or phrases were offensive and how society used them, responded to them, and dealt with them – and who was and was not allowed to speak them. In particular, I uncover the particularly *Australian* dimensions of this story. The words we choose to use can reveal much about the way we think and the society that we live in. Many accounts of the history of swearing and offensive language typically focus on Britain or the USA. We know much less about the fascinating story of Australia's bad language.

While we borrow much of our bad language from elsewhere, there are many uniquely Australian swear words and 'colourful' idioms. We also invest different significance in certain words, and our use of them can vary from the way a word or expression is used elsewhere. There are very particular Australian stories to be told about the history of offensive language in this country, and about how such language has been used and understood.

Bad language has long been entwined with mythologies about Australian identity and character, as I'll also show in this book. Swearing and the particular ideas and attitudes that have attached to it across time, including its imagining within popular culture and its use as a source of Australian humour, can be revealing of these mythologies, and of what might be considered to be 'typical' Australian values and characteristics. Put simply, the story of bad language in Australia can lead us to reflect on what it means to be Australian.

WHAT IS BAD LANGUAGE?

This book defines 'bad language' as including both swearing and discriminatory language such as epithets and slurs. Words that might not be considered particularly offensive to our modern-day sensibilities (for example, *bloody*, *damn*), but which outraged some sectors of the community in the past, are included. The term *bad* here, of course, should be placed mentally in scare quotes to acknowledge that the 'badness' or 'wrongness' of language is a social and cultural construction and is very dependent on context – hence the importance of understanding the history around these words.

There are many terms that are used in talking about bad language. Language can be judged as 'obscene', usually when talking about sex or body parts or functions (*shit*, *fuck*), or 'profane', usually when talking about blasphemous language (*damn*, *Christ*), although 'profanity' has become a much more encompassing term for swearing. The words discussed in this book have all been considered at various times to be 'offensive', 'profane', 'vulgar', 'abusive' and/or 'blasphemous'. These kinds of labels are often used interchangeably in many contexts and can be somewhat arbitrarily applied. For the most part, I use 'swearing' or 'profanity' as all-encompassing terms for those words, from *bloody* to *fuck*, that are used as an emphasis, or to shock or abuse someone. Historically, these words have been variously subject to censorship and punishment, but many of these words are now acceptable in Australian speech to varying extents.

This book broadens out the scope of bad language from swearing and profanity to also consider the kind of language that has been used to target, stereotype and label particular groups and individuals in society. This language has only become taboo more recently, but while it may have remained uncontested until well into the 20th century, it has long been used to disempower and marginalise certain groups. The book thus includes the history of terms related to race, class, ethnicity, sexuality and gender, arguing that if we are to understand how language has been used historically in Australia to reinforce particular identities and to exert social and cultural power, such terms must be considered.

Derogatory slurs and epithets have become the bad language of the last few decades, and this book traces the story of how these words originated, how they were deployed in various ways within public discourse and personal encounters, and how they continue to shape politics and social interactions and culture today. It can be difficult and confronting to write about, and to read, these words. However, I argue that understanding how they have been used in the past and how they became invested with social power – and in turn resisted and rejected – is important in illuminating not only our past but also our present. These words are not reproduced in this book to cause offence or harm, but rather to deepen our critical understanding. Nevertheless, the reader should be warned that there are a number of these words discussed in this book.

WHY WE SWEAR AND USE OBSCENITIES

Why do we swear? Scholar of psycholinguistics Timothy Jay has written that swearing is a 'rich emotional, psychological, and sociocultural phenomenon'.[5] Swearing can be used to insult, joke with, or bond with someone. It can express anger, frustration or happiness, or show allegiance. Swear words perform a number of important functions in our speech. Sometimes we use them as an interjection, or we might use them to affirm or emphasise, or as an insult. Think of some of the multiple ways a word such as *fuck* might be used: the literal *fuck* (sexual intercourse), saying *fuck off!* to another person, or declaring that the planet is *fucked*.

Most studies agree that swearing is highly emotional. The most common emotions expressed in swearing are anger and frustration.[6] Some studies have even suggested that swear words may originate in a different part of the brain from other speech.[7] Swearing in fact links to many parts of the brain; because of its emotional power, it can connect to the right side, which processes emotion, but because we need to consider when and where we swear (except in instances where we are highly emotional), we also often use the left side at these moments – the more rational side of our brain.[8]

Studies suggest that swear words make up about 0.3 to 0.5 per cent of typical conversation, although they argue that this probably underestimates the use of such language in everyday speech. Most estimates suggest the 'average' person uses between 80 and 100 swear words a day. Swear words are thus a common feature of speech. Studies usually agree that bad language is a feature of just about everybody's speech, although cultural and social norms can affect our individual usage.[9]

A 2009 study revealed that the most common American swear words are *fuck, shit, hell, damn, goddamn, Jesus Christ, ass, oh my god, bitch* and *sucks*. But gender and age affect the commonly preferred words. The same study also revealed that swearing peaks in a person's teenage years, and declines thereafter.[10] A list of the most frequently used Australian swear words would likely be somewhat different from an American list: while *fuck* and *shit* would almost certainly be at the top, *bugger, bastard, dickhead* and *wanker* might all get a guernsey. Alongside the most frequently used swear words, there are also those that we typically find the most offensive. Linguist Ruth Wajnryb, writing in 2004, identified the 'big six' most offensive swear words as *fuck, cunt, cock, arse, shit* and *piss*.[11] Of these, it is estimated that *fuck* and *shit* account for some 50 per cent of actual swearing in public.[12]

While society often demands that children be protected from bad language lest it corrupt them, the reality is that children quickly learn to swear early in life, and they swear often, although typically using less strong words. In an American study conducted over the course of a year, it was discovered that adults engaged in 3190 utterances of taboo words including words such as *fuck, hell, damn* and *bitch*; children between the ages of one and 12 made 1187 utterances, including *fuck, shit* and *oh my god*. The younger children used words like *poop, stupid* and *jerk*, while older children used stronger words such as *fuck* and *bitch*. Overall, children's top ten most used taboo words were *shit, fuck, oh my god, stupid, damn, jerk, suck, crap, hell* and *bitch*.[13] Writer and children's folklore specialist June Factor's 2000 dictionary of Australian *Kidspeak*, collected from various sources including interviews with children, records terms such as *bullshit, cunthead, dickshit, fucker, prick* and *ratshit*, among many others, attesting to the popularity of swear words with young people. As she notes, '[v]ulgarity is a treasured mode of speech performance for a large number of young people, [and] a form of linguistic subversion'.[14] There is no scientific evidence that supports the idea that profanity causes any kind of harm to children, although abusive language more generally *can* potentially do harm. Rather, our own beliefs around swearing that connect it to, for example, immorality, make us feel we must protect them from it.[15] Children are of course drawn to this language, not least because they know that adults disapprove of them using it.[16]

If swearing is learned early in life, so are the rules around it.[17] We quickly learn that some words are considered 'naughty' and 'rude', and we begin to understand when and where we can get away with using them (if at all). Most people want to conform, hence we will often use particular styles of speech (or registers) depending on who we are talking to: for example, we probably use bad language quite differently if speaking to our friends or to our boss at work.

There are many myths about swearing. One of them is that swearing is a sign of a lack of education and a poor vocabulary. In fact, linguists point out that 'a voluminous taboo lexicon could be seen as an indicator of healthy verbal abilities'.[18] As we'll see, people over time shaped this myth as a way to attach bad language to particular social groups and to rob them of social power.

Another myth, which has some basis in fact, is that swearing, and our perceptions of it, are often gendered. However, this is not because there is something inherent in men or women that make them swear more or less – rather, our society and culture create particular gendered expectations and stereotypes around swearing. Women are typically expected to swear less, and less strongly if they do. They are also likely to be criticised, chastised and judged to a much greater extent when they swear or use bad language.[19]

Studies have shown that generally women tend to conform to these gendered expectations. For example, women use less powerful swear words such as *hell* and *bloody*, while men are more likely to use stronger words such as *fuck*. But this is changing over time – a recent British study suggests that women's use of *fuck* has increased five-fold since the 1990s.[20] Women are moving away from this stereotype of swearing less and/or more mildly. Nevertheless, they are still more likely to be judged harshly for swearing.

In any given culture or language, certain words will be taboo – but there are no universal, absolute taboos across all cultures. As linguist Keith Allan writes: 'Nothing is taboo for all people under all circumstances for all time.'[21] Some Indigenous Australian cultures have different customs about what is taboo with respect to language and what isn't. English-language taboo terms may not have the same level of offensiveness, or be used to the same effect, within Indigenous conversation.[22] Most notably, taboo terms are often linked to kinship relationships – that is, what one can or can't say to a particular person depends on your family relationship with them.[23] Marcia Langton, anthropologist, public intellectual, and descendant of the Yiman and Bidjara Nations, further explains that swearing also functions as an integral part of Indigenous dispute processing and conflict resolution, and this has been often misunderstood by white Australia.[24]

A BRIEF HISTORY OF OFFENSIVE LANGUAGE

Linguist Geoffrey Hughes writes that 'people swear by what is most potent to them'.[25] What is considered to be 'most potent' changes across time, although taboo has often focused on the religious (*hell*), the sexual (*fuck*), and the excretory (*shit*). More recently, racial, sexist and other discriminatory epithets have become our most taboo and controversial terms.

The first recorded instances of swearing in any language date from Ancient Egypt, around 1198–1166 BCE, with the threat that those who failed to make an offering to the gods would have to copulate with a donkey.[26] Examples of swearing can be found in classical Greek and Latin (a favourite curse of the Romans was *By Hercules!*[27]), and we also have evidence of swearing from medieval Europe. By the time we get into the medieval period, much of what was considered to be taboo was religious, reflecting the primacy of Christianity in Western Europe. Christians feared their souls being damned, and this made curses that involved damning a person's soul to hell especially powerful.[28]

From the Middle Ages onwards, we can trace a slow shift from oaths, or religious swearing, to obscenities that deal with the excretory and the sexual.[29] Oaths were still a favourite for a long time, and were considered taboo by many well into the modern era. However, over time, they slowly lost their religious baggage to simply become mildly offensive and, for much of the 20th century, were considered to indicate one's class and educational status.

Queen Elizabeth I (1533–1603) was a notable swearer, and her favourite curse was said to be *God's wounds*, considered a strong blasphemy at the time, as it referred to the wounds inflicted on Jesus when he was crucified. *God's wounds* was therefore sometimes shortened to *zounds*, an example of what is known as a 'minced oath'.[30] All swearing generates 'disguised variants'.[31] In short, we look to replace taboo words with polite euphemisms. *Zounds* and *gadzooks* (*God's hooks*) have long ago fallen by the wayside, but we still might hear *darn* (from *damn*), *fudge* (*fuck*), *gosh* (*God*), and the more Australian *crikey* (*Christ*) and *strewth* (*God's truth*), although many people won't necessarily know the relationship to the original profanity.

While the period of the English Civil War was marked by the dominance of Puritanism (Oliver Cromwell banned his troops from swearing, as well as engaging in other 'immoral' actions), during the Restoration, swearing and sexual language flourished.[32] By the 18th century, though, profanity began to be increasingly censored in printed sources. The word *fuck*, for instance, appeared in Nathaniel Bailey's *Universal Etymological Dictionary* in 1721 but did not appear in Samuel Johnson's influential *A Dictionary of the English Language* in 1755.[33] From the 18th century, the rise of the bourgeoisie meant that good manners, refinement and demonstrations of civility were seen as indicating a person's social and moral worth.[34] Consequently, profanity was increasingly considered unacceptable. Many English-language euphemisms for swear words date from the 19th century, when concerns with politeness and civility in language reached their peak.

Censorship and the practice of disguising swear words became increasingly common from the 18th century onwards. Writers such as Charles Dickens, who often wrote about the working and criminal classes, never used a word stronger than *drat*, generally preferring to stick to euphemisms in his writing.[35] From the 18th century, print also employed various evasions and disguises to avoid printing swear words, ranging from asterisks and other typographical substitutions (for example *f**k*), to word substitutes such as *blankety-blank* and *four-letter word*. Of course, the reader nearly always knows what is meant in such instances, so the effectiveness of such censorship in helping to keep minds 'pure' remains questionable but it does serve to signal disapproval. We see this today when television and radio broadcasts continue to 'bleep' out words, even though it is nearly always obvious what the person is saying, and social media 'live-tweeting' guarantees we can otherwise discover what was said.

From the 18th to the 19th century, the English language began to undergo a process of standardisation, underpinned by the rise of print, which required common standards, and the rise of the idea that education and literacy were for all. Dictionaries were one of the key reference works to help standardise language, and to prescribe what was appropriate and correct usage. Slang and 'vulgar' language were either labelled as such or excised altogether from Standard English in this period (as we saw above with Johnson's dictionary), reinforcing the 'deviance' of such language. This view only began to shift in the later 20th century.

Imperialism and colonialism, another defining feature of the 18th and 19th centuries, brought Europeans into contact with other peoples. A drive for land and resources had profound effects and was underpinned by a language and science of race and difference.[36] Racialised language, insults and slurs became more common and prominent features of the English vocabulary, reinforcing and communicating ideologies of white supremacy and colonialism. It was considered acceptable, and so was not 'bad' language per se – at least to those who used it.

It is at this critical juncture of the late 18th century that Australia was chosen as the site for a convict colony. The more riotous, contested and multi-vocal British society of the 16th and 17th centuries was giving way to a Britain of empire, respectability and civility. Ideas about language and its purpose would be transferred to the new colonial society taking shape in the Antipodes.

As the 19th century went on, bad language would help to shape ideas about what it meant to be Australian, adhering to particular constructions of the typical Australian as white and male. The bushman, the bullock-driver, the gold-digger, the digger at war: all these archetypal 'Australians' would be linked to profanity, especially within popular culture imagery, helping to make such language celebrated. At the same time, ideas of respectability would make the use of bad language, especially by groups without power in Australian society, such as women, the working classes and Indigenous people, something to shun and condemn. These conflicting attitudes towards bad language have lasted until well into the 21st century.

Broadly speaking, through the 20th century, the shift from religious swearing to obscenities continued. The word *fuck* became one of the strongest swear words of the century, and in some ways one of the most iconic: the focus of censorship efforts through the first half of the century, and a word of protest, subversion and comedy through the second. Most dictionaries didn't even begin to include *fuck*, despite its long history in the English language, until the 1970s.[37]

But swearing quickly became an established part of popular and elite culture from the end of the 1960s. The power of bad language was mobilised to challenge authority and to liberate. The feminist movement, for example, used swearing to mark its challenge to patriarchal power. Swearing for Indigenous Australians was used as an act of sedition, as Marcia Langton termed it in 1988, that challenged structures of oppression.[38] While swearing is now omnipresent in popular culture, efforts to control and censor it have evolved but not entirely disappeared.

SLURS AND EPITHETS

Slurs and epithets are now the taboo speech of our time, reflecting social and political shifts in attitudes. Slurs have been defined as 'derogatory expressions that target certain group members on the basis of descriptive features such as their racial or sexual identity'.[39] According to one scholar, slurs are primarily about wielding power and inflicting psychological damage: 'Slurs generally emerge in environments where there are perceptions of conflict, competition, or extreme anxiety caused by the presence of an outside group, usually in physical, political, social or economic space.' They can be used to gain advantage, and can represent an effort to exert social control by those who hold social power.[40] Slurs function differently from swear words – we don't use them as an emotional exclamation, for example – but they also fall into the category of taboo language and are highly contentious.

In recent decades, we have seen efforts to 'reclaim' certain words as a means of empowerment. Probably the most well-known example of this is the 'n-word', generally now considered to be one of the most taboo words in the English language. African-Americans have reclaimed this word in a variety of ways – with variant spellings that aim to transform its meaning and the use of it in popular music forms such as rap and hip-hop, often employed within lyrics that challenge and defy authority. In instances of reclamation, words remain taboo, however, to anyone except those doing the reclaiming, and even then, some suggest that reclamation can only be truly powerful if it occurs alongside other forms of political protest.[41] In more general use such as in the media, if this word must be referred to, it is now often disguised in some way, often as 'the n-word', or with asterisks obscuring some of its letters. In some recent instances, the word has only been alluded to rather than presented in disguised form, indicating that the taboo continues to strengthen.

Slurs and epithets have a long history in Australian English, and they reveal the dark underside of our colonial history. Sexist language was well established in the English brought to Australia. Ideas about the 'other' informed the first encounters between Indigenous Australians and the invaders, later to evolve into a language of racism that formed part of the structures that discriminated and oppressed. Many groups have been the target of slurs, from ethnic groups to redheads. While the level of disempowerment varies, such slurs underpin how language can marginalise and vilify. Bill Ramson, editor of the first edition of the *Australian National Dictionary* (1988), said of Australian English that it provided 'evidence of [Australia's] racism, sexism, and inhumanity', and indeed there are many Australian slurs and insults we should not be proud to admit are Australian. Nevertheless these *are* part of Australian English, and their history is revealing of how Australianness has been defined and redefined across the years.

*&^$

In January 2019, a 74-year-old Sydney man named Danny Lim, much loved by Sydney residents and famous for his street protests, was arrested for wearing a sandwich billboard with the word 'CVN'T' on it. There was a public outcry in response to the heavy-handed way in which the police arrested him. It was not the first time Lim had been arrested: he had been charged in 2016 for a similar sign that said 'Tony [Abbott, Prime Minister] You CVN'T'. While Lim was initially fined for his 2016 breach of offensive language laws, the judge later dismissed the charges on appeal, arguing that the word was 'not necessarily offensive' and noting that Australians were more likely to consider *cunt* less offensive than inhabitants of other English-speaking countries.[42] The case highlighted the way in which laws around offensive language and behaviour are still used to silence protest. Lim chose swearing as a way to challenge authority – in this case to question the policies and morality of the Abbott government. But authorities continue to use laws around bad language to police and control potentially disruptive and dissenting elements in society, a point I return to in the concluding chapter.

The outcome of this particular case speaks to the changing, but still ambivalent, attitudes we have around particular words – in 2019, few 'average Australians' were likely to be offended by *cunt* being used in this particular context. But interestingly, like Sidney Baker writing over 70 years before, the judge also believed that Australians were more relaxed in their attitudes towards offensive language than other speakers of English, and were not likely to invest much serious meaning in their use of it. Community attitudes are shaped by, and help to shape, the stories we weave around bad language and its meanings.

We all have our own unique journeys with, and attitudes to, bad language. For some of us, bad language is just a part of our everyday speech, used without any sense of shame, and isn't worth thinking too much about. For others, bad language is something we feel uncomfortable using and so we avoid it a lot of the time, especially when in the company of others. And some of us could just not imagine ever swearing.

My own journey with bad language has been something I've reflected on in researching and writing this book. My family was probably like many others. My parents occasionally swore (usually in Danish, their first language), my older brother swore a lot. But while most parents reprimand their children for swearing, I experienced something of the opposite. I went to a Catholic convent school until the age of 13 and we got in trouble if we said any swear word, including *damn* or *Jesus*. Swearing was considered to be a sin, and I took this very seriously. This led to me telling my parents off, in no uncertain terms, whenever they swore. Up until my mother died a few years ago, she still sometimes substituted *sherbet* for *shit*, especially when she was around me!

I am still not much of a swearer, particularly when I'm in company. But being a lexicographer, and especially working on this book, has led me to discuss swear words – of all kinds – around the workplace and in general conversation, as well as dealing with and thinking about discriminatory language. We grapple with offensive language all the time in the context of editing and writing dictionaries, and this means keeping a close watch on the changing attitudes that people have towards such language and thinking about how we treat it in ways that are sensitive while being true to the evidence of the way words are used.

I've also found myself talking about this book with a number of different people, and the range of attitudes I've encountered towards swearing and bad language has been fascinating to observe. People hold very different views and understandings of bad language. For example, some people are certain that class still very much matters when it comes to swearing; many younger extended family members are happy to use the 'c-word' on social media, while others, mostly of an older generation, remain horrified by it and are convinced that the word is still highly taboo.

In this book, I turn to exploring both the realities of bad language and the attitudes towards it across time. Historian Greg Dening in his book *Mr Bligh's Bad Language* writes that: 'Language is notoriously difficult to recapture in history or in a courtroom. An inflection, a look in the eye, a turn of the lip could make even words like "scoundrels, damned rascals, hell-hounds" terms of endearment and familiarity, not insult. Or the words could cascade over hearers so constantly that they would not be heard at all.'[43] Yet we can still listen closely to the past to find traces of the all-important context that reveals to us the many lives of bad language in Australia. And we can use these traces to learn something about ourselves.

PART ONE

ESTABLISHING BAD LANGUAGE IN THE COLONIES, 1788–1880

1

CONVICTS AND BAD LANGUAGE

In 1821, the Reverend Robert Cartwright, an Anglican minister who had arrived in Sydney in 1810, provided testimony to the Bigge Commission, which was investigating how effective transportation was in deterring crime. Cartwright was asked whether he thought the conversation of convicts was worse than that of common labourers in England. He replied that he believed it to be 'much worse', and that convicts were 'much addicted to swearing and use the most horrid kinds of oaths'. He added, 'I think this cannot be otherwise from their association with every kind of vice'.[1]

Cartwright's testimony reveals two important things about language in the early convict colonies. The first is that bad language was very much a feature of the early settlements of New South Wales and Van Diemen's Land. The second is that figures of moral authority, such as this clergyman, believed that bad language was a clear marker of convicts' moral failings. The image of the convict as full of vices was propagated often through the early years of the colonies and it profoundly shaped the nature of convict society.

But the early colony's bad language was more complicated than this. It was a way for convicts to challenge authority and express identity; suppressing and punishing it was a means of asserting control over them. Bad language was intimately tied up with status, social class and identity in the newly established colonies, and its story reveals much about the nature of early colonial society.

A TRANSPORTED LANGUAGE

Around 162000 convicts were transported to the Australian colonies between 1788 and 1868, and around 22000 of these arrived before 1822. The colonists brought their words with them, and English was established as the common language. This was the English of the late 18th century; it captured the diversity of British regional dialects, and it also featured the distinctive slang and strong language of marines and sailors who had a role in the early settlements, as well as the underworld slang of convicts. Words travelled with the Europeans to the colonies, but they also came to acquire new meanings and power once there. The colonies were established at the end of the 18th century, a period governed, as historian Alan Atkinson writes, by an oral culture. But it was also shifting to one that would be governed by rules, paper and imperial order.[2]

Convicts were a diverse lot, and not all of them would have been familiar with the language of the British underworld with which they were associated. Nevertheless, the 'criminal classes' of London were considered to have their own language, often referred to as 'flash' or 'cant'. This language was a source of endless fascination at the time and was written about and recorded in dictionaries as part of a general rise in interest in slang or 'deviant' language. Cant served various functions, but the increased popular interest in and representations of cant language underpinned an 'othering' and criminalisation of the 'lower orders', especially those regarded as 'vagrants'.[3]

Francis Grose's *Classical Dictionary of the Vulgar Tongue* was published in 1785, just a few years before the first settlement at Port Jackson. Grose was born in 1731, and he had an interest not only in words but also in antiquities and drawing. These latter interests resulted in him compiling a registry of medieval buildings (and their remains) in the 1770s. He moved on to recording 'vulgar' language, but also documented English 'provincial' speech. While including many terms from earlier 'canting' dictionaries of the 17th century, Grose's dictionary purported to be a lexical snapshot of the great variety of people who lived in London, including soldiers, seamen, and the 'lower orders' such as cock-fighters, tradesmen, and women who worked in the sex trade. Whether Grose's dictionary reflects authentic speech of the time is perhaps questionable, although it is believed he collected at least some of the terms on 'numerous nocturnal trips from his favourite Holborn tavern into the nearby slums'.[4] He includes some colourful terms in his collection: for example, he describes the art of picking pockets as *figging law*, a parson as a *snub devil*, and a 'stupid fellow' as a *cod's head*.

The 1786 edition of Grose contained few obscenities, but the 1796 revision included the word *cunt*, printed as *c**t*. Reflecting the misogyny of the period, he defined it as a 'nasty name for a nasty thing'. In 1811, after Grose's death, a new version appeared. This 1811 *Lexicon Balatronicum* included a number of new entries, including some profanities. *Bugger* was defined as 'a blackguard, a rascal, a term of reproach', *bloody* was defined as 'a favourite word used by the thieves in swearing', and *kiss mine arse* was glossed as 'an offer ... very frequently made, but never ... literally accepted'.

In Grose's dictionary, women were often defined in ways that sexualised them or that condemned their sexuality, as slang dictionaries of the period often did. For example, *dairy* was defined as 'a woman's breasts', *romp* was a word for a 'forward wanton girl', and 'lewd women' at 'bawdy-houses' were *game*. To *dock* was to 'lie with a woman'. *To box the Jesuit and get cockroaches* was a bizarre naval term for masturbation (and can be interpreted as a religious slur). It was defined by Grose as 'a crime, it is said, much practised by the reverend fathers of that society'. Crime was another topic his lexicon covered thoroughly. A *gentleman's master* was a highway robber, and a *scrap* a 'villainous scheme or plan'.[5] Grose's lexicon thus includes more general slang as well as underworld cant. Its focus on the popular topics of sex and crime is typical of such dictionaries. The collection gives us an insight, however mediated, into some of the language (as well as the prejudices and preoccupations) of the period. Another dictionary compiled a few years later gives us even better insight into the words convicts used.

James Hardy Vaux was a 'gentleman convict' transported to New South Wales in 1801. He returned to London in 1807, only to be sentenced to transportation once again in 1809. In 1811, he was sent to Newcastle, then a place of secondary punishment. He wrote a memoir, published in London in 1819, which included an extensive glossary of cant. Vaux's *Vocabulary of the Flash Language* lays claim to be the first 'Australian dictionary', although we must acknowledge the earlier compilation of Dharug wordlists (1790–91) by Lieutenant William Dawes, with the assistance of Eora woman Patyegarang.

Vaux dedicated his lexicon to Thomas Skottowe, a justice of the peace and commandant of the Newcastle settlement. In his dedication, Vaux wrote about how he had 'in the course of a chequered and eventful life … intermixed with the most dissolute and unprincipled characters'. As such, Vaux had become, he claimed, 'familiar with their language and system of operations'. He hoped that Skottowe would find the vocabulary amusing, but also that it would be 'useful in your magisterial capacity'.[6]

Vaux's dictionary included entries found in pre-existing cant dictionaries but as one analysis of his work has demonstrated, even these entries are distinctive enough for us to argue that he was most likely familiar with these words from personal experience and brought to them his own understanding and knowledge. Further, many of the entries had not appeared in any earlier collections, suggesting Vaux's importance to cant lexicography.[7] And so Vaux's dictionary is an invaluable document recording some of the underworld vocabulary the convicts brought with them. While the language recorded by him is not 'Australian' – insofar as it arrived with convicts who already used these words – it does give us insight into the kind of words with which convicts were familiar.

Vaux's vocabulary does not include terms that we would consider to be swear words: it omits *bloody*, *bugger* and *damn*, for instance – all common curses of the period. Many of the terms he includes instead refer to the various dimensions of criminal society – for example, *beak* for a magistrate or *high-toby* for the 'game' (as Vaux describes it) of highway robbery. He also includes some colourful slang terms, such as *fly the mags* 'to gamble, by tossing up halfpence', *joskin* 'a country-bumbkin', and *slop-feeder* 'a teaspoon'.

But in a different sense Vaux's vocabulary *was* representative of language that the non-convict population, especially those in power, found unacceptable, if not offensive. Using such language excluded those who could not understand it (that is, the authorities). If convicts called shoes *hopper-dockers*, a door a *jigger*, and a dog a *jugelow*, those who supervised them could find themselves at a loss to understand what was being said. A secret language used by convicts was potentially subversive, and many in authority believed that such a language could encourage criminality through its very secrecy. Flash language maintained convicts' identification with not only a criminal way of life but also with each other. It therefore had a purpose for convicts, while being a source of concern for those who sought to control them and keep order.

Did convicts perpetuate this language once they were in the colonies, especially as time went on? Vaux suggests that they did, and perhaps within the relatively 'closed' community of a place of secondary punishment, a common 'secret' language had some value. There are a few contemporary observations on colonial flash language that suggest that for the first years of settlement at least, it had some currency and was known to, if not spoken by, convicts.

Watkin Tench, an officer of marines who provides some of the most vivid images of life in Port Jackson, commented on the use of flash language. His observations are worth quoting in full:

> A leading distinction, which marked the convicts on their outset in the colony, was an use of what is called the *flash*, or *kiddy* language. In some of our early courts of justice, an interpreter was frequently necessary to translate the deposition of the witness, and the defence of the prisoner. This language has many dialects. The sly dexterity of the pickpocket; the brutal ferocity of the footpad; the more elevated career of the highwayman; and the deadly purpose of the midnight ruffian, is each strictly appropriate in the terms which distinguish and characterize it. I have ever been of opinion, that an abolition of this unnatural jargon would open the path to reformation. And my observations on these people have constantly instructed me, that indulgence in this infatuating cant, is more deeply associated with depravity, and continuance in vice, than is generally supposed. I recollect hardly one instance of a return to honest pursuits, and habits of industry, where this miserable perversion of our noblest and peculiar faculty was not previously conquered.[8]

As is clear from Tench's observations, flash was regarded by the authorities as something that marked out the convicts, perpetuated their vices, and prevented them from reforming. Naval surgeon Peter Cunningham, in his account of the colony published in 1827, similarly wrote in a disdainful tone that the 'slang phrases current in *St. Giles's Greek** bid fair to become legitimized in the dictionary of this colony … the dross here passing as genuine, even among all ranks'.[9]

Accounts such as those from Tench and Cunningham were being sold to a British audience and were of interest at least in part *because* of the way in which they sensationalised the nature of the colony. How much they attest to a reality remains a question. Contemporary newspapers do not say much about the ongoing currency of flash, nor do we see many flash words entering the common Australian English vocabulary, with a few notable exceptions such as *swag*. Nevertheless, there are some hints that it lingered for a while, or at least was of some interest to the colonial population. That Vaux's guide to the flash language was considered handy is attested in a notice printed in the *Hobart Town Gazette* in 1821: Mr Williamson, a solicitor, offered a reward of five shillings for the return of a volume of Vaux containing the dictionary that had been 'lost or mislaid'.[10] Colonial familiarity with Vaux is also suggested in another description of a police incident in Sydney in 1832. A woman named Mary Connor was described as 'throwing all the hard words in Hardy Vaux's dictionary at her mistress' head' and as a punishment was being 'sent to try Gordon's Villa [the female factory run by Ann Gordon] for one month'.[11]

If there is only limited evidence of convicts continuing to use flash language as time went on, there is plenty to suggest their use of abusive or what was then sometimes called 'forcible' language. In the trial transcripts of the Old Bailey courts, where many convicts were sentenced, we can find glimpses of the spirited language of those who were transported (as well as those who were the targets of their crimes), and the crimes that got them sent away. Sophia

---

* A synonym for flash referring to the London area of St Giles that was notorious for its crime.

Lewis, who would be transported on the First Fleet, was charged in 1786 with stealing a handkerchief, a coat, a silk purse and several other items, and her companion, William Cox, was charged with receiving the stolen coat. Their trial was held in October 1786, and both were sentenced to transportation. Lewis was given seven years; Cox 14. Lewis had enticed a man named Thomas John Burrell to drink a glass of wine with her, and then to accompany her home. Once Burrell was undressed and in bed, Cox entered the room. Burrell testified that Cox had then declared, 'you bloody b[ug]g[e]r, what do you do here?' and the confrontation escalated from there.[12] In another case, John Tate, who was sentenced to transportation and a seven-year sentence, was found guilty of stealing a handkerchief from a man named Henry Beswick. Beswick, on catching Tate, declared 'damn your bloody eyes, you will suffer for this', and was described as 'using very bad expressions'.[13]

Convicts were certainly familiar with a range of strong words, as would have been the sailors and marines who came on the First Fleet. However, we have fewer ways of reconstructing the naval language of the 18th century than we do that of the language of convicts. Grose's dictionary captured numerous marine terms, suggesting that cant, slang and sailor talk were all considered part of the 'vulgar tongue' of the 'common people'. William Falconer's *An Universal Dictionary of the Marine*, published in 1813, records mostly technical naval terms, and we don't get a sense of the strong language sailors undoubtedly used.[14] Those who worked on the sea spoke a 'dialect and manner peculiar to themselves'.[15] How much of this language transferred to the convict colonies is unknown, but at the very least, the presence of sailors and naval men in early Sydney would have reinforced a world where strong language (if not a unique slang) was commonplace. One study of American maritime speech in this period has traced the use of swear words by sailors in the Atlantic world – *damn, son of a bitch* and *bugger* were particularly popular.[16]

And there is also the case of William Bligh, who became governor of the fledgling Antipodean colony in 1806 after a career as an officer of the Royal Navy. His temper and use of bad language were notorious even before he arrived in New South Wales.[17] Bligh quickly came into conflict with a rising colonial elite (especially the pastoralist John Macarthur), and he won few friends in the colony with his tendency to use abusive language, including towards members of the New South Wales Corps. A curse he was known to have used was *God damn you*, and he insulted people by calling them *villains, wretches* and *tremendous buggers*.[18] When the rebels were put on trial in London after the Rum Rebellion, the 1808 military coup that sought to remove Bligh from power, Bligh's language became a point of some contention: had he in fact damned the Privy Council and the Secretary of State, as the rebels alleged? Bligh denied the charge. He admitted that he might have said, 'Damn it, get out of my way', but said he never would have damned the Secretary of State or the Privy Council.[19] Bligh's disastrous experience in the colonies can at least in part be attributed to his temper and intemperate language.

So the early colonists, from convicts through to the most powerful figures of authority, brought with them a familiarity with bad language, as well as, for some of them, the flash language of the London underworld, and a mix of other influences such as the lexicon of sailors and the navy. Flash language was only partially applicable to the conditions of precarious settlements on the other side of the world and so this language fell from use over time, or at least became marginalised. But bad language in the form of swearing and abusive language would thrive in the colonies.

DISCIPLINE, MORALITY AND LANGUAGE

Language in the early colonies was considered to be, Alan Atkinson writes, 'the pivot of good discipline'.[20] Language considered insolent and challenging to authority could threaten the stability of the fragile community, and so convicts were subject to punishment for using it. Bad language was also regarded as an insult to personal honour.[21] From 1806, Governor Philip Gidley King put orders in place that prevented convicts from using abusive or insulting language towards military personnel.[22] Once convicts began to be placed on assignment, it also became an offence to insult employers or overseers. Such insolence could be punished with whipping or other corporal punishment, transportation to a place of secondary punishment, or hard labour. From 1825, colonial Justices of the Peace could punish male convicts who engaged in 'misbehaviour or disorderly conduct', including the use of improper language, with ten days on the treadmill, 50 lashes, solitary confinement for seven days, or confinement and hard labour for three months.[23] Matthew Adey was one such convict; a newspaper report indicates he was returned from assignment to spend ten days on the treadmill after he called his mistress 'a grumbler'.[24]

The records are full of incidents of abusive language and so we can reconstruct some of this fledgling society's bad language and how it was used. Some of the first trials in the settlements involved offensive language. In 1788, convict Samuel Barsby was sentenced by Judge-Advocate David Collins to 150 lashes for calling sergeants of marines 'bloody buggers'.[25] William Frazer, another First Fleet convict, was disciplined for saying 'You may kiss my Arse', when reprimanded for trespassing too close to the soldiers' huts.[26] The first murder trial to be held in the Sydney colony also happened in 1788, and featured bad language. Four men were charged with murdering a man named Thomas Bulmore. The dispute began over a convict woman, Mary Phillips. Bulmore had, according to one witness, gone to Mary's hut, and demanded to be let in. On going in, he found another man there (James Baker, one of the accused men). Bulmore said of Baker that he was a 'cowardly dog, and no man' and also accused him of standing there 'like a woman in petticoats'.[27] The language here was not only abusive but clearly impugned Baker's manhood, suggesting something of the code of masculinity of the time. The two then fought, and Bulmore died of his injuries. All the men present were subsequently found guilty of manslaughter and sentenced to 200 lashes – the others, although they didn't touch Bulmore, were punished for not having stopped the altercation.

Other such incidents also capture the flavour of the language of the day and how it was used. At the Moreton Bay settlement (now Brisbane), a dispute took place between John McIntosh, principal overseer, and the settlement's commandant, over the conduct of a prisoner named John Cunningham. The prisoners loathed McIntosh, who was renowned for his brutality.[28] In the dispute, McIntosh wrote a petition to Governor Darling informing him that he was resigning. McIntosh said that the prisoner had asked him: '"Who are you, you b[ugge]r." I made answer that I would let him know who I was. He replied, "You may kiss my a[r]se, you b[ugge]r, I'll settle you", and made use of a great deal of opprorious [sic] language.'[29]

Another incident at Moreton Bay involved a man named William Perfoot, who was killed by another convict, John Brungar, in 1828. Both worked in the gaol gang, and the two got into a dispute over the fact that Perfoot's pick was apparently lighter than Brungar's, and Brungar had wanted Perfoot to give it to him. The overseer told Brungar that he couldn't have it, and so Brungar struck Perfoot on the head with the pick:

Brungar pulled it out and threw it away as if nothing had occurred, took up a shovel, and said, 'That's the way to serve the buggar'. Daly roared out 'Murder, murder, hold him, hold him!' Crout seized Brungar round the arms, and Brungar dropped the shovel and said 'That's for jacketing* of me'. Perfoot, who appeared quite dead, was carried away to the hospital on a barrow.[30]

Secondary offenders (that is, a person who committed a crime in the colonies) were often the ones most likely to be described as 'rascals' and villains, and were considered those most likely to use bad language. The gaoler at the Newcastle penal settlement, Morris Landers, gave evidence in January 1820 that the prisoners were 'very much' given to swearing and quarrelling.[31] In a list of prisoners who were punished at Newcastle from July 1818 to the beginning of January 1821, most were charged for refusing to do work, and some for insolence. None were specifically charged with using offensive language per se, but one charge reminds us that language was potentially incendiary: Stephen Curran was given 50 lashes on 20 September 1820, for the crime of 'Disobedience in uttering expressions to create mutiny'.[32]

What is most striking in many of these accounts of insolence is the way convicts used bad language as a way to challenge authority. Their defiance runs through these insults, even when they were liable to be punished. Linguistic subversion could even be found in physical form on their skin. Many convicts had tattoos – at least 37 per cent of convict men, and 15 per cent of convict women had at least one tattoo.[33] Authorities recorded the details of these tattoos, as they were useful for monitoring and identifying convicts.

---

* A flash term defined by Vaux as 'removing a man by underhand and vile means from any b[e]rth or situation he enjoys, commonly with a view to supplant him'.

But tattoos could be a way of expressing individuality and asserting agency for some, not least when they were of offensive words. One convict, William Langham, was tattooed with the words *fuck me*;[34] another, Robert Dudlow, had a tattoo of *cunt* on his right hand (recorded by the authorities with the 't' scratched out, and 'indecent word' written next to it).[35]

If discipline, order and control were one pivot around which bad language turned, the other was morality. While the push for respectability really only began in earnest from the 1820s, from the first days of settlement there were those who wished to reform the convicts by encouraging them to stop using bad language.

Reverend Richard Johnson was a clergyman who travelled with the First Fleet, and the subject of his very first sermon at sea in 1787 was profanity. He declaimed to his convict audience:

> Our Lord assures us, that for every idle word that men shall speak they shall give an account in the day of judgement! How dreadful then will be the case of those persons, who during their whole life have employed their tongues in cursing, swearing, lying and all manner of vile and unclean conversation. Oh! think of this in time, and tremble and repent, and learn to use your tongues to better purpose in future![36]

For several days afterwards, Johnson believed, he 'scarcely heard an oath from any of them'.[37] The issue of language would continue to occupy him. In 1794, his 'Address to the Inhabitants of the Colonies, Established in New South Wales and Norfolk Island' was published in London. The address was an entreaty to the people of the colonies to follow the word of God and attend religious services. Johnson complained that '[t]oo many of you can find time to jest, to talk obscenely or profanely, read and sing idle songs', and would be better off reading the Bible. He warned the population off swearing, especially blasphemy, which he believed was all too prevalent in the colonies. This was language 'only fit for incarnate devils'.[38]

By the time of the Bigge Commission in 1820, an investigation into the state of the colony and whether transportation was really effective in punishing convicts, many in authority were complaining of the convicts' immorality. Samuel Marsden saw nothing in the settlements, he attested, other than evidence of convict vice, drunkenness and debauchery.[39] William Howe told the commission that he believed the convicts were unlikely to be capable of being reformed.[40]

Commentators continued attacking colonial moral character into the 1830s. When Quaker James Backhouse toured Australia over several years in the 1830s to survey the convict system, he reported to Governor Bourke that he believed that 'the use of profane language' might 'rank next to that of drunkenness' as evils that were promoting 'bad morals' in the community.[41] And in 1837, landowner James Mudie, who was particularly scathing of the convicts and resentful of emancipist power, described the language of convicts as 'too horrid for repetition'; convicts were, he argued, generally 'profligate, treacherous, dishonest and mutinous'.[42] These kinds of commentaries were coloured by the moral sensibilities of the period, as well as by a desire on the part of some colonists to end transportation and increase the rate of free settlement. But does it say anything about the realities of convict life and behaviour?

Historian Grace Karskens' work on life in early colonial Sydney, and in particular the area of The Rocks, reveals that convicts' lives were similar to those of English people of the 'lower orders' more generally. Gambling, fighting and drinking were all common features of everyday life. This was part of their culture, identity and community, however unsavoury it might have seemed to those who aspired to or claimed greater respectability. Violence and abusive language were undoubtedly real features of convict life, but, as Karskens argues, this culture can be seen as a means of resisting one's circumstances through defiance and disorder. Fighting could be a form of public entertainment.[43] Drinking was a way of coping with life, and in popular culture 'a way of defying exhortations to sobriety, regularity, time-discipline and relentless work'.[44]

While a distinctive culture existed in communities like The Rocks, where we can catch glimpses of the chaotic and lively culture of the 18th-century working classes, it is important to note that the rest of the colonial population, especially soldiers and sailors, were probably little better in their behaviour, or different in their values, at least as far as the use of bad language goes. Rather, punishing bad language was a way to stigmatise and control convicts. Once convicts moved into assignment, and from there into freedom, there was not much to distinguish many convicts (especially ex-convicts) from the free settlers. As we'll see in the next chapter, free settlers were just as likely as convicts and ex-convicts to be charged with public obscenity and abusive language from the 1830s onwards.

UNRULY WOMEN

The use of offensive language by women was considered particularly subversive of prevailing beliefs about how women were supposed to conduct themselves. Convict women by the very fact of their convict status were considered to be of dubious moral character, and were commonly labelled 'whores' or 'strumpets'. Convict women were often described by authorities as being 'lewd' and 'bawdy' in their language and gestures.[45] Women who engaged in sexually provocative behaviour, used foul language, and drank to excess were considered unsettling to the social order.[46] James Mudie described convict women as the 'pest and gangrene of the colonial society', and their language as 'disgusting even when heard by profligate men'.[47] These kinds of views of the convict women led them to be more closely controlled and monitored than male prisoners.[48]

Yet, as historians have consistently shown in recent years, the majority of convict women made the best they could out of the new circumstances in which they found themselves. As Karskens observes, convict women were the invisible householders, workers, businesswomen and tradeswomen integral to the growing economy of the colonies.[49] The women of The Rocks displayed attitudes and behaviour similar to that of men – they could be noisy and unruly, and were capable of violence, used profane language, and cared little for time discipline.[50] This was how they survived in a difficult world.

Women used fighting and bad language as a means of resisting the control and surveillance they were often subject to.[51] On board the First Fleet ship *Friendship*, for example, Elizabeth Barber told a ship's officer that he could 'come and kiss her C[unt] for he was nothing but a lousy Rascal'.[52] It is noted in the records that Barber was punished by being placed in leg irons on several occasions during the voyage.[53] The use of the word *rascal* is as interesting as the use of *kiss my cunt*; in this period *rascal* implied a person was of low social status, so this insult carried powerful connotations and challenged the social status of the officer Barber was insulting.

From around 1804, 'female factories' were used to house and imprison women before they were sent out on assignment. They could also be sent back to the factories for insolence and bad behaviour, including bad language. Women from female factories were considered especially prone to using offensive language. Such language – along with song and gesture – was used to mock figures of authority.[54]

One incident involving bad language, reported in the *Sydney Herald* in 1834, captures both the way women convicts were controlled and the way they defied authority. A colonist, writing to the newspaper, extensively criticised the language used by convicts from the female factory who were currently being assigned to colonists as servants. When the writer had remonstrated with one of the women who was, according to him, 'making use of obscene language', she responded by telling him to '—' and said 'if you don't like it, send me to the Factory, where I want to go. You can't flog me, you — it's only three months'. The newspaper's decision to disguise the words leaves us in the dark as to exactly what this woman said and how strong her language was, but we can assume that it was highly offensive. The colonist told her that 'if she did not cease such vile language, I certainly would endeavour to gag her. She dared me to do so, and said "it was more than the Governor could do".' Two other women then joined in abusing him and one of them observed, according to his account, that 'if all the prisoners in the Colony were of her mind, they would turn out, and cut one half of the — settler's [sic] throats'. The writer complained to the newspaper's editors that this was 'a specimen of the behavior of the female convicts in the interior', and he argued that they wouldn't act in such a daring manner 'if the punishment in the Factory was more exemplary'.[55]

The incident described in the *Herald* nicely captures the way convict women showed their contempt for the authorities through using bad language, but also illustrates the moral superiority the (presumably) free and male colonist tried to assert over them. There is plenty of evidence to suggest that convict women were hardly the only people in the colony to speak like this, even though they were the ones most taken to task for their language. Men enjoyed exercising power over them, using language as a means of condemning them and countering the threat of their challenges. Lieutenant Ralph Clark, a marine, complained of the language convict women used – he had never heard such language, he claimed – and denounced them as 'damned whores' and a 'disgrace to ther [sic] Whole Sex'.[56] As a marine and a man, he was able to lay claim to bad language himself without it undermining his character or having much consequence, unlike the women he condemned.

SUBVERSIVE WORDS

As we've seen, a range of words made up the profane vocabulary of the convicts, as well as those who came free to the colonies. Common words in circulation included *bugger*, *bloody*, *bastard*, and we have some evidence of words such as *fuck* and *cunt* being used. Expressions now obsolete such as *damn your eyes* were much used. Let's look at the story of some of these.

Bugger was a fairly ubiquitous word in the speech of the early colonists. It can be used in a number of different ways, of course, with different meanings. When the early settlers used it, it was mostly in the sense of 'a term of abuse or contempt for someone'. In this vernacular sense, first recorded in 1694, it was an insult. After this period, from the middle of the 19th century, we also see it being used in a less offensive and more affectionate way (for example, 'silly bugger'). *Bugger* in both senses has continued to be a key word in the Australian English vocabulary of insults and has also developed as a general exclamation of frustration.

Where does *bugger* come from? According to *Oxford English Dictionary* (*OED*) etymologist Anatoly Liberman, *bugger* has its origins in:

Old French *bougre*, which in the Middle Ages meant
'heretic,' from *Bulgarus* 'Bulgarian.' The Bulgarians were
Orthodox Christians, specifically Albigensians, and various
sins, including bestiality, were imputed to them. Those
rumors spread and were busily cultivated in Southern
Europe before, during, and after the Albigensian Crusades
(1209–1229).[57]

Bugger meaning 'heretic' gave way to the 'homosexual' sense by the
16th century and was recorded as a more general term of contempt
from the late 17th century. Spelling variants include *bouger* and
bougre, and we sometimes see these spellings in early Australian
colonial records. *Bugger* likely continued to carry some connotation
of effeminacy in its use in the 18th and 19th centuries; it was an
insult that called into question the recipient's manliness.

Damn was a blasphemy or religious curse, and while it is no
longer considered much of a swear word today, it was considered
to be strong language in the 18th and 19th centuries. *Damn* 'used
profanely' (as the *OED* terms it) is a word first recorded in 1589
and has its origins in the Latin *damnare*. By the 18th century, it
was a common curse word. Historian Paul Gilje, writing about
Anglo-American maritime culture, suggests that for a sailor the
use of this word – taking the Lord's name in vain – could be seen
as a way of 'proclaim[ing] his command of his own destiny'.[58] We
could imagine this may well have similarly inspired a convict's use
of the word, insofar as there might be an attempt to grasp some
power in a situation where power was so limited. The first recorded
evidence of the curse *damn your eyes* comes from testimony in an
Old Bailey court trial from 1732, and is an expression very well
attested throughout the 18th century. *Damn rogue* and *damn rascal*
were common insults of the period. A word such as *rascal* implied a
person had low social status, adding to its level of insult.

We saw earlier that Grose's dictionary of the vulgar tongue included many terms for women, especially those who worked in the sex trade or were considered to be sexually 'loose'. This was part of the way sexist language was encoded in this period. A common appellation for convict women was *whore*, although for the speakers of the time it was not considered offensive in the way that it might be today. Samuel Johnson's dictionary, published in 1755, and a major development in the codification of English, defined *whore* as '[a] woman who converses unlawfully with men; a fornicatress; an adultress; a strumpet'.

Whore is found in late Old English, referring to a sex worker, and from the 13th century also used for 'an unchaste or lewd woman', to quote the *OED*'s 1924 definition, yet to be updated. Both senses were still in use by the 18th century. According to Grose, however, *whore* was not the worst insult that a woman could incur – *bitch* was considered to be the most offensive. He defines *bitch* as 'a she dog, or doggess; the most offensive appellation that can be given to an English woman, even more provoking than that of whore'. The Old Bailey archive reveals some use of the word *bitch* by those convicted at the time, although nothing in these records suggests it being more or less offensive than any other insult of the period. Many negative connotations were (and are) attached to *bitch*, including the sexualised insinuation of a female dog in heat that also implied a person driven by their 'primitive' urges.*

Words such as *bugger, damn* and *whore* suggest the range of bad language transplanted to the Australian colonies. *Bugger* was used as an insult and a challenge. It was often used by convicts towards figures of authority, as well as in arguments with each other. *Bugger*

---

* There are numerous 'dog' insults, mostly aimed at men, such as *cur* and *mongrel*. In Australian English, *mongrel* is a strong insult, and there are a number of uses of *dog* through the 20th and 21st centuries with negative connotations.

may well have helped to define aspects of colonial masculinity through its connotations. *Whore* functioned differently, insofar as it determined who and what was respectable and shored up the gendered hierarchy of power that operated in the colonies. *Damn*, by contrast, was the ubiquitous swear word that reminds us of the continuing importance of blasphemy in 18th- and 19th-century swearing.

LANGUAGE AND COLONIALISM

The year 1788 marked the beginning of the European invasion of the continent and the subsequent dispossession of Indigenous people. The first colonists arrived at an area already occupied by probably over 30 Indigenous groups, including the Dharug and Eora peoples of the Sydney region. Encounters between the existing occupants of the land and the new arrivals involved both violence and peaceful interaction. Historians Tracey Banivanua Mar and Penny Edmonds write of settler–Indigenous relations in early colonial Australia that 'contact, conciliation and conflict would always be closely intertwined'.[59] English was established as the primary language of the colonies, and ultimately displaced many Indigenous languages – but through these early years English existed alongside a significantly large number of Indigenous languages and dialects.

For the Indigenous people of the Sydney region, the intruders were, at least initially, perplexing. By 1790, Grace Karskens tells us, the Eora had several names for the new and uninvited arrivals, most notably *Berewalgal*, 'people from a distant place'.[60] While not used offensively as far as we know, this word reminds us of how Europeans were the 'other' to the people who already occupied the land. Communication between the Sydney people and the invaders was a challenge and depended not only on attempts to speak to each other – there was a need for gesture and action to try and communicate across the linguistic divide.[61] This divide meant that few Europeans could fully understand the nature of Indigenous society and culture.

The invaders attempted to learn some of the Sydney Language, which included Dharug and Eora dialects. We therefore have some record of the language, or at least some of its vocabulary, mostly in the form of wordlists or mentions in the accounts of men such as Watkin Tench and Judge-Advocate David Collins. Wordlists were also compiled by Lieutenant William Dawes from information given to him by a young Eora woman, Patyegarang. Patyegarang developed a close and trusting relationship with Dawes, teaching him her language. The Sydney Language was 'functionally dead' by the late 19th century, and although now extinct, a reconstructed version of Dharug is spoken and used by Dharug people today.

As might be expected, there are only a few traces of any specific offensive words in the language spoken by the Sydney people, not least because the context of their use remains unknown. We know some words relating to body parts and functions: for example, *guni* 'excrement', *ganadinga* 'copulate', and *bura* 'testicle'. David Collins recorded *wuruwuru* meaning 'go away' (and used by the Sydney people when they first saw Europeans), and Watkin Tench recorded *guninbada* – 'eater of human excrement' – as an insult. Another list also records *wumidjang*, defined as 'a term of reproach with which the Aboriginal people are highly offended. It is sometimes used by the women and the men always punish them for using it.'[62]

The Sydney people also began to pick up offensive words from the English language, if the observations of the colonists are to be trusted. In his 1794 address to the colonists, clergyman Richard Johnson chastised people for using bad language not only because it would damn their souls, but also because it would corrupt those people he called 'poor unenlightened savages'. 'Already some of them have been taught to speak such language ... and though they do not yet understand the meaning of the words they use', he declared, 'they can utter oaths and blasphemies almost as readily as their Christian instructors.'[63] Some years later, pastoralist Robert Dawson noted in his 1830 account of the colony, *The Present State of Australia*, that the Aboriginal people had begun to learn what he described as the 'low slang language of abuse' from convicts.[64]

Some of these terms became part of the New South Wales Pidgin language that evolved through contact, and that the settlers and Indigenous people used to communicate with each other. New South Wales Pidgin, sometimes described by colonists as a form of 'broken English', was in fact a language and an essential medium of communication between Indigenous people and Europeans in the first decades after invasion. While most words were borrowed from English, words were also borrowed from the Sydney Language, and as European settlement expanded, from other Indigenous languages. Curses and swear words from English that formed part of the Pidgin vocabulary include terms such as *bladirog* 'bloody rogue!', *kas* 'curses!', *maiwod* 'my word!', *maioath* 'my oath', *dammaiai* 'damn my eye(s)!', and *no bladifia* 'no bloody fear!'[65]

The 18th century saw the ongoing evolution of a language of racial difference that informed the perceptions and language of the settlers, and shaped their interactions with Indigenous people. Racial language in the early years of settlement was more redolent of 18th-century European sensibilities that sometimes took a more romantic view of indigenous peoples across the globe, rather than the harder racial attitudes of the 19th century. Regardless, the arrival of Europeans had devastating consequences for Indigenous people in the areas in which they settled.

The names Europeans ascribed to the Indigenous people they

encountered included *Aborigine* (first recorded 1803), *Aboriginal* (as a noun, first recorded in 1826), *Indian* (first applied to Australian Indigenous people by Joseph Banks in 1770), and *native* (as a noun, first used of Australian Indigenous people by James Cook in 1770 and used adjectivally in many compound terms through the first decades of settlement such as *native settlement, native camp* and *native name*). While used descriptively, these terms underpinned the nature of colonialism. For example, the use of the word *Aborigine*, which quickly established itself in the colonial vocabulary, obscured the fact that the continent was occupied by a large and diverse number of Indigenous groups, speaking their own languages and dialects, and with distinctive cultural and social beliefs. While *Aborigine* would become established in Australian English as a name given to the Indigenous peoples of Australia, it was a term that in the 18th century was used for indigenous peoples of other places, as was *native*. Europeans often saw the indigenous peoples of the countries they colonised in similar ways, and the language they used reinforced these common approaches to understanding (or not) these peoples, their cultures and their societies.

Indigenous people, like many other indigenous groups in countries that came under British control, were often regarded as 'primitive', 'uncivilised' and 'savage' by Europeans. *Savage*, as a noun to describe Indigenous Australians, was first recorded in 1792 used in an address by Richard Johnson, the clergyman who chastised the colonists over their use of bad language. The term *cannibal* was also used, first recorded in 1804. The word *wild* was also used in a number of terms used to refer to Indigenous people from the 1820s, including *wild native, wild blackfellow* and *wild tribe*.

Skin colour too was used as a designation, with *black* first used as a noun in Australian English in 1795, and the term *blackfellow* in 1798. The diminutive *blackie* (or *blacky*) is first recorded in the Australian context in 1827, although interestingly in a passage by

Peter Cunningham that suggests Indigenous people had the upper hand over the settlers, and were using bad language to condemn them: 'The instant *blacky* perceives *whity* beating a retreat, he vociferates after him – "Go along, you dam rascal".'[66] For a settler to be cursed and called a *rascal* by an Indigenous person was likely to be considered a particularly egregious insult.

Wordlists and other evidence demonstrate that words for describing settlers and Indigenous people formed part of the core vocabulary of the New South Wales Pidgin language. These terms included *blakman* and *waitman* borrowed from English, and *wadyiman* 'non-Aboriginal person' and *balagaman* 'Aboriginal person' borrowed from English by way of the Sydney Language.[67]

The language used to describe and label Indigenous people, then, served to set in place a racialised language of otherness that would subsequently play a significant role in shaping Australian society, and have a profoundly negative impact on Indigenous Australians. The power of racial language was evident from the inception of colonial Australia. This was not considered 'bad' language at the time – there was no transgressive or taboo element to such language and so it was not considered to be offensive, at least by the Europeans. But such language shaped the world the colonists were creating that Indigenous people were being inexorably drawn into.

*@$%

When Alexander Harris came to the colonies in the early 19th century he described parts of Sydney as being like 'St Giles and Wapping in one' – two of the most notorious districts of London.[68] The labouring population of the New South Wales colony he believed to be 'universally lost to all sense of moral duty and religious obedience'.[69] Language was seen at least in part as both a cause and a symptom of this apparent moral laxity in the colonial population.

But Australian colonial society was rapidly changing. As the number of free settlers increased, opposition to transportation grew, and those who arrived in the colonies as convicts increasingly sought to leave behind their convict origins and rid themselves of the 'convict taint'. For this reason alone, their language began to change. The middle of the 19th century would see a growing preoccupation with manners and respectability. Colonial society would also become increasingly linguistically intolerant.[70] We now turn to the story of what happened to bad language as settler society began to grow.

2

RESPECTABILITY AND ITS DISCONTENTS

In 1873, a Victorian newspaper commented on the problem of young colonial men and their language: 'The use of filthy language in either the streets or private houses is looked upon with disfavour. It is not respectable in Victoria in 1873 to make blackguard boasts and allow streams of blasphemy to flow from a vile tongue.'[1] By the 1870s, respectable society in the Australian colonies was distancing itself from any behaviour that it considered to be immoral and indecent: the use of bad language was a marker of such behaviour and so it should be condemned and avoided at all costs.

The Australian colonies expanded rapidly through the middle decades of the 19th century. By 1860, the settler population numbered 1.15 million.[2] Urban centres such as Sydney and Melbourne flourished, but so did some of the problems that came with cities in the 19th century, such as poverty and disease. Settlers moved across the land, dispossessing Indigenous people, often violently. These were the realities. As colonial society sought to overcome its convict origins, it became preoccupied with respectability. This was driven not only by a desire to leave behind the 'stain' of convictism, but was also bound up with broader social and cultural shifts that saw manners, self-discipline, character and propriety become increasingly important to an expanding 'genteel' middle-class culture. These were the aspirations.

The question of who you were and how you presented yourself was one that preoccupied many in colonial society, especially because your social origins might be murky. In such a context, how you behaved became more significant; manners, etiquette, speech and dress all became important signs of respectability. Such concerns were amplified in a period of rapid change. Manners – which included not using bad language – helped to 'define [one's] social position in an unstable world'.[3] These concerns over class and social status were not confined to the Australian colonies,[4] but they did take on particular local inflections, as we'll see.

Bad language was part of a broader colonial discussion about respectability and class: what they meant, and even more importantly, how they could be performed in everyday life.[5] As Australian society grew in size and complexity, the need for regulation and social and moral order – for people to behave themselves – increased. Much of the debate surrounding bad language turned on discussions of profanity in *public*. The main concern was not so much what was done (or said) in private, but rather how people presented themselves and behaved in public. If language was a marker of respectability and gentility, it could also threaten to expose a *lack* of respectability.

Alongside, and integrally connected to, the notion of respectability was that of being 'civilised' – taken in this period to include standards of behaviour around manners, modesty and speech, and the adoption of British values, education and belief systems. Through the 19th century, the British increasingly spoke of their 'civilising mission' throughout their empire, and this held true in the Australian colonies. Even as Indigenous people were being dispossessed and killed, there was a desire to find ways to 'civilise' them.[6] Some advocated an approach to dealing with the Indigenous population they believed was more humanitarian, especially the removal of Indigenous people to reserves and missions, where they could be educated in Western ways. Language – speaking (proper) English – was considered to be one marker of being civilised, and so the policing and disciplining of language – for example, through forcing Indigenous people to speak English – played a key role in exerting power over the Indigenous population.

But if the colonies were aspiring to attain respectability, civilisation and order, they faced ongoing challenges to that order. The impact of the gold rushes, rapid urbanisation, a remnant convict (and ex-convict) population, crime and widespread alcohol abuse – all of these posed threats to good order. Despite having left convict days behind them, the colonies had a lingering reputation for immorality that was difficult to overcome. If order was desired and desirable, disorder still seemed more common and more visible, and nowhere more visible than on the streets of growing colonial cities nor more audible than in the sound of public bad language.

POLICING AND REPORTING BAD LANGUAGE

As the colonies expanded, policing and the law were important means of keeping order, shaping the fabric of colonial society and reflecting its preoccupations.[7] The criminalisation of bad language (including profanity and abusive language) served to make individual speech and behaviour a public and legal concern, but also signified the kind of ordered society that colonists were trying to forge.

The colonial press played an important role in making bad language a public concern. Frequent discussions of swearing (and, more generally, morality and behaviour) in newspapers helped to shape and communicate the social and cultural norms that were developing. And in reporting on crime and its punishment, they also became a vehicle for showing people how to behave and what might happen to them if they broke the law.[8]

Through the middle of the 19th century, there was a great deal of public concern about offensive language. If the number of court cases is any indication, such concern peaked in the years of the gold rushes that began in 1851.[9] This fact is unsurprising, perhaps, as the colonial population swelled with an influx of people looking for quick wealth. Most of these newcomers were men (a gender imbalance continued in the colonies right through the middle of the century) and unattached – the exact type likely to care little about the niceties of language or proper behaviour.

The first *Vagrant Act* in New South Wales, passed in 1835, made no specific reference to bad language (although convicts could still be punished for insolence). But the colonies were rapidly changing, and there was an increasing demand, as the number of free settlers increased and as many emancipists sought to leave their convict identities behind, to 'clean up' the streets.[10] Under vagrancy legislation introduced in New South Wales in 1849, a person could be arrested for using 'any profane or obscene language to the annoyance of the inhabitants or passengers in any public street or place'. Amendments in 1851 broadened the scope of the legislation to include 'any obscene song or ballad', as well as the writing or drawing of 'any indecent or obscene word, figure, or representation'. It also criminalised the use of 'any threatening, abusive or insulting words or behaviour' in a public street, thoroughfare or place. A person could be punished with a fine of five pounds, or imprisoned for three months.[11] While the exact nature of language deemed offensive was not specified in the legislation, it was generally interpreted to mean words that threatened, or that could undermine dignity or reputation.[12] Other colonies passed similar legislation: for example, in Western Australia, a Police Ordinance of 1849 decreed that a constable could apprehend without warrant any 'loose, idle, drunken, or disorderly person whom he shall find disturbing the public peace'.[13]

Discussions in the colonial press generally supported laws relating to public behaviour, arguing that vagrancy legislation would help to improve public spaces. In 1850, one colonial commentator complained that 'in no place in the world was such disgusting language used, as in the streets of Melbourne'.[14] These complaints were echoed in other urban centres. Underlying much of this discussion was an attempt to manage and control the working classes, whose behaviour was typically much more visible and public.[15]

Historian Michael Sturma's careful study of court records in New South Wales through this period reveals that at the Parramatta courts, there were 55 prosecutions for obscene language in 1852, 95 in 1853, and 200 in 1854.[16] Some of the cases he describes give us insight into the way bad language offences came about, as well as an idea of the language that led to charges. A woman named Mary Salsbury was charged for using obscene language towards Mudgee's chief constable, who deposed that he had found her lying drunk in front of a public house. When he tried to pick her up, she told him 'to kiss her arse'.[17] Another woman, Mary Ann Fleming, was charged with calling her husband a 'bloody bugger' while in a public house.[18] William and Margaret Burke were charged for calling each other 'a bloody old bitch' and 'a bloody old bugger' when a constable passed by their home.[19] Blasphemous language also featured in some of these court cases: Thomas Dowan, an ex-convict, was sentenced to four days in Parramatta gaol for using the expression 'Holy Jesus',[20] and Elizabeth Sicwood was fined three pounds for swearing 'by the Bloody Holy Ghost'.[21]

The colonial press was, unsurprisingly, more circumspect in its reporting of bad language, but the words are often fairly obvious. An account of a murder case in *The Australian* in 1834 included a number of insults that were used in exchanges with the deceased, with the dead man condemned as 'a b[lood]y old soldier' by one Mary Malony; according to one witness, he had called Malony 'a b[itc]h'.[22] A Tasmanian newspaper in 1835 reported that Charles Turner, a constable, had complained of William King, described as 'a flash waterman', as having threatened 'to knock his b[lood]y head off, and calling him a trap,* and other disgraceful names in his capacity of a constable'. King was fined five shillings for his 'flash language'.[23] An 1845 police report noted that a man named Lear had been charged with disturbing the peace; he had called a constable, Robert Smith, 'a d[amne]d rascal'.[24]

Despite public concerns raised by the gold rushes, the cases identified above suggest that domestic and local disputes were a potent and frequent source of bad language offences, and that women were as likely to use bad language as men were, including swearing at each other. For example, in one instance, a woman's female next-door neighbour called her a 'bloody whore and a bloody bitch'.[25] Young women were no exception to this: in another case, a 12-year-old girl named Catherine Bell was charged with assaulting an older woman, Mrs Clara Cane. Their fight involved Catherine throwing water over Clara, as well as calling her an 'opprobrious name' and using 'disgusting language'. A witness, Bell's sister, claimed that Cane had first used 'language of a disgusting nature' to Bell.[26]

Discussions of obscene language cases in the colonial press frequently linked the use of such language to alcohol, and many colonists were charged with drunkenness along with using offensive language.[27] A man named John Wood was accused by the landlord of the Retreat Inn in Pentridge, Melbourne, of having used 'language of a grossly obscene description'; Wood was sorry for his behaviour, which he attributed to being 'in a "state of beer" at the time', reported the *Melbourne Daily News*.[28] Alcohol undoubtedly loosened the tongue for many, but these reports also indicate the

---

*   A slang word for a policeman.

way alcohol and bad language were linked to each other, and to failings of character, in public discussion.

Sturma observes that many of the cases in this period were initiated by civilians (as opposed to police constables) and were often precipitated by minor disputes over things such as business and money. With a flood of people coming into the colonies and few other ways of settling differences between them, litigation was a way to deal with such conflicts.[29] One case found in the court records involved a dispute over the repair of an umbrella, with the accused, an ex-convict, telling the wife of the accuser to 'go and fuck herself'.[30] Another case, this one reported in the press, involved a cabman named William Millhouse who had used bad language towards a minister, Reverend W Bedford. Millhouse was accused of demanding more than his fare at the end of the journey and then swearing violently when the higher payment was refused, saying 'd[amn] his eyes if he'd be imposed on … and other improper expressions'. However, when questioned, Bedford was unable to say that the defendant had actually used any derogatory words towards him, or insulted him, and so the charges were dismissed.[31] What is also clear, and as shown in the case of Millhouse, is that there are examples of those who worked in what we would today call 'service roles' refusing to behave in what might be considered a suitably deferential manner, reflecting the working out of social and class status in the socially mobile world of the colonies, as well as the strong position of workers in a time of high demand for labour.

Sturma speculates that there was more to these cases than just a rising sense of respectability and propriety, although this was clearly important. Tensions between social and national groups, he argues, can also be discerned. Ex-convicts were often accused of using bad language, reflecting a desire on the part of the free settlers to assert their superior respectability and status, and to keep former convicts in their subordinate place. Some newspaper evidence supports this, with a number of cases making mention of convicts and emancipists. For example, in 1850, a woman named Emma Woollen charged a ticket-of-leave holder named William Knightly with having used 'very indecent language towards her'.[32] A number of cases also revealed Irish ethnicity as a common target of abuse: for example, one woman was recorded as calling another woman a 'bloody Irish Immigrant Bugger'.[33] Attitudes towards the Irish in the colonies reflected both the racialised light in which they were viewed, as well as associating them with the worst qualities of the working classes and condemning their Catholicism.[34]

We can discern in these various offensive language cases that those who were charged were rarely repentant and commonly defiant. We could thus interpret that using offensive language was a working-class challenge to genteel propriety and a sign of rebellion against authority as much as anything else. For example, a man named Charles Murray was arrested by a district constable for using 'the most scandalous and indecent language he ever heard', and in the presence of women. When appearing before the magistrate, Murray responded – we can only imagine scornfully – that the constable must be 'a pretty delicate chap [to be so offended]'.[35] Constables were frequently regarded with little respect. Indeed, colonial newspaper editors conceded that some offensive language charges had dubious motivations, because police constables were themselves of questionable character. A Hobart newspaper suggested in 1835 that constables in the town were likely to 'construe any words into bad language for 2s. 6d'.[36]

DEFINING OFFENSIVE LANGUAGE

So what *was* the language that could lead to charges? What exactly constituted offensive language was something much debated and contested in various cases heard before the magistrates. We've seen already from the court records that words that typically incurred charges included *bloody*, *bugger* and *bitch*. Yet there were a number of words that were less obviously offensive and so their actual 'criminality' was subject to debate – although we rarely find out exactly what these were. One case in Sydney had the magistrate determine that the language used by the defendant 'was more entitled to be termed jocose than obscene', and so dismissed the case[37] – but we aren't enlightened as to what the words actually were. Other cases were similarly noted as having been dismissed because the language in dispute was ultimately deemed by the magistrate as not obscene.[38] An example of this is the case of William Garwood, whose charge was dismissed by the magistrate because he had only called constables 'rogues and vagabonds' and nothing stronger.[39]

One particular case gives us some insight into the fine distinctions that could be made in determining what constituted offensive language. In 1857 an older man, one John Fitzpatrick, was brought up on charges. A constable deposed that the defendant had used the words 'b[lood]y wretches and b[lood]y traps' towards the police. The magistrate did not, however, consider these words to be obscene. Another constable then said that the words had in fact been 'b[lood]y b[ugge]r and b[lood]y wretches'. This *was* deemed to be offensive, and so the defendant was found guilty and fined.[40] What is notable here is the evidence that the word *bugger*, as a term of abuse levelled at a person (notably a constable), was deemed to cross the line into obscene language – *bloody* was not, nor was *wretch* or *trap*.

Contestation over whether the use of particular words was offensive enough to warrant charges was not the only way in which the legitimacy of these language cases was challenged. The very wording of the legislation could be debated. For example, in 1852, a publican was charged under the *Vagrant Act* with using 'obscene and indecent language'. The defendant's attorney, Nichols, noted that the defendant was charged with using 'obscene and indecent language, in lieu of obscene *or* indecent language'.[41] The bench dismissed the case. The following year, the same attorney who had appeared for the publican argued the exact same point when a woman was similarly charged with obscene and indecent language. Nichols again quibbled over the wording of the charge, arguing that it was a tautology to be charged with both, and so asserted that the charges should be dropped. This case, like the earlier one, was in fact dismissed, as the magistrate conceded that he had no power to emend the statute.[42]

Whether obscene words should be uttered in court was also a matter of some debate. In one case it was deemed unnecessary for a constable to tell the magistrate the exact language: 'the oath of the constable that obscene language was used, is deemed quite sufficient to convict a man and send him to gaol, without taking the trouble to ascertain what were the objectionable expressions complained of'. The writer reporting on this case for the colonial press suggested that this action would help to protect the 'refined audience' that might hear the language. But the writer expressed concern, however, over another case where an Irish constable laid a charge against someone for having told him to 'go to blazes' – language clearly considered tame enough to be reprinted in the press, and so hardly likely to be considered strong enough to incur charges.[43]

Legal scholar Elyse Methven's study of 19th-century offensive language cases in Australia suggests that it can be difficult to know exactly what words were considered to be highly offensive as they often didn't make it into the court proceedings. An increasingly common practice for dealing with offensive language in the court-room was for the prosecuting officer to write the word or words on a slip of paper that was then handed to the defendant in the dock to be affirmed or denied, and then passed to the bench.[44] Her study concludes that oaths such as *Christ, damn, Jesus* and *by God* were overall less likely to be censored in the courtroom, suggesting their relative tameness, even in the 19th century.[45]

Language considered to be mocking of religion could fall under the obscene language statutes, but this was contentious, indicating the somewhat ambivalent attitude to actual blasphemy in colonial society. One correspondent to the *Sydney Morning Herald* took up the issue of a report of someone singing a 'profane parody of the Lord's Prayer' in a public street. The letter-writer pointed out that the singer had indeed breached the *Vagrant Act* and could have been taken into custody, but hadn't been.[46] In 1870 the case of W Lorando Jones garnered much coverage in the New South Wales press. Jones gave speeches publicly in Parramatta Park on Sunday afternoons.[47] He was charged with blasphemy under an old English statute, on the basis of having used words 'giving illus-trations of the immorality of certain passages in the Bible'.[48] Jones was accused of calling the Bible 'the most immoral book that has ever been published'. The prosecutor argued that his language had been 'an offence against Christianity'.[49] He was subsequently sen-tenced to two years' imprisonment and a fine of £100 (although he was released a month later, on the basis of agreeing to keep the peace, and in response to public complaints).[50]

Jones's case was an important one in the history of colonial censorship, as well as bad language; while it was not a case of offen-sive language per se, it brought into focus the question of the true nature of blasphemy – not just taking the Lord's name in vain, but disputing contemporary tenets of Christianity. This was a time in the colonies when secularism was on the rise, but religious ideas were also being explored and debated.[51] The Jones case also raised a dispute around the issue of freedom of speech, one the colonies debated vigorously. A writer in the *Brisbane Courier* queried whether Jones should have been denied a freedom 'which we claim for ourselves'.[52] The New South Wales parliament subsequently debated the nature of what constituted blasphemy, reaching the conclusion that it should be defined as 'the use of language calculated to lead to disorder'.[53] Again, the preoccupation with a social order that could further distance the colonies from their convict origins guided the debate, rather than any actual concern with offences against God. Finally, in December 1873, a bill was passed preventing prosecution of the offence of blasphemy, in the sense of saying something negative about the Bible and/or aspects of Christianity.[54]

So while prosecutions of offensive language were undoubtedly a feature of colonial Australia, there was also much debate about what it actually constituted. These cases reveal much about the preoccupations of colonial society, but also show a significant concern with creating and maintaining public order, a topic we now turn to.

ST GILES AND WAPPING IN ONE

Many of the cases described above suggest that a major concern for colonial society through the middle decades of the 19th century was bad language *as spoken in public* – more so than any explicit preoccupation with sin or immorality. The sound of swearing in the streets was considered to be an affront to those colonists who aspired to respectable status, and it was believed that it had a potentially corrupting effect on the young and the vulnerable who might be exposed to it. It also threatened to entrench the reputation of the colonies as places of disorder.

Colonial observers frequently commented on the prevalence of profanity in the Antipodean colonies. As we saw at the end of the last chapter, Alexander Harris, in his 1847 book *Settlers and Convicts*, observed that the 'low-life' section of Sydney was like 'St Giles and Wapping in one' – two of the most notorious underworld areas of London. But he also declared that regional areas were terrible: touring the bush, he recorded hearing phrases such as 'd[amne]d scoundrel', and 'd[am]n him'.[55] A writer in the Sydney newspaper, *The Colonist*, similarly commented in 1837 that anyone arriving in the colonies would likely be shocked by the common use of profane language. He condemned such language in no uncertain terms, observing that:

> It can only be that morbid love of slang and flash, that false idea that there is something valorous or fine in rapping out a manly oath, which has unfortunately taken but too strong a hold on the minds of our native youths, that has caused this vice to disgrace Australia, and to give to her sons their present bad pre-eminence in the rank of profane swearers and blasphemers.[56]

While instances of swearing were observed and condemned in both city and bush, urban centres were arguably considered more problematic because respectable people could be too easily exposed to that language and it was audibly apparent. A report in Sydney newspaper *The Monitor* in 1826 commented that one of the many 'nuisances' of the town was 'the disorderly assemblages on the Sabbath Evening, in some of the principal thoroughfares, of characters of the lowest description, who amuse themselves, by outraging the ears of modesty and decency with the most disgusting expressions'.

The corner of Pitt and King streets was considered especially bad, 'with their obscenity … chiefly directed to the congregations returning from the respective places of worship'.[57] People also complained about Bourke Street in Melbourne: 'Oaths, blasphemies, the sound of smashing glass, the screams of frightened women, and the brutal exclamations of drunken men, confusedly fighting with each other, woke all the echoes of Bourke-street at that midnight hour', complained one letter to the editor of the Melbourne *Argus* in 1868.[58]

By the middle of the century, there was frequent discussion in the press about the problem of swearing in streets and public spaces. The *Sydney Morning Herald* reported in 1850 that obscene language was a common occurrence on the streets in some areas of the city.[59] The Mayor of Sydney vowed that he would do whatever he could to 'put a stop to the intolerable nuisance by which the ears of respectable persons were every day assailed'.[60] The *Geelong Advertiser* lamented that same year that it was 'a fearful fact that the first word many of the children in our town learn to lisp is an oath'.[61] And an 1857 complaint in a Victorian newspaper lamented the 'blasphemy and obscene language' being 'heard in the streets in open day'.[62]

Yet it is clear that it was not just the poorer classes who used bad language, even if they continued to be associated with it in the public imagination. Another police case reported on in the colonial press around the same time reveals that some of those who were considered respectable had little time for moral proprieties with respect to language. The *Sydney Gazette* reported that a minister named Richard Hill had made a complaint against an unnamed defendant described as a 'respectable individual'. Hill complained that this person had used 'profane and blasphemous language in the public street'. When Hill admonished him, the defendant had 'treated him with a considerable degree of derision'. Hill stated that he was not so concerned about himself but was worried about the way this behaviour offended against public morals. The magistrate agreed, thanking him 'for his general exertions to check the spread of offences against good order and morality', and charged the defendant a fine of 30 shillings ('five shillings for each oath, the complainant having deposed that he had sworn at least six').[63] In the 1859 case of a 'respectable looking woman' named Mary Wakefield being fined for using obscene language, it was observed that such language was a 'growing evil' in Hobart.[64] Perhaps what was particularly perturbing about Wakefield's case was that she presented herself as respectable yet her speech marked her out as not so – this made her social status problematic. As mentioned earlier, the outward markers of respectability were all that one could use to estimate social status in an uncertain colonial world.[65]

Bad language as used by and towards women was a particular topic of concern and commentary, reflecting the evolution of ideas about how women should behave and the increasing expectation that women should ensure respectability. In 1850 a Queensland newspaper reported on the case of a woman who had been squabbling with her neighbour and was charged with using 'threatening and obscene language' towards her. The reporter decried the 'prevalence of obscene and filthy language in public places', and was especially unhappy with the 'common quarrels and recriminations of feminine belligerents'. He not only thought that magistrates and police should help to control such behaviour but 'the husband of the offending party might advantageously exercise his authority and settle the dispute in a summary manner'.[66]

In another instance a woman was not just described as having been charged with 'abusing and resisting the constable in taking her on a warrant [and] for using obscene language', but also with 'being a common scold'.[67] The offence of 'common scold' was a common-law charge originating in English law, and one often used to control women considered to be 'public nuisances'. Through the early to middle decades of the 19th century, there are numerous instances of women being charged with this offence, and newspaper accounts often mention some kind of abusive language being part of the reason for the charge. A number of cases involved disputes between neighbours: for example, Eliza Smith and Mary Lugg were accused in 1849 of being common scolds after their neighbours complained of their constant quarrelling and their use of the 'most obscene and blasphemous language'.[68] Another case involved an unnamed woman being charged as a common scold because she constantly used 'abusive filthy language' towards three particular individuals and in the process made herself a nuisance to her neighbours. The newspaper reported that the woman had used 'a novel mode of annoyance' to convey her bad language – a speaking trumpet.[69]

Many cases of women using obscene language were brought before magistrates in the 19th century. These women were considered to be 'disgusting the ears of decency'.[70] But we can also catch glimpses of them defying authority. One woman, Mary Kenny, was brought before a magistrate in Hobart for 'employing towards [Serjeant (sic) Holton] language, not only threatening and uncomplimentary, but decidedly unladylike, obscene and disgraceful'. Holton testified to both Kenny's violence and her use of 'filthy language'. Another woman, Mary Murphy, appearing on behalf of Kenny, argued that Holton had in fact started the argument. The newspaper report on the trial noted that under cross-examination, Murphy was more than a match for Holton, with her testimony leading to much laughter, especially when she pointed out that Holton had said Murphy might do well with the magistrates because she was good looking but the prisoner (Kenny) would be punished because she was plain. The case was dismissed.[71]

That 'respectable' women could be exposed to the evils of bad language was an ongoing cause for concern. In 1848 an article in the *Sydney Morning Herald* decried the actions, or lack thereof, of police in Pitt Street. The writer observed that in passing through that street they had been compelled 'to witness "sights and scenes unholy," and to hear language which could be heard nowhere else but in the very lowest streets of Wapping … Virtuous females may be grossly insulted, and their ears be polluted by the most filthy, blasphemous, and obscene language.' But the writer felt that this behaviour was too often ignored by police.[72]

It was unclear whether bad language could only be an offence if actually heard by others and in public. In 1850 one woman was brought up on charges before the police bench, with the apprehending constable noting that the woman had used the offending language within her own home. A question was therefore raised as to whether the fact that she had used the language there – 'her house was her castle, and no law could prevent her there making use of any language she might think proper' – meant she could be found guilty. The magistrate responded that no matter where the person might be, 'if [the language] was in so loud a tone as to become an annoyance to the inhabitants or passengers, as was the case here', that person was guilty. The woman was subsequently fined ten shillings.[73] But while the woman was found guilty, this was because others (strangers) had heard her, not because of any intrinsic 'evil' attached to the utterance of bad words. This case again reinforces the conclusion that the real offence of swearing in colonial society lay more in the violation of social norms and the disturbance of public order than any real moral concern about the intrinsic 'badness' of uttering swear words. This period thus entrenched ideas of bad language as linked to both a broader concern with public order and the personal virtues of character. For colonial society, especially one shedding its dubious convict origins, appearance, behaviour and speech mattered.

A QUESTION OF CIVILISATION

Violence was all too common on the pastoral and settler frontiers.[74] But if violence was the norm in how settlers treated Indigenous people by the 1830s and 1840s, some Europeans called for an approach they thought was more humanitarian – something advocated across areas of the British Empire. The Aborigines Protection Society was established in Britain in 1837 to lead the way in protecting Indigenous peoples across the Empire.[75] Underpinning protection was the 'civilising mission': the belief that making Indigenous people adopt European customs was the best way to save them from inevitable extinction. This idea was perhaps 'Britain's most powerful tool of self-legitimisation' in relation to its treatment of Indigenous peoples.[76] 'Protection' was, in this period, largely carried out through the activities of Christian churches. Missionaries and other humanitarian advocates travelled and worked in the Australian colonies, attempting to save the souls of Indigenous peoples for God. Language was critical in this process. Missionaries took an interest in Indigenous languages, some recording and learning these languages for the purpose of converting Indigenous people to Christianity and for translating religious texts. But bad language was a matter of some concern also: Indigenous people had to be protected from its corrupting and sinful effects.

If settlers saw themselves as 'civilised' in relation to an Indigenous 'savage', many missionaries believed settlers to be the greatest corrupting influence on Indigenous people, as was their bad language. This began with the view that convicts, especially those they saw as beyond redemption, were a malign influence. Peter Cunningham, for example, observed in 1827 that Aboriginal people had an excellent command of 'the Billingsgate slang they certainly have acquired in perfection, and no white need think of competing with them in abuse of hard swearing'.[77]

Lancelot Threlkeld, a missionary who went to work with the Awabakal people around Lake Macquarie in the 1830s and who recorded their language, decried the bad effect of the settlers, including the use of what he called 'indecorous language' around them.[78] German missionary Johann Handt also complained of white men cursing in the presence of Indigenous people while he worked in the Wellington Valley, reproving one Indigenous person who used such language by telling him 'that it was bad language, at which God was angry, and only that of wicked white men'.[79] Another German missionary, Jakob Günther, also noted of the Indigenous people in the area that 'what they know of English is chiefly the language of wickedness'.[80]

One of the most confronting missionary accounts relating to Indigenous use of bad language comes from George Augustus Robinson. In 1841 Robinson wrote in his journal about two young girls in his camp, Pinggumyere and Narracort, who had been held by some hut-keepers in the neighbourhood for the purposes of providing sexual and other services. He describes these young girls as using 'obscene, scurrilous and blasphemous language', which he also described as being spoken 'with the most perfect indifference, apparently quite unconscious of what they were repeating'. In his journal he recorded them saying 'well done fuckumall, go it fuckmoll, goodnight fuckwik', and then noted that 'fuckumall and fuckmoll was oft repeated'. He believed 'no better evidence is wanting to stamp the infamous character of the white ruffians who prowl about the country insinuating poison into the minds of these depraved beings'.[81] Robinson writes about the incident to complain of the effect of language and to call for the benefits of Christian education. The story also reveals how hut-keepers often sexually exploited Indigenous girls and women, an occurrence all too common in rural areas.[82]

Another disquieting account comes from a Queensland

newspaper in 1863. Here it was reported that the newspaper had received many letters on what it called the 'disorderly conduct of the blacks'. The editor noted: 'Being ourselves frequent witnesses of the disgusting exhibition of batches of drunken blackfellows, often in a state of nudity, yelling, and howling, mingling with their own lingo the bits of English blasphemy they have learned from the "civilised" whites, we can bear testimony to the truthfulness of our correspondent's descriptions.' The writer suggested that while it was not bad enough to justify the formation of a vigilance committee, he suggested that a mounted police patrol 'with the special duty of watching over, controlling, and over-awing the natives, exerting every means to discover and to bring to justice those guilty of the crime of supplying them with grog'.[83]

Missionaries were preoccupied with the goal of converting Indigenous people to Christianity and the desire to 'save their souls'. To this end, language mattered. Threlkeld taught the people in his mission not to use bad language, and reported a young boy as warning another to 'not say those words, they are bad … for he who is above is angry with those who use them'.[84] One Anglican missionary in the Wellington Valley, Reverend Watson, reported on how Indigenous people had come to recognise the evils of swearing. In 1833 he reported that a young man, Booley, had reproved a stockman who had sworn at his cow that he 'wont [sic] go to heaven if you swear'. Watson reported that Booley had arrived 'much in the habit of swearing, but after a short time I have heard him frequently reprove other Natives for that wicked practice'.[85] His journals reveal that Indigenous people had adopted bad language, with frequent observations on their use of such language (although he doesn't specify its nature – occasionally he writes that he has heard 'the worst language that was possible'[86]). His records also indicate that alcohol was sometimes attributed as the cause of such language.

Those Indigenous people who lived in or near urban centres were increasingly viewed as a vagrant population to be contained within particular spaces.[87] There was no desire to have the Indigenous population anywhere near where white people lived. Indigenous people could be, and were, charged under the *Vagrant Act*, and bad language could prompt those charges. For example, the *Melbourne Daily News* noted the arrest of a young Indigenous woman believed to be 'of unsound mind' in January 1850, who was charged with using 'obscene and disgusting language' in Queen Street. As she couldn't pay the fine, she was sent to gaol.[88] The punishment of bad language in both urban and rural areas thus reflected the larger colonial attempt to control the lives of Indigenous people.

BLOODY AND OTHER COLONIAL OATHS

A regime of censorship, largely based on self-censorship and ideas about propriety, evolved through the 19th century. As with the court cases described above, we have limited access to the full range of bad language that might have been in use in the colonies. In the printed record, words were typically either avoided altogether or disguised in some way. In such a context, it can be hard to discern exactly what the colonial bad language vocabulary consisted of. Yet we know the language existed and was liberally used. Indeed, one commentary on such language in New South Wales observed that the 'vernacular is singularly rich in expletives, no man considering that he has done his duty either to society or himself if he finishes a sentence of twelve words without the incorporation of five dissyllables, each like the others, all beginning with b'.[89]

The word that was perhaps most identified with this period, and with the Australian colonies, later became known as the 'great

Australian adjective', *bloody*. The word *bloody*, according to the *Australian National Dictionary*, used as an intensifier 'ranging in force from "mildly irritating" to "execrable"', is found in early colonial records from the beginning of the 19th century. Convicts and settlers alike used *bloody*, often to express frustration. The phrase *my bloody oath* (or just *bloody oath*) is also recorded from the middle of the century.

Bloody (in the sense of an adjectival intensifier) dates to the 16th century, and by the 18th century was in common colloquial use. The *Oxford English Dictionary* (*OED*) writes that 'for many speakers [it] constituted the strongest expletive available'. Although some have argued that it has a religious connection, referring to the blood of Christ, the *OED* rejects this origin, suggesting instead a possible connection to the 'drinking habits of aristocratic rowdies' of the 17th century, as the first examples of its use are found in the form *bloody drunk*. Regardless of its origin, Melissa Mohr writes that *bloody* was the definitive expletive of the 18th century in England, adding that it was typically associated with the lower classes.[90]

Bloody gained its Australian associations through the 19th century, and indeed the *OED* argues that the process of normalising *bloody* began in the Australian colonies. Early colonists and visitors to the colonies frequently commented on the ubiquity of the term. George Robinson noted in his *Journals* that his wife had observed to him how common the word was: 'The fire they said was bloody; the wood was bloody; the water, the place, their eyes, and limbs, even the food they eat – it was all bloody.'[91] But it is Alexander Marjoribanks' commentary on the word (already quoted in the introduction and repeated here) that constitutes one of the most famous early observations on the language of the Australian colonies. As a visitor, he was perhaps particularly attuned to observing and identifying what were developing as characteristic features of the society and culture of the new Antipodean colonies. For him, language was one such marker:

> The word bloody is the favourite oath in that country. One man will tell you that he married a bloody young wife, another, a bloody old one, and a bushranger will call out, 'stop, or I'll blow your bloody brains out.' I had once the curiosity to count the number of times that a bullock driver used this word in the course of a quarter of an hour, and found that he did so twenty-five times. I gave him eight hours in the day to sleep, and six to be silent, thus leaving ten hours for conversation. I supposed that he had commenced at twenty and continued till seventy years of age ... and found that in the course of that time he must have pronounced this disgusting word no less than 18 200 000 times.[92]

Bloody was undoubtedly ubiquitous in the colonies and we have a great deal of evidence of its common use (and we saw it was also borrowed into New South Wales Pidgin). Was it actually used more frequently than back in Britain, or were 'respectable' colonists just more likely to be exposed to hearing it in the more mixed society of the colonies?

The discussion around *bloody* raises the question of whether certain offensive words were considered to be more common in the colonies and if the language of the colonies was particularly bad and/or distinctive. Some of the colonial observations suggest as much, but they were frequently aiming to tell sensationalist stories for British consumption. Yet the language itself reflects a self-perception that a markedly 'bad' language was evolving in the colonies. *Colonial language* and *colonial slang* both became terms in use through the middle of the 19th century, referring to a distinctive language developing in the Antipodes. The term *my colonial oath* and *my colonial* were variants of the common, and largely Australian, exclamations *my oath* and *my bloody oath*. Expressions such as *my colonial oath* were, according to one commentator writing in 1870, 'colonial colloquialisms of the class most affected by bushmen and diggers'.[93]

Colonial oath was also a term understood to be synonymous with (any) swear word, and suggested that language in the colonies might have been considered especially contrary to the idea of respectability associated with the British metropolis. One description of an obscene language charge described the language the defendant had used as 'very colonially obscene',[94] emphasising the role the colonies played although failing to explain just what was so much worse about the language used in this instance.

One other term is worth mentioning: *ornamental blasphemy*. The term came to have a short period of popularity in the Australian colonies through this period. Possibly coined by Mark Twain in *The Californian* – 'It has done nothing but bring down upon me a storm of abuse and ornamental blasphemy' – the term was picked up and used through the late 1860s and 1870s in Australia. It alludes to the idea that the words referred to were used merely as an affectation or for show. Several offensive language cases in the Australian colonies described the accused as using 'ornamental blasphemy'.[95] But its life in the colonial vernacular was short.

DIGGERS AND BUSHRANGERS

'Between drunken bullock-drivers, flash expirees, and half crazed gold diggers', opined one commentator in 1852, 'it is scarcely possible for a respectable woman to walk the streets of Melbourne, either morning, noon, or evening, without having their ears shocked with the most disgusting and blasphemous expressions.'[96] As we've seen, colonial society was in flux through the middle decades of the century. The presence of convicts and former convicts, the impact of the gold rushes, bushranging 'outrages', and a rising concern about criminal urban youth were all seen as threatening the colonial social order being carefully constructed through these decades.

The start of the gold rushes in the middle of the century prompted fears of disorder, immorality and crime, with concerns about bad language being expressed as part of a general, albeit mostly middle-class, discussion about the influence the influx of miners was having.[97] A highly mobile population was seen to be potentially disruptive and threatening to colonial social order.[98] As we saw earlier, the number of court cases dealing with offensive language increased after the gold rushes began. The culture of the diggers of the gold fields was often described in similar ways to convict culture – as marked by 'drunkenness, gambling, rioting, and blasphemy' as one person described the diggings at Turon, New South Wales.[99] It was noted in 1852 that Victoria had passed a bill that would not only prevent unauthorised mining on Crown lands but would also suppress gambling and the use of obscene language, suggesting the ubiquity of both of these 'habits' and their link to the diggers.[100]

Descriptions of the gold fields in the contemporary press often included commentaries on their language, usually linking it to a central feature of the diggings: the sly-grog (unlicensed alcohol) shop.[101] For want of anything else to do, diggers frequented the sly-grog shops, got drunk, and were then prone to use bad language and become either victims or perpetrators of crime and violence. 'Grog shops' helped to create the problem, one writer complained, for they 'vomit out their besotted occupants brimfull of blasphemies and obscenity; the staggering drunkard is watched, waylaid, robbed, and maltreated; the proceeds all gotten are ill spent; gambling precedes thieving, tossing up coppers for pound notes leads to fighting and to robbing again and so the round of vice circles continually'.[102]

Some colonial commentators were shocked by the behaviour of people at the diggings. Naturalist and illustrator Louisa Meredith, who travelled to the mining town of Ballarat in the 1850s, was horrified to see men and women dirty and drunk, 'cursing and screaming'. She observed that the impression of Ballarat she was left with was that 'all my preconceived opinions and expectations of the misery, brutality, filth and degradation, known to prevail in the digging settlements, were outdone' by the reality.[103] In 1852 author and historian James Bonwick, after touring the diggings, wrote about their 'moral state'. He acknowledged that the men were 'out of the pale of civilized life' but he found them, despite this, generally 'courteous'. Nevertheless, swearing was 'an almost all prevailing vice' encouraged by the 'wild and uncomfortable life' of the gold fields.[104]

The gold fields were frequently depicted as places that corrupted 'decent' men by those who harboured suspicions about the effects of the rushes on colonial society. The *Sydney Morning Herald* reported in 1853 that respectable men quickly abandoned their normal behaviour once at the diggings. This included adopting bad language, argued the writer: 'The language spoken, the oaths uttered, the horrid blasphemies, shouted loud and deep, are some of the most shockingly revolting nuisances to be encountered among such a population.'[105] In Western Australia, where the gold rushes commenced in the 1890s (and where convictism also lasted the longest), there was a continued commentary on the prevalence of a population of diggers who have a 'habitual inclination to blasphemy, swearing and drunkenness'.[106]

The language of the gold fields was indeed distinctive, ranging from technical terms such as *heavy gold* (gold in heavy lumps) to terms that reflected the impact of gold on Australian culture such as *digger's wedding**. But we have little verbatim evidence of what bad language was actually used on the gold fields, even though diggers were associated with it. Traveller and author Raffaello Carboni, who was present during the Eureka stockade events, noted in passing the 'hard swearing' that was 'prompted by gold-thirst, the most horrible demon that depraves the human heart'.[107] Often commenting on the presence of the Vandemonians (former convicts and hardened criminals), he notes them as having 'low, vulgar manners and hard talk, spiked at each word, with their characteristic B, and infamous B again; whilst a vile oath begins and ends any of their foul conceits'.[108] Such men were also notoriously hard drinkers. But such characters also made up the police that became so despised on the gold fields and whose heavy-handed policing of digging licences was a factor in the Eureka uprising. As historian Clare Wright observes, the police were drawn largely from the 'flotsam of ex-Vandemonians and other layabouts'[109] – that these men were no better, or even worse, than the gold diggers and yet attempting to exercise power over them was unacceptable.

Diggers quickly became part of an emerging popular culture of colonial Australia. In a study of gold field ballads, literary scholar Philip Butterss concludes that in them 'diggers are not generally shown swearing themselves, but they *are* portrayed as familiar with and unabashed by such language'.[110] Popular novels of the period also often depicted diggers as fond of bad language – much more so than the average respectable 'gentleman'. Anthony Trollope's 1877 novel *John Caldigate*, partly set in Australia, features several diggers from the gold fields – although not the only swearers in the

---

*   Bruce Moore writes in *Gold! Gold! Gold! The Language of the Nineteenth Century Australian Gold Rushes* (Melbourne: Oxford University Press, 2000), 34: 'Successful diggers often paraded their success with lavish weddings, including carriage drives through the streets of a major city.'

novel, they are the most associated with such language. While not unsympathetically portrayed, Australian diggers are, in Trollope's description, 'inquisitive, familiar, and with their half-drunken good humour, almost repulsive'.[111]

Another figure seen to threaten the fragile social order of colonial society was the bushranger. Bushranging began during the convict period, and the first bushrangers were escaped convicts. Living beyond the law was made easier with sparse settlement. Bushranging continued through the middle decades of the 19th century, fed by the poverty experienced by some, especially those working on the land, during the gold rushes.[112] It was marked by a hatred of squatters and banks, but, as sociologist Pat O'Malley points out, also the police and magistrates, who were seen as their tools.[113]

Bushrangers were outlaws and as such we might expect that they made use of potent bad language. Charles Duigan was charged with horse-stealing in 1869; the victim of the crime described how Duigan 'made use of some disgusting language'.[114] Daniel 'Mad Dog' Morgan, a bushranger active in the 1860s in the Riverina area in south-western New South Wales, was also described in a contemporary press report as having used the word *damned*, and swearing 'a fearful oath that he would blow the brains out of every man on the station' during a shootout.[115] A court case involving bushranger William Troden, alias Podgey, described his robbing the manager of a station and threatening him with the words 'Bail up, you b[lood]y b[astard]s, or we will blow your b[lood]y brains out.'[116]

The most famous bushranger of all, Ned Kelly, brought his own style of colourful language to his Jerilderie Letter, written in 1879 as an explanation and justification of his actions, including the killing of three policemen. His deep contempt for the Victorian police is captured in his vivid description:

... and is my brothers and sisters and my mother not to be pitied also who was has no alternative only to put up with the brutal and cowardly conduct of a parcel of big ugly, fat necked, wombat headed, big bellied, magpie legged, narrow hipped splaw-footed sons of Irish bailiffs or English landlords which is better known as officers of justice or Victorian police who some calls honest gentlemen.[117]

Bad language was certainly used by bushrangers, but it also became part of their mythology. Bushrangers became the stuff of Australian legend. Their bad language, a mark of their rebellious and dangerous nature, was part of the public's fascination with, and even sympathy for, them. The bushranger took up a place in a lengthening line of male Australian users of bad language, and as they became part of the tapestry of colonial popular culture, they signalled a shift to a view of bad language that suggested that there was something attractive – perhaps even positive – about it.

*@#%

The colonies struggled to shake off a reputation of immorality and disorder, and bad language seemed to be connected to the legacy of convictism and the threat of the lower orders. But something was shifting. By the turn of the century, while bad language was still discussed as a moral issue, it had also become a marker of Australian identity and masculinity. Australian characters such as the convict, the digger and the bushranger fed an emerging popular mythology and culture that celebrated bad language, recasting it as a potential positive marker of Australianness.

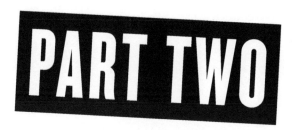

PART TWO

MAKING BAD LANGUAGE AUSTRALIAN, 1880–1920

3

BULLOCKY AND THE BUSH

In 1897, writer and journalist WT Goodge's poem 'The Great Australian Adjective' was first published in *The Bulletin*. The poem, which quickly became popular and was reprinted several times in subsequent years, connected swearing to bush mythology with its depiction of 'the sunburnt — stockman' with a '— nag' that isn't able to get him across a river.[1] The poem's title became the great euphemism and descriptor of its disguised word: *bloody*. It also associated the bush and an idea of Australian cultural nationalism with bad language, an association that would exert a strong hold on the popular imagination for a long time to come.

Important developments shaped the history of bad language in Australia through to the end of the 19th century and into the early 20th. 'Good' language – language free of profanity and slang – continued to mark social status and class, but there was also an emerging discussion around just what 'Australian English' might be, and its role in shaping an idea of 'Australianness'. What were the distinctive qualities of English as it was spoken and used in Australia? This question was of considerable interest. Reflecting a spirit of growing cultural nationalism, Australian English was increasingly associated with irreverence, humour, and a spirit of anti-authoritarianism. Australian English was for many linked to the use of colloquial language and slang but, as we'll see, also to swearing, at least by men. In particular, it became popularly associated with a range of 'quintessentially Australian' male figures such as the bullock-driver and the bushman. The 'typical Australian' of this mythology was, as historian Russel Ward would write in 1958 in his *The Australian Legend*, a man who 'swears hard and consistently, gambles heavily and often, and drinks deeply on occasion'; he is also 'one who endures stoically' and is 'a "hard case"'.[2] Bad language became an integral part of this Australian 'legend'.

Popular culture played a significant role in all of this. Swearing could be a source of playful humour and the marker of certain types of writing, even as it was censored. As print culture flourished, euphemisms abounded – but the many euphemisms used to substitute for words such as *bloody* and *damn* not only reflect the impact of censorship, they also attest to a creativity of language, making this period one in which we discover the use of a great variety of euphemisms and 'mild' swear words. Public defences of swearing were also mounted, both on nationalist grounds as well as on the basis that there could be justifications for it, such as the need to express emotion in a difficult situation. Bad language was becoming thoroughly Australianised.

THE COLONIAL SWEARER: THE BULLOCK-DRIVER

If there was one Australian character most associated with swearing in this period, it was the bullock-driver. Bullock-drivers, essential to the colonial economy, no doubt actually used bad language (they often asserted that such language was an 'absolute necessity'[3]), but they also became iconic figures associated with swearing in colonial Australian culture. An early description – dating from 1856 in the *Melbourne Punch* – observed 'that in the use (and abuse) of expletives and opprobrious epithets the model bullock-driver defies all competition'.[4]

Bullock-drivers quickly came to set the gold standard for swearing to which all were compared: for example, an 1864 diatribe about the ills of the Melbourne Cricket Club complained that in order to be a member it was necessary to 'swear like a bullock-driver',[5] and in 1885 it was noted that a certain thing was 'as necessary as blasphemy [is] to a bullock-driver'.[6] The Australian lexicon also expanded with terms that reflected this notorious language: the word *bullocky* to refer to bad or coarse language was in use from the 1860s, and variants included *bullockese, bullock language* and *bullock-driver language.*

The bullock-driver quickly established himself as a popular cultural figure, often appearing in humorous stories, as well as colonial ballads and verse. An early colonial ballad celebrating his notorious language featured in the collection of Charles Thatcher. Thatcher was an Englishman who toured the Victorian goldfields writing and collecting ballads and songs, publishing them in 1864. His ballad 'The Lady and Bullock Driver', included the verse:

> Bullock drivers of course you all know,
> Are queer specimens of humanity,
> The words from their mouths too that flow,
> Evince a most horrid profanity.

The ballad tells the tale of an 'uncouth' bullock-driver named Dick who is warned by his master that he will be given the sack 'if my wife you offend with your guiver*'. Dick sets out with the wife on their journey. When the bullocks get stuck in mud and need to be cajoled to move, they are 'stunned by such wond'rous civility' as Dick now shows them: 'And of course they would not pull at all /

---

*   *Guiver* is an Australian English slang term that generally means 'an affectation of speech or behaviour'.

For they missed his colonial curses'. The bullock-driver in his despair turns and says to the wife, 'I say, mum, will you be so kind / As 'low me to damn that 'ere Poley?'[7]

Many popular stories and songs similarly played on the reputation for 'language' that bullock-drivers had earned for themselves. In one story, for example, a character named 'Horrible' claimed to be 'the "language" champion of the Barcoo ever since he swore at the dry skeleton of a bullock, which had been dead for two years, until it got up and jumped a fence'.[8] Often, he was contrasted to the 'green' 'new chum', fresh from the mother country, typically depicted as shocked by the bad language in use in the colonies. In the popular ballad 'Getting Colonized', for example, one such new chum was described as 'horror-stricken' when the 'ribald bullock-drivers swear; / And shocked by curses loud and deep'.[9] One writer published his experiences of being a newcomer under the name 'Bow Bells' in 1861. He was struck by the bad language of the bullock-drivers immediately on his arrival in the colonies. When he asked them why they swore so much, he was instructed that 'all new chums had to lay aside their prejudices, and address their bullocks with the prefix b[lood]y or they could never do any good with them'.[10]

Joseph Furphy's novel *Such Is Life* appeared in 1903, immortalising the bullock-driving life and culture. Furphy had spent time working with bullock teams,[11] and he captured the flavour of their language in his depiction of the experiences of his narrator, Tom Collins. Most of the swearing in the novel is disguised, but the characters themselves discuss their own propensity to swear. As one bullock-driver, Cooper, observes: 'I got a curse on me. I got it through swearin' and Sabbath-breakin'. I've tried to knock off swearin' fifty dozen times, but I might as well try to fly'.[12]

AN 'AUSTRALIAN LANGUAGE'

The late 19th century saw the evolution of a cultural nationalism in the Australian colonies. In much writing of the period, Australians were imagined as 'young, vigorous, independent and egalitarian'.[13] While this construction of an Australian identity included loyalty to the British empire,[14] it clearly distinguished itself from the 'Old World'. *The Bulletin*, an Australian periodical published from 1880, and edited until 1903 by JF Archibald, was particularly important in this process. While its pages contained diverse views, the causes it often championed included secularism, democracy, and mocking capitalists and wowsers,[15] with a large dose of racism and misogyny thrown in. Cultural historian Tony Moore argues that *The Bulletin* appealed to a wide readership, across the social classes.[16]

The Bulletin used a lot of vernacular and slang as a way to mark the new society of the colonies. This attracted criticism from some quarters. For example, one newspaper sniffed that 'cheap blasphemy couched in nasty phrasing, ought not to be regarded as the best literary pabulum to offer Young Australia'.[17] But *The Bulletin* and its colloquial style proved to be popular with many, was widely read, and was an influence on Australian cultural production through to the First World War. It also helped to establish a mythology of Australian English that fused it with the idea of slang and informality.

Many of the writers of the 1890s – who often wrote for magazines such as *The Bulletin*, which became known as the 'bushman's bible' in this period[18] – mythologised the bush, drawing on folk traditions and building on the tales of characters such as the bullock-driver and the British migrant 'new chum', and promoting values such as mateship. This was despite (or perhaps due to) the fact that many of these writers lived in the city. One of the appeals of the bush mythology was its power as a unifying myth that avoided addressing class and other divisions in Australian society.[19] In these stories, the bushman was turned into a cultural hero.[20] His use of bad language was part of what made his character distinctive, and in turn tied into a vision of a distinctive Australian society and culture.

While the term *Australian language* was first used with reference to Aboriginal languages, as it is again today, from 1869 it was also used to refer to Australian English.* Australian English was an identifiable variety of English by the late 19th century, with people noting a distinctive, if often criticised, accent, as well as lexicon. While much of the lexicon of Australian English in fact consists of words for plants, animals, and other characteristic aspects of the Australian environment, it was, and is, popularly associated with slang. In the 1890s and through into the 20th century, the idea that the Australian English vocabulary was informal, irreverent, and largely made up of slang took hold, boosted by magazines such as *The Bulletin*, whose writers helped to popularise and even coin many slang words.

The association of the term *Australian language* with a certain style and idea of cultural nationalism extended to the idea of the *Australian language* as bad language – that is, swearing. The first recorded use of the term as synonymous with swearing dates from 1891, and refers, unsurprisingly, to bullock-driving: English novelist Morley Roberts in his account of travelling around Australia commented, 'I tried to back the bullocks, but they scorned me utterly, in spite of the Australian language I used.'[21] References to the *Australian language* as bad language helped to reinforce the idea of Australian English as informal and colloquial (and for some, less desirable than 'proper' British English), but also helped to reshape ideas about swearing.

---

* *Australian English* itself is a term not recorded until 1881.

An increasingly ambivalent, rather than condemnatory, attitude towards profanity can be discerned in Australia by the end of the 19th century. Moral concerns certainly continued and often still dominated most public debate around bad language. But as Australian cultural nationalism developed, the idea that bad language was somehow quintessentially Australian – and reflective of 'innate' Australian qualities such as irreverence and contempt for authority – is apparent.

So how did this shift come about? As we saw, the bullock-driver was an iconic 'colonial swearer', and his swearing was seen to be if not acceptable at least understandable given the intransigence of the animals he was dealing with. Men who worked and lived in the bush could generally be considered 'acceptable' colonial swearers. The 'acceptable' colonial swearer was also always a man, as swearing came to be strongly associated with white Australian masculinity.

Women had no claim to swearing; indeed, they were expected to continue to be the guardians of respectability and propriety. This perhaps also reflected the ambivalent cultural position women more generally held. While women certainly participated in the emerging national culture of the period – for example, writers such as Ada Cambridge, 'Tasma' (Jessie Couvreur) and Louisa Lawson – their relationship with the masculine bush mythology was complicated.

The bushman was regarded by some contemporary commentators, like Englishman Francis Adams, as the 'typical Australian' – '[t]he one powerful and unique national type yet produced in Australia'.[22] One shearer was said to be able to 'condense within ten minutes solid cursing more blasphemy than any other man … ever heard'.[23] Another character who featured in a popular ballad was a 'shed-boss' on a sheep station who was described as a 'language-man' who 'went a-swapping swear-words round at the office-door' with a shearer.[24] Bad language in these contexts could be celebrated, and even tinged with nostalgia, tied to a yearning for a life in the bush that might already be passing away. Bad language was to one writer but a 'remnant of the old rough days of bush and bullocks', and it would 'gradually disappear before increasing culture'.[25]

The bushman's language was regarded as particularly, even uniquely, inventive. One account of the typical bushman's speech, written in 1898, provided a lengthy description of its qualities. It was:

> a queer compound of unlike elements. Catch-words out
> of music-hall or Christy Minstrel songs, gags out of opera
> bouffe, patter, cant terms, queer verbal mosaics of profanity
> and indecency, bits of aboriginal phrases, technical terms of
> the most bizarre perversions of meaning, phrases from the
> card table and the miner's camp, and novel inventions from
> the stations – English and American and Australian slang
> – all this in a mass makes English as it is spoken (for this is
> never written) in the West one of the most expressive and
> picturesque of *argots* for those who understand it, one of the
> most incomprehensible and topsy-turvy for those who do not.
> … He has further a vocabulary of expletives and interjections,
> unmeaning in the sense of having no definite meaning for
> the words as such, though the phrase means something
> to him and his mates. His curses in due form are another
> branch of this language, and they have a racy flavour of their
> own in some instances, though it is impossible to deny that
> more frequently they are just stupid brutality and profanity.
> Anyhow, there he stands, the typical bushman, the one unique
> type that Australia has yet produced, and the analogue of
> whom at his best and his worst I do not suppose is to be
> found on earth.[26]

This description clearly identifies the language of the bush with the use of slang and cant, as well as 'expletives and interjections'. But it also celebrates both the language and the bush as positive things – they are imagined as unique and distinctive.

As is clear, certain types of person came to be associated with bad language; by the end of the 19th century, these types were considered to be fundamentally Australian. It was a short step then to regard Australian swearers as superior to other nationalities. This idea would flourish during the First World War, but we can trace evidence of this attitude before the war. In an 1898 newspaper account of a Tasmanian travelling in the Canadian Klondike region, it was observed that 'Americans are terrible fellows to swear, but their blasphemy lacks the poetical variety and fluency of expression of the Australian.'[27] A year later, an observation was made of some workers in the Flinders Ranges arguing that 'for pure and undiluted blasphemy, hair curling curses, and the length, strength and variety of their oaths, I think the Australian stockman, when his temper is up, can take the fancy bread from even the Yankee sailor, or the British soldier'.[28]

BAD LANGUAGE ON THE PRINTED PAGE

Print culture and its infrastructure – bookshops, publishers, periodicals – were flourishing in the colonies by the end of the 19th century.[29] The readership for books and magazines was growing, and more venues for Australian writing were appearing. The bulk of most people's reading was still imported from Britain, but a distinctive Australian literary culture was also beginning to be produced.

Print and popular culture was a domain in which bad language could be used, or, through its censorship, imagined and debated. As we've seen already, colonial swearers such as the bullock-driver and the bushman were as much a product of the creative imagination as a reality. Print played an especially important role in reshaping bad language and attitudes towards it. It did this in at least two distinct ways. Firstly, it helped to create the sort of characters we have already met – those who regularly used bad language – and so built and reinforced particular associations between bad language and the bush, bad language and men, and so forth. Secondly, as we'll now see, because of concerns over bad language in print and its corrupting potential, a variety of ways of presenting such language – primarily through disguise and euphemism – came into use. This generated a linguistic creativity that still alluded to, and allowed the imagining of, bad language while recognising that the original words were not approved of. Print thus brought into circulation certain words, including euphemisms and mild oaths, giving them legitimacy and currency, and making them popular.

The most common swear words found in print through this period were *bloody* and *damn*. These words typically appeared in disguised form. They would be presented as, for example, *d—n*. Dashes and asterisks were common disguises, although for most readers, it would be easy enough to figure out what the word was. The very practice of disguising words through typographical means – the use of a dash or an asterisk – gave rise to its own lexicon. For example, there was use of the euphemistic *dash* and *dashed* for *damn* and *damned*, and the word *asterisked* was used to replace any censored word.

Beyond the use of dashes and asterisks, a range of words could be inserted to disguise or replace an unacceptable swear word. An 1889 newspaper simply put *(blasphemy)* where a word should appear;[30] another inserted *(blanky)*.[31] *Blanky*, along with *blankety* and *blankety-blank*, were commonly used to disguise bad language in print. Less common but nevertheless in use was *blanker* as a disguise for *bugger* (as in, for example, *you blank blanker* and *silly blanker*). Author and artist Percy Clarke, in his book *The New Chum in Australia* (1886), used the terms *adjectival, adjectival substantive,* and *adverbially adjectival substantive. Adjectival* (also *adjective, adjectively*) was a well-attested replacement for *bloody*.

Joseph Furphy's novel *Such Is Life* (1903) took the art of the bracketed disguise to another level. Most of the swear words in his book about bullock-driving appear in brackets and include *(adv.), (adj.),* and *(verb)*. However, he added to these *(ensanguined)*, a clear allusion to *bloody, (fourfold expletive)* for emphasis, and *(sheol)*. This last was Hebrew for *hell,* and appeared in the Revised Version of the Old Testament that was in use in the late 19th century. But it was also a humorous slang word/euphemism for *hell,* appearing in *The Bulletin* and in various comic items in the press. Language was important to Furphy. The vulgar language of the novel, even or perhaps especially in disguised form, was essential to its style and to the manufacturing of a kind of 'bush' authenticity. Furphy was so concerned that the typists who were dealing with his manuscript before its publication would tidy up his language, he purchased a typewriter so that it could be typed under his watchful eye.[32]

Disguises and euphemisms arguably helped to make writing more playful and were a source of creativity in and of themselves. For example, *The Bulletin* imagined a bullock-driver exclaiming 'Pull, you blanketty dash asterisks … Pull, you slummocky fag ends of blanky creation.'[33] Henry Lawson, in his poem 'The Captain of the Push*' made extensive use of euphemisms, acknowledging in verse that he couldn't employ the 'real' language his character would use:

---

* *Push* is a term for a gang, especially of larrikins.

> And the language that he muttered I should scarcely like to
> tell
> (Stars! And notes of exclamation!! blank and dash will do as
> well).[34]

Australian popular writers through the late 19th and into the early 20th centuries varied in their use of almost always disguised bad language. For example, popular Australian writers Guy Boothby and Ada Cambridge used hardly any or none at all. Writers who aimed to focus on Australian rural life, or who focused on particular aspects of Australian history such as the convict period or bushranging, were much more likely to make use of bad language because of the popular associations between their subjects and profanity. Of course, their portrayal of characters as users of bad language only served to reinforce and amplify the association. Male writers generally had some licence to make use of bad language; it was much less acceptable for a female writer to do so. A variety of writers, then, brought bad language into print, and in the process helped to connect bad language to a distinctive Australian culture. We'll now take a look at a few of these.

Marcus Clarke (1846–1881) wrote about the language of both the city and the bush. While we'll take a look at the language of the city and its underworlds in the next chapter, here it is worth mentioning one of his most important cultural contributions: *For the Term of His Natural Life*. Clarke's famous book, first published under the title *His Natural Life*, appeared as a serial in the *Australian Journal*, a monthly magazine, from March 1870 to June 1872, and was then published in book form in 1875. The serial story about the travails of Richard Devine (who takes the name Rufus Dawes), as he is falsely accused of murder and sent to the Australian colonies as a convict, was enormously popular both in Australia and abroad.

His Natural Life is both melodramatic and sensationalist, depicting the horrors of penal servitude in Van Diemen's Land. Clarke makes some use of bad language, especially to highlight the 'evil' nature of the novel's main villains, although he does not necessarily always attribute it to convicts. Lieutenant (later Captain) Maurice Frere, the least likeable character next to the cannibal convict Gabbett, frequently swears. He is an inveterate user of *damned*, and Clarke frequently describes him as letting forth 'a succession of oaths'.[35] Another character who is a figure of authority in the colonies, Captain Burgess, Commandant at Port Arthur, is also depicted as fond of swearing. He is described as having a 'weakness for blasphemy, and was given to condemning the convicts' eyes and limbs with indiscriminate violence'.[36] He ends up being responsible for the death of the 'good' (that is, religious and moral) convict, Kirkland. In the book, convicts also make use of convict slang, such as *stow yer gaff*. And they use swear words, typically *damn*, which was disguised in early editions as *d—n*. The most prominent female convict character to feature in the book, Sarah Purfoy, is depicted as becoming corrupted with age. When she is encountered later in the story, Clarke writes that Sarah was middle-aged, 'and with it had come also that indescribable vulgarity of speech and manner which habitual absence of moral restraint never fails to produce'.[37]

Bad language was clearly linked to character in Clarke's book. For Clarke, convictism is an evil system that corrupts people, including figures of authority. The use of swear words was a sign of that corruption, if not its cause. Yet the sensationalist depictions of the violence and terror of the convict penal system were to be revelled in, and the allusion to swearing no doubt titillated readers. Stage adaptations, notably that by Alfred Dampier, also made use of some bad language, although such language was fairly limited. The strongest word to be found in a surviving script is *damn* ('d—d impudence'; 'Damn your impertinence!') but it is unknown whether the word was spoken on the stage or what kind of response there might have been to such a word being spoken aloud.[38]

While Clarke linked bad language to Australia's convict past and still connected it to ideas of morality, others who focused on contemporary bush life embraced bad language with much less moralising. Their subjects were the rural working men who were making Australia through a hard life on the land. Steele Rudd (Arthur Hoey Davis, 1868–1935) was one of the most popular Australian writers of the late 19th and early 20th centuries with Australian readers. His stories, notably the collection of stories *On Our Selection*, focused on farm life on a small tract of land, and featured 'Dad and Dave'. Rudd's stories were published in *The Bulletin* from 1895, with *On Our Selection* appearing in 1899. One critic observes that the speech of outback families is 'reproduced quite naturally as rough and ready'. A 1903 edition of *On Our Selection* includes, spelled out, words such as *damn* and *hell*. Dad is frequently exclaiming things such as 'damn your insolence' and 'you damned whelp'.[39] He also uses expressions such as 'curse you', 'well I'm blowed', 'by crikey', and 'by cripes'.[40] Notably, however, in the 1903 edition *bloody* is replaced with a dash, indicating its continued unacceptability in print through the turn of the century.

Journalist and short-story writer Price Warung (William Astley, 1855–1911), who often wrote about early Australia and convict life, also used a variety of swear words in disguised form in his writing. In one of his books, *Half-Crown Bob and Tales of the Riverine* (1898), the word *hell* was presented as 'h–ll', *damn* as 'd—n', and he made good use of the euphemistic *dashed*.[41] Elsewhere in the book, he used a dash but inserted *(bullockese)* after it, and also used *(bullockese)* and *(more bullockese)* as replacements for swear words. So, a sentence in one of his stories might appear as: 'He swore he would stoke the furnace with the (bullockese) carcasses of the (more bullockese) deck-hands!'[42]

Many of these books reinforced the use of bad language by and between men. It was (white) men who could get away with the use of bad language, and their use could be seen as humorous and expressive of positive Australian values (hard work, working in the bush, and so on). The writing of Rudd and Warung are typical examples of cultural works that reinforced this link.

Writers such as Clarke, Henry Lawson, Rolf Boldrewood and CJ Dennis (discussed later) were all very popular with many Australian readers.[43] But they also voraciously read overseas authors: Charles Dickens, Walter Scott, Jules Verne, Arthur Conan Doyle, H Rider Haggard, Zane Grey, and the popular romance writer Ethel M Dell were some of the most popular and widely read authors of the period 1890–1940.[44] Did these writers also use bad language? Some did, of course – notably those such as Grey, who wrote in a genre such as the Western – yet they did not tie bad language closely to an idea of national identity, as many of the Australian writers did.

By the end of the 19th century, Australian readers encountered a great deal of disguised profanity in the various novels and magazines they read, especially from the writers and genres most associated with stories about Australia. While the words were far more commonly disguised rather than reproduced in their original, uncensored form, it was often clear to the reader what the words were. Combined with the shift towards associating bad language with both humour and some kind of emerging 'Australianness', a range of words were beginning to become more acceptable as the 20th century dawned.

THE PROLIFERATION OF EUPHEMISMS

In an 1890 issue of the newspaper the *Australian Star*, in a regular column named the Western Sketch, a humorous story featured a character who, in order to prove to a prospective boss that he can swear (deemed necessary to the job), holds forth with a string of invective:

> Why, you tallow-chopped, pudding-faced, pumpkin-headed son of a salt sea cook, can I swear? Why you cord-jammed, dod-gasted, rotten-livered, blankety-blanked, ram-jammed, rotterdammed, amsterdammed, cramjammed, sanguinary ruddy, gore-blistered —.[45]

None of these words, save the final, censored, one was in fact a swear word. But the string of mostly made-up words in this story evoked the sense of a string of expletives. Popular writing had to be creative in how it communicated the nature and effect of swearing, and euphemisms were one way to do this.

Censorship in print – at this stage largely self-imposed – led to a whole range of colourful and creative replacements to complement the euphemisms already in common use. A variety of euphemisms are recorded as being in use in the Australian colonies from the middle of the 19th century. Numerous euphemisms disguised blasphemous curses. *Jesus* (as an exclamation) could be disguised as *Jimmy Jee* or *jings*. *Cripes*, *crimey* and *chrimes* all disguised *Christ* – but Christ's most popular replacement (and an exclamation that came to be popularly associated with Australians) was *crikey*, first recorded in Australia in 1835. Variants and elaborations on *crikey!* include *cricker!*, *crikes!*, *crikie jack!*, *holy crikey!* and *my crikey!*

Some euphemisms were so well entrenched in their use that they were mostly disconnected from the word(s) they originally derived from. *Crikey* is a good example of this, as are *strewth* and *blimey*. Evidence for the popularity of *strewth* proliferates from the 1890s, but its origins in the blasphemous exclamation *god's truth* (*gawdstruth*) is long forgotten and this was perhaps even the case in the 1890s. Similarly, the origin of *blimey* in *god blind me* (*gorblimey*) has long been obscured.

Bloody – by this period 'Australia's oath'[46] – produced a large number of euphemistic variants. These include *bally*, *bleeding*, *blessed*, *blimey*, *blinding*, *blurry* and *bully*. *Ruddy* could also substitute for *bloody*, and *gore-stained* alluded directly to the literal meaning of the word (stained with gore). In Britain, the word had strong class connotations and was generally avoided. After George Bernard Shaw's notorious use of *bloody* in his 1914 play *Pygmalion*, *Bernard Shaw* and *Pygmalion* were both used as substitutes for *bloody* ('not *Bernard Shaw* likely') and it became known as the *Shavian adjective*.[47] Euphemisms for *damned* include *blowed* (used from the 1840s) and *jiggered*; *damn* could be substituted with *hang*, and *damn it* with *blow it*. Euphemisms for *bastard* include *blankard*, first recorded in 1921.

Stronger words could also be found in disguised form, and a number of these can be traced in print more definitively from the period of the First World War onwards. *Bullswool* (first recorded in 1871), *bullsh* (1919), and *bulldust* (1923) are all Australian euphemisms for *bullshit**. Sexual words, including disguised ones, really only begin to make their way into print in any form during the 20th century, and so there were very few euphemisms for a word such as *fuck* in 19th-century popular print culture (although of course euphemisms for *damn!* could be read to express a similar

---

* Baker in *The Australian Language* (1945) also records a number of others, some of which may have evolved in this period, including *cowsh, heifer dust, bumfluff, bovril* and *alligator bull*.

sentiment). *Flaming* was in popular use and its origins may be as a disguise for *fucking*, but it could also have originated as an allusion to the flames of hell. *Flogging* was around from the 1920s onwards, and is more clearly a euphemism.* The backslang form of *fuck*, *kay-cuff*, is recorded in the *Sydney Sportsman* in 1900, marking a rare allusion to *fuck* in popular print in Australia in the period before the First World War.

Many of these euphemistic replacements became what is sometimes referred to as a 'mild swear word' or 'mild oath'. Mild oaths and curses can be traced in popular usage of this period, often appearing in print. These include oaths such as *strike me dead*, *strike him blind*, and *my kerlonial oath* – all of these were used by Henry Lawson. More obscure mild oaths and exclamations that were in (some) circulation in the colonies in the late 19th century include *dash my wigs!*, *my cabbage-tree!*, *Od's fish!* (from *God's flesh*), *Dicken!* and *my Jimmy!*

That such euphemisms had at least some spoken use is attested in an 1885 Australian etiquette manual that dedicated a section to what it called 'vulgar exclamations', with the warning that:

> No lady should make use of any feminine substitute for profanity. The woman who exclaims 'The Dickens!' or 'Mercy!' or 'Goodness!' when she is annoyed or astonished, is as vulgar in spirit, though perhaps not so regarded by society, as though she had used expressions which it would require but little stretch of the imagination to be regarded as profane.[48]

---

* Most euphemisms for *fuck* and *fucking* are recorded after the Second World War and include *fogging*, *frig* and *frigging*.

The advice proffered in *Australian Etiquette* reminds us that the tolerance extended to the male Australian swearer was not extended to women, who were expected to continue to display linguistic purity at all times.

AUSTRALIAN BASTARDS

The 'b-words', writes linguist Anna Wierzbicka, are stereotypically associated with Australia.[49] We have already observed the ubiquity of *bloody* in the 19th century, as well as the many 'b-euphemisms' that made their way into print if not spoken use. But here we take a closer look at a profanity, popular through the late 19th century and into the 20th century, and which also became strongly marked as being particularly Australian in its use through this period. It is another one of the 'four Bs': *bastard*.

Bastard has, in Australian English, been used both as an insult and an exclamation, could be used with affection, and has come to denote a certain quality of 'Australianness'. The *Australian National Dictionary* currently defines it as 'used variously of a person: sometimes derogatory (but without any suggestion of illegitimacy), frequently good-humoured, if sometimes edged'. *Bastard* continues to be used, although less so than once was the case. On the whole, though, *bastard* was never quite as unacceptable as *bloody*, and can be found in print in this period.

Bastard, in the sense of an illegitimate child, is an English term with a long history, first recorded in the 14th century, and borrowed from French. It appears as a term of abuse towards a person, especially males, from the 17th century and, by the 20th century, in a weaker form also directed at inanimate objects. Australians enthusiastically embraced *bastard* as a term of abuse, but as the *Australian National Dictionary* makes clear, it was also increasingly used in a good-humoured, even affectionate way. The word has, especially in its 'affectionate' sense, come to be particularly associated with Australian English. As an English writer observed in 1932 about Australia, 'If a man calls you a bastard, don't get sore – it don't mean nothing.'[50]

The first Australian evidence recorded for *bastard* as a term of abuse can be found in all its printed glory in a South Australian newspaper in 1872. The newspaper reported on an incident that had resulted in charges. A woman named Margaret Quin, wife of Laurence Quin, was charged with threatening to stone John Quin, her brother-in-law, and his children. John reported to the magistrate that he had encountered Laurence and Margaret on the way home from church. Margaret allegedly said to him: 'You blind, perjured, ninnyhammer,* have you a stone in your hand? You will die with a stone in your head. Go on you blind bastard.' It was reported that she had used other 'bad' language as well. But it was also reported that John had indeed threatened Margaret's life with a stone beforehand. Margaret denied ever using the terms 'ninnyhammer' or 'bastard'. The magistrate subsequently dismissed the case.[51]

The period of the 1890s solidified the place of *bastard* in Australian culture, with the term appearing in the pages of *The Bulletin*. Most notable perhaps was Henry Lawson's poem 'The Captain of the Push' which included the line (as spoken by the Captain): 'Here's the bleedin' push, me covey – here's a bastard from the bush'. In turn, a poem called 'The Bastard from the Bush' may have circulated, modelled on 'The Captain of the Push'. Its exact provenance is unknown although it has been attributed to Lawson; it has certainly enjoyed a long life in Australian bohemian circles.

---

*　The term *ninnyhammer* is an old English slang term (dating back to at least 1590) for a fool or a simpleton, but also could be used for someone being accused of being a cuckold.

'The Bastard from the Bush' was a much bawdier kind of poem that included words such as *fuck* ('Then he made the introduction, "Here's a covey from the bush / F[uck] me blind, he wants to join us, be a member of the Push!"').[52]

The increasing use of *bastard* in the first decade of the 20th century was noticed by those who disapproved of bad language. In 1907 one commentator complained that young men were far too fond of the 'vile accusation'. He saw it as highly offensive because of its suggestion of illegitimacy, but noted that the young men he complained of in fact argued that it was simply used out of habit 'without thought, intention, or belief of any such conditions attending the births of those to whom they apply it'.[53] By the time of the First World War, *bastard* was established as a term of affection as much as an insult in Australian English.

'LANGWIDGE', HUMOUR, AND SHIFTING ATTITUDES TO BAD LANGUAGE

Edwin Greenslade Murphy, writing under the name 'Dryblower', was a journalist, resident in Western Australia, who wrote for the Kalgoorlie *Sun* and Perth *Sunday Times*. He was well known for his satirical and humorous writing. His piece published in *The Sun* in 1903 was written as a response to an exchange in the Western Australian parliament in which the state's treasurer, James Gardiner, used the word *bloody* in a response to the auditor-general, Spencer. The poem replicated and commented on Gardiner's language:

> But Gardie, too, can swear as if
> His dray was in a muddy pool,
> Informing Spencer in a tiff
> He must not play the — fool.

The last verse emphasised Gardiner's attitude that 'all who dare to contradict / Can simply go to — hell'.[54] While the poem clearly was an attempt to lampoon the combative nature of the state's treasurer, it also used Gardiner's rough language to make a humorous point. The language was not used to shock the reader, only to emphasise how it reflected Gardiner's personality. The verse also celebrated Gardiner's language in some respects – his rivals' speech was described as 'flatulent and floody'. Notably, the use of 'floody, too' in the poem to rhyme with '— few', clearly emphasising to the reader that the disguised word used repeatedly in the poem was *bloody*.

Greenslade's poem drained bad language of its shock value and made it something more amusing than problematic. Many anecdotes and jokes around this period complemented *The Bulletin* and popular writers in shaping a culture that tolerated and celebrated bad language. One typical example is this 1894 joke:

> Scene, tram. Clergyman remonstrates with young Australian re his frequent and lurid blasphemy. 'Where on earth did you learn to swear so?' 'Learn it: I never learnt it – it's a (blanky) gift.'[55]

By the turn of the 20th century, humour, profanity and Australian-ness were coming together.

The use of the term *langwidge* to refer to swearing became common in the late 19th and early 20th centuries, and further reveals the humorous turn in discussions of bad language. While sometimes used in a quite straightforward way – for example, in press discussions of court cases – its use more often alluded to a comical pronunciation of the word *language*. Using the word *langwidge*, rather than 'blasphemy' or 'obscenity' for example, often lightened the tone of discussion and distanced such discussion from what might be considered 'chargeable' or socially unacceptable bad language. The term probably also intended to invoke a 'Cockney' pronunciation of the word *language*, something that was often used to suggest broad/working-class Australian accent and speech and used to much effect by a number of popular writers.

Alongside the normalising power of humour, by the second decade of the 20th century, there was considerable discussion in the press and elsewhere about what motivated the use of swear words, and whether there was really much cause to be overly concerned or outraged by them. Attitudes towards, and explanations of, bad language were beginning to shift. Popular culture depictions were important to this, but so were the emergence of psychological-style defences of swearing. These defences marked an important step in the evolution of discussions and understanding of bad language. A 1901 newspaper commentary was typical, arguing that the 'mental effect' of profanity was 'that of a pleasant feeling of relief from a painful stress'.[56] There is no real moral condemnation here, only an acknowledgement of the psychological efficacy of swearing.

A variety of similar defences and explanations for profanity were put forward in the early years of the 20th century. Some operated on the principle that there was no bad intent behind the use of bad language. In 1903 a discussion of swearing in Queensland acknowledged that people living in the bush had a 'voluminous vocabulary of expletives in common use'. But the author also asserted that such language was 'meaningless' and 'effective – especially when applied to a wayward horse or a lazy bullock team'. Any attempt to curtail swearing was likely to be doomed to failure, argued the writer, not least because it would be an affront to 'the liberty of the subject and a check to industrial enterprise'.[57] A 1910 defence condemned swearing as a 'bad habit' but thought there were reasons, 'even among the cultured', for its use: 'In the stress of the social round the harassed and annoyed man who has missed a train or ferry often finds the "langwidge" of Quakerdom quite inadequate.'[58] In 1913 a newspaper writer commented that '[i]f blasphemy is a crime, I am afraid that we are all more or less criminals. For who is there amongst free-tongued Australians who does not upon occasion find exercise for and relief in language which the unco' guid* might – possibly – call profane?'[59] All of these commentaries suggested that there were valid circumstances where swearing could be necessary.

The criminality of offensive language was also being questioned with more frequency than before. For example, a 1913 discussion of a case involving a man who was arrested and charged for saying 'Charlie Lindwall is the best [bloody] man of the family' prompted the writer to observe that '[bloody] is an oath, but it has no relation to indecency'.[60] And one commentator suggested that while 'foul language in the streets' was a 'wretched nuisance', it was better to leave it to 'the influences of education and culture rather than to those of the policeman and the magistrate'.[61] Defences of swearing, at least in certain circumstances and with reason, were now commonly to be found, and as we'll see later, the experience of the First World War would intensify the frequency of these kinds of explanations.

^ & * $

In 1908 *The Bulletin* ran a competition calling for a new national song for newly federated Australia. The writer CJ Dennis won it with 'The Austral-aise'. He later expanded his song from four

---

*   *Unco' guid* is a Scottish term referring to those who were very strict in morals and manners. It was famously used in a 1786 poem 'Address to the Unco Guid' by Robert Burns.

to seven stanzas. In the 1915 edition of *Backblocks Ballads* in which the poem was reprinted, Dennis acknowledged his debt to WT Goodge's 'The Great Australian Adjective' in writing 'The Austral-aise'. The poem/song proved to be enormously popular. Tipping a nod to the famous French national anthem (and revolutionary song) 'The Marseillaise' and sung to the tune of 'Onward Christian Soldiers', the poem has a — on just about every line. The 1915 edition also provided a note saying that one could replace the dash in your imagination with *blessed, blooming* or 'any other word … that suggests itself as suitable'. Here is a taste of it:

'Ow's the — nation
Goin' to ixpand
'Lest us — blokes an' coves
Lend a — 'and?
'Eave yer — apathy
Down a — chasm;
'Ump yer — burden with
Enthusi — -asm.*

Dennis, as we'll see later, brought together the popular masculine ethos of the bush with the larrikin life of the metropolis. We now turn to exploring the bad language of the city.

---

* The last line quoted here with its 'enthusi-bloody-asm' provides a good example of another feature of swearing that featured in the printed record: infixing or tmesis – placing *bloody* or another swear word (in a later period, *fucking* would be common), as an intensifier within another word. *Abso-bloody-lutely* and *fan-bloody-tastic* are common such usages in Australian English.

4

THE PERILS AND PROFANITY OF THE CITY

In his book *Town Life in Australia*, published in 1883, Richard Twopeny expressed concern about what he called 'Young Australia' who, he argued, made 'a specialty of swearing'. While he acknowledged that there was no bad intent behind it, the ubiquity of swearing did result, he believed, in a 'comparative want' of gentility in Australia.[1] If the late 19th century saw an emerging mythology of the bush inform a sense of an Australian identity, the reality of colonial Australia included a growing urban population, industrialisation, and the development of a commercial culture and a more modern and dynamic society. The city also shaped the Australian imagination, although it suffered from comparison with an increasingly idealised bush.

Swearing was intimately linked to the city, as much as the bush. But while the bullock-driver and the bushman could swear with justifiable reason and were celebrated in popular culture, such tolerance was rarely extended to the city swearer. Indeed, swearing in the city was a source of concern and anxiety, arguably bound up in the anxieties that marked attitudes towards the perils of urban life and, more broadly, concern about the rapid changes resulting from modernity.

THE LANGUAGE OF LARRIKINS

What we might think of as youth 'gangs' can be identified in Australia before the word *larrikin* came into use: for example, in the 1850s there were complaints made of the behaviour of the 'cabbage tree mob'. But it was the young ruffians known as larrikins who would prompt the greatest amount of anxiety on the part of 'respectable' Australia through the closing decades of the century.

The word 'larrikin' first appears in print in 1867 and was quickly taken up both to describe a particular phenomenon of youth behaviour, as well as used by these young people to describe themselves. It comes from the British dialect word *larrikin*, 'a mischievous or frolicsome youth', which in turn was formed from 'larking about'. A variety of collocations appear in print by the early 1870s: *larrikin class*, *larrikin element*, *larrikin mob* and *larrikin tribe*; the phenomenon of *larrikinism* was also identified and, from the later 1870s, *larrikinish* was used to denote a certain type of behaviour. The feminine form *larrikiness* was in use by 1871. As is clear from this lexical productivity, the culture of larrikins quickly became widespread in colonial Australia and was frequently discussed. While *larrikin* would shift to a more positive meaning largely as a result of the First World War, in the 19th century 'larrikinism' was nearly always negative in its connotations.[2]

What underpinned such a concern with youth? Firstly, there were the demographics. The number of young people in the Australian colonies swelled from the 1860s through to the 1890s. And most of them lived in fast-growing cities such as Sydney and Melbourne. Secondly, as historian Melissa Bellanta identifies, there was a link between larrikinism and the growth of unskilled labour during times of rapid economic change.[3] For many young working-class Australians, economic opportunity was limited and jobs (when they could find them) provided only limited satisfaction. The culture and community of larrikinism offered an escape from this. And then there is the appeal to the young of the larrikin culture itself. Larrikins developed their own distinctive urban youth culture that drew on popular culture forms such as vaudeville, and that placed value on 'flash' dress and performance.

The contemporary press reported extensively on the behaviour and culture of larrikins, often whipping up a kind of moral panic. Reporting on larrikins and larrikin 'pushes' (gangs) was often sensationalised, writes Bellanta, but as she also makes clear, violence *was* integral to larrikin culture and should not be overlooked or downplayed. This included both racial violence and violence towards women.[4]

When the press complained of larrikin behaviour, journalists often reported on the offensive language larrikins used. Much of the concern was about language used in public spaces. Larrikinism was a phenomenon closely associated with public space.[5] It was the fact of this behaviour (including language) happening in full view and earshot of 'respectable' members of the public that provoked particular moral outrage. Such behaviour threatened to make public areas places that respectable people could not venture into. An 1872 report on larrikins gathered on Brisbane Street in the centre of Launceston in northern Tasmania, for example, observed that their 'blasphemy and obscenity … would put proverbial Billingsgate* in the shade'. People, especially respectable women, feared to walk anywhere near there as a result, the paper reported.[6]

Descriptions of larrikins' bad language became a way to show how they differed from those who considered themselves

---

*   Billingsgate in London has a famous fish market that historically was notorious for its abusive language; the term *Billingsgate* was used to mean 'foul language, abuse', and is recorded in Francis Grose's 1785 *Dictionary of the Vulgar Tongue*.

respectable. Language was understood as a sign and symbol of larrikin contempt for authority, as well as their questionable moral
character. Perhaps, though, we can also read this language as a way
in which young people expressed resistance to the institutions that
oppressed them, especially in a world that offered them limited
opportunities for social advancement. Defiance of authority was
often clearly a significant part of the larrikin attitude: for example, one incident in Adelaide involved a group of young larrikins
who travelled to the house of prominent politician and business-
man Thomas Elder and assailed him with 'a disgusting torrent of
mingled blasphemy and obscenity'. When a constable showed up
to get them to stop, they 'appropriate[d] some of the choicest selec-
tions of their vocabulary for his special benefit'.[7] But while defiance
of authority was later embraced as a distinctively Australian virtue,
primarily due to the way this value was incorporated into the character of the First World War digger, late 19th-century descriptions
of larrikin defiance saw little to celebrate.

The speech of larrikins – and their culture generally – was a
source of fascination and discussion, as well as condemnation. One
writer described larrikin speech as a 'curious mixture of "loudness,"
blasphemy, lewdness, slang, and vulgarity'.[8] In another account,
the writer declared that 'in the whole course of my experiences
amongst sailors, navvies, shearers, diggers, and "knockabout" men,
I never heard such disgusting blasphemy [as that of larrikins] –
such a filthy prostitution of the English language'.[9] The typical
larrikin was seen to swear and use obscenity more effectively than
just about anybody, including the celebrated bullock-driver:

> In the matter of picturesque language the average Australian
> larrikin can hold his own against all comers. Let one of these
> lords of the street and terrors of the way get fairly anchored
> against a post at a street corner, and he can fire off more

lurrid [sic] profanity in ten minutes than any up-country bullock-driver could find use for in ten months and he does it all with an ease and abandon which proves him to be a past master at the business. There is no apparent straining after effect at all, but a terrible tonguester carefully holds up a post or a public house wall with his back, and lets out a torrent of oaths and general obscenity from one side of his dirty mouth, even filthier than the stream of vile tobacco juice which he squirts from the other.[10]

Another account echoed this comparison with the bullock-driver, writing that a larrikin's language was considered as being likely to 'excite the envy of an experienced bullock-driver'.[11] But unlike bullock-drivers, who were seen to contribute something to society through their hard work, there was not much to redeem or celebrate when it came to the larrikin, who was generally considered to be an idler. One writer bluntly labelled larrikin language 'the language of the scum'.[12]

Female larrikins were also described as users of bad language. Words used to describe their behaviour generally included 'brazen'.[13] As historian Leigh Straw notes, by virtue of keeping company with male larrikins, such women were automatically regarded as having loose morals.[14] Yet while popular depictions presented female larrikins in ways that questioned their morality and respectability, Bellanta suggests that we could consider larrikin girls as being even more transgressive of authority and respectability than larrikin boys.[15] They, more than male larrikins, were challenging the existing norms and standards of feminine respectability through their behaviour and speech.

We don't have much evidence of exactly what kinds of swear words larrikins used, although we can imagine that they would have made use of the full vocabulary around in colonial Australia, as well as the slang of the underworld (discussed below) that had at least some currency in this period. In terms of what was reported in the press, various newspapers mention the use of the 'sanguinary expletive', *bloody*, as well as what one writer described as the 'epithet … which questions the illegitimacy of their birth',[16] that is, *bastard*.

Larrikins also featured in popular culture. Writer Edward Dyson's *Fact'ry 'Ands* (1906), much of which had already been published in the pages of *The Bulletin*, depicted larrikin life in the city. Unlike many other writers of the period who focused on the bush, Dyson's book directed attention to the lives of working-class people who worked in factories; it was full of slang, and dialogue was rendered in the 'Cockney accent' style popularly used to depict an Australian working-class accent. His book includes expressions such as *pigs to you, strike me dead*, and euphemisms and mild curses such as *bloomin', struth, bally, blighted* and *blasted*. Insults include a man being called a *lyin' 'ound* [*hound*], and a woman *you pig's sister* and a *dirty stop-out*. Louis Stone's 1911 novel about larrikin life, *Jonah*, also employs much Australian vernacular, with some tame swear words appearing. Larrikin characters use words and expressions such as *my oath, gorblimey, strewth, bloomin', bastard, bitch* and *damned*.[17] Stone uses language to reflect the working-class identity of the characters, as well as their dubious morality.

Profanity was a part of larrikins' defiant performance, and their embracing of such language had the power to outrage those who believed they should be ashamed of their behaviour. One writer was particularly affronted that larrikins jokingly called their obscene language 'Bad French'; that they did so attests to the fact that larrikins regarded their language as an intrinsic part of their cultural performance.

There was a great deal of press devoted to discussing larrikins and their behaviour, as well as how to deal with them – 'despotism and a cowhide' was what one writer declared preferable.[18] South Australia was the first colony to introduce legislation to control them in 1872.[19] This law targeted boys under the age of 16 and included making the use of indecent language and the singing of obscene songs into chargeable offences. Western Australia passed a *Larrikin Act* in 1880 to deal with what it called the 'troublesome disease' of larrikinism.[20] New South Wales passed similar legislation in 1882, targeting boys under the age of 18, and making offences of 'profane' graffiti, vandalism, cruelty to animals, and indecent exposure, amongst other things.[21] Overall, during the 1880s and beyond, there was a concerted official effort to 'clean up the streets', deter loitering, and increase surveillance of 'undesirable' elements.[22] A process of 'disciplining' and 'ordering' public spaces was under way.

LANGUAGE AND THE CITY

Much of the discussion about larrikinism continued a tradition of concern about public spaces in the Australian city, and how they should be controlled and ordered. As we've just seen, criticisms of larrikins and their language were often related to the fact that 'decent people' could not walk the streets 'without having [their] ears filled with a mixture of blasphemy and obscenity'.[23] Bad language formed a pollution on the streets that threatened good order.

Through into the early 20th century, there was a simmering anxiety about the effect of bad language in public, what it was doing to colonial society, and what it revealed about that society. One Sydney commentator opined that the 'language of the streets grows ... worse and worse'. Compared to 20 or 30 years previously, he argued, it had changed from what he described as 'the comparatively "clean swear" of bygone days' to 'an unspeakably filthy form of gutter verbosity'. He urged those in authority – clergy, magistrates, schoolmasters and police – to do everything they could to 'suppress this lingual plague', and that punishment 'should be meted out to these offenders who seem to think that blasphemy and obscenity are indispensable twentieth century accomplishments'.[24]

Tied into this preoccupation with the 'language of the streets' was a persistent anxiety about vagrancy. Around the turn of the century, further vagrant laws were introduced to deal with what were then described as 'idle persons or vagabonds' considered a threat to good order and progress. Scholars have shown how 'vagrant' was a capacious label that could be used to target anyone considered to be potentially disruptive to public order.[25] Offences against public order, as Leigh Straw makes clear, were also tied into debates and anxieties around drunkenness, the containment of the sex trade, and ideas about respectability and citizenship.[26] Through vagrancy laws and public discourse, ordinary men, women and children came to be 'categorised, criminalised, and condemned'.[27]

Working-class women were often targets of these offences against public order. Crime historian Alana Piper and criminologist Victoria Nagy's study of female prisoners in Australia from 1860 to 1920 reveals that the bulk of women's offences were minor, often including 'disorderly, indecent or riotous behaviour' and obscene or abusive language.[28] Working-class women who engaged in drinking, riotous behaviour or sex work were seen to be transgressing particular norms about what was regarded as appropriate female behaviour.[29] As a result, the authorities surveilled working-class women especially closely, and often arrested and charged them. They also became subject to common depictions in the press that stereotyped them with the use of such descriptors as *undesirable, riotous, notorious, detested* and *dreadful*.

Women were thus especially likely to be condemned for bad public behaviour in ways that linked it to their character. For example, one woman was described by a newspaper as a 'termagant' and a 'virago' for screaming and swearing in the streets of Perth.[30] Targeting bad language was just one way to mark out people who the 'respectable' classes – those with social, economic and political power – wanted to control. Along with behaviours such as drunkenness, bad language was an audible marker of a lack of respectability, even depravity, and had to be silenced. This was a period where 'undesirables' found their lives subject to surveillance, discipline and intervention, even as they sought to use bad language to continue to defy authority and retain their agency.

Working-class women of this period suffered from the way they were depicted, but it is important to note that, as Alana Piper reminds us, women had some agency in all of this. For example, a distinctive drinking culture existed that helped to bond working-class women together socially.[31] This harks back to what we saw of the way the culture and community of The Rocks during the convict period provided a means of survival in a difficult world.

Yet despite the best efforts of the respectable classes to target particular social groups as bearing the most responsibility for bad language and behaviour, they could not entirely escape the charge that it was the colonies as a whole that suffered from the swearing habit. Some commentators argued that *all* Australians were guilty of using excessive bad language. One colonial commentator observed that the 'educated of the middle classes, and many of the upper classes' were just as likely to indulge 'in strong and sometimes blasphemous language', although he did qualify this by saying that this language 'never reaches the foul and disgusting level … attained by a great majority of the deserving poor and hard working men'.[32] Another commentator similarly lamented that bad language was 'a very fashionable vice in these enlightened days … daily uttered in the highest and the lowest places, from the Senate-house down to the tap-room'.[33] All of this reflected an underlying belief that

Australian society as a whole was somehow hopelessly degraded – it could not escape its convict origins. Such a belief, hinting at the ongoing anxieties of settler Australia, persisted alongside the emerging nationalist view that saw colonial society as stronger and more vigorous than that of the mother country.

WOWSERS, ALCOHOL, AND THE PROBLEM OF BAD LANGUAGE

A Salvation Army captain visiting the Australian colonies in 1896 observed that 'there was no more God-defying people in the world, for blasphemy and loose talk were used here to an alarming extent'. He reported that he 'had heard men swearing, children swearing, and – he would say it – ladies swearing. And not only were oaths heard amongst the working people, but the very fashionable might at times be heard cursing the Almighty who gave them breath.'[34] The colonies were thus still viewed by some as a 'hotbed' of bad language. If on the one hand this was starting to attract positive connotations in some quarters and in some popular depictions, there were many who continued to condemn such language, especially when used by the 'wrong' sort of swearer.

A variety of condemnations were made of swearing, often on the basis that it was tied to (public) drunkenness. The typical targets of such criticisms were the working and less 'respectable' classes whose drinking was far more likely to be in public spaces (including pubs) than the upper classes, who typically kept their drinking and other potentially problematic behaviours behind closed doors.[35] But it should be noted that the 'respectable' working class also carefully sought to distance itself from the 'less respectable'. They prized sobriety, cleanliness, the absence of bad language, and good moral character highly, in part because of the very precarity of their hard-won respectable status.[36] The ability to manage one's alcohol consumption was seen at the time as one of the 'great dividers between the respectable and the rough'.[37]

Many charges of offensive language were linked to excessive consumption of alcohol, as a quick survey and sampling of cases reported on in the press reveals. John Buchanan, under the influence of drink, assaulted the owner of a pub and 'made use of most obscene language'.[38] James Donovan was charged with both drunkenness and with using profane language the police magistrate characterised as a 'mixture of filthy obscenity and blasphemy'.[39] Another case involved a couple named John and Johanna Bruce, who were found on Dover Road 'using the most filthy language towards each other in a loud tone'. John Bruce claimed that he had been drinking, and expressed regret for his behaviour; Johanna Bruce had three previous convictions for drunkenness and obscene language.[40]

Bad language was often linked with alcohol consumption within broader public commentary on working-class habits, reinforcing this association in the public imagination. In 1885 one letter to the editor of a Brisbane newspaper complained about the people who came out of public houses 'mad with drink'. Fighting took place, and 'the oaths and filthy and blasphemous expressions could and must have been heard as far off as the dry dock, and nearly as far off, if not quite as the Victoria Bridge [Brisbane]'.[41] Another letter to the editor, this time to the Hobart *Mercury*, complained that the residents of West Hobart were being subjected to badly behaved drunks: 'the howling and screeching of drink-sodden women and men in a nearby house, and interlarded by strings of vile curses and hideously filthy blasphemy'. The letter-writer, who signed himself 'A Disgusted Property-Owner', called for more 'efficient police protection'.[42]

Religious condemnation of bad language was also common through the end of the 19th century and into the 20th, as there continued to be a strong moral connection drawn between sin and swearing, although this was slowly starting to shift. A 1909 advertisement for a talk at the Clifton Show Pavilion in Queensland's Darling Downs by the Church of Christ noted that the talk was dedicated to the topic of 'Obscene language, blasphemy, slanguage, filthy and suggestive talk condemned'. Families were invited to attend the talk, which was to be held on a Sunday evening.[43] In 1912 a newspaper reported that a Presbyterian minister, David B Hutchison, had recently delivered a sermon entitled 'A Dangerous Tongue', in which he condemned profanity, as well as gossiping, lying and saying unkind things. He argued that:

> The way to have a clean tongue is to have a clean heart, for no unclean thing can come from him whose heart is pure. Another dangerous tongue is the blasphemous tongue. It is a vulgar tongue because it shows evidences of lack of refinement. It is foolish, because it makes no speech better. He who uses blasphemy in his speech soon loses the respect of his fellow-men, because such a man is breaking one of the commandments.[44]

And in the same year, it was reported that a minister delivered a sermon condemning the consumption of alcohol because it caused men to use 'oaths, blasphemies and curses' around their children.[45] It was this connection between sin, drink and bad language that especially preoccupied moral reformers around the turn of the century.

The temperance movement had considerable popularity in Australia through the end of the 19th century, especially with middle-class Protestant women. The Women's Christian Temperance Union (WCTU), an American organisation that had a global reach, established itself in the Australian colonies in the 1880s.[46]

Temperance campaigners often focused on trying to remedy the behaviour of men who drank and who, as a result, compromised their family and work responsibilities.[47] Class status for these women was drawn from asserting moral values and emphasising character. Many scholars interpret the temperance movement as an attempt to impose middle-class values and ideology on the working classes, especially men, who were regarded as a threat to respectability.[48] Temperance campaigners had some notable legislative successes, including having the legal drinking age in Western Australia raised from 18 to 21 in 1923, and the introduction of six o'clock closing times for pubs in five states during and just after the First World War.[49]

For some Australians, including those who wrote for *The Bulletin* and tabloid sheets such as the Sydney *Truth*, these campaigners became figures of ridicule.[50] The use of the word *wowser*, likely coined by the editor of the Sydney *Truth* newspaper, John Norton, in 1899, helped to prevent temperance campaigners and others who were regarded as being 'publicly censorious of others and the pleasures they seek' being taken seriously. (There is a popular folk etymology that says *wowser* derives from the first letters of the slogan *we only want social evils righted* [or *removed*], but there is no early evidence that supports this; there is a possible origin in British dialect *wow* 'to whine; to grumble, to make complaint' but the Norton origin in an alliterative headline, 'Willoughby "wowsers" worried', seems more likely.[51]) Much of the early evidence for *wowser* is linked to the way such *wowsers* condemned the consumption of alcohol. CJ Dennis provided a witty definition in his *Backblock Ballads* (1918), defining the wowser as 'an ineffably pious person who mistakes this world for a penitentiary and himself for a warder; a kill-joy'.[52]

A number of words formed on *wowser* appear through the early 20th century, indicating its rise in popularity within the

Australian English vocabulary and within popular discourse. They include: *wowseress* (a female wowser, 1910), *wowserette* (a female wowser, 1910), *wowserine* (a female wowser, 1911), *wowserdom* (1906), *wowserish* (1906), *wowserism* (1904), *wowseristic* (1907), *wowserland* (1910), *wowserly* (1907), *wowsery* (1911), and *wowsey* (1903). The evolution of *wowser* into a core term in Australian English reveals something about the fact, discussed in the previous chapter, that the boisterous, rowdy behaviour of men was being elevated over a different, more moral and respectable, and perhaps most importantly, feminine popular identity and mythology for Australia.

RECORDING THE LANGUAGE OF THE CITY AND ITS UNDERWORLD

If Marcus Clarke is best known for his tale of convict days, he was also feted in his time for writing lurid depictions of city life. By the 1870s Australian cultural production was taking off. The bush might have captured the Australian imagination, but as cities grew, so did the number of authors who wrote about them. Writers sought to depict the horrors and delights (real and imagined) of the city. Marcus Clarke, who moved in Melbourne's literary bohemian circles, was one of these writers, writing about his home city at a time in which it was the fastest growing metropolis in the Australian colonies and one of the most dynamic in the British Empire.

In stories about Melbourne published in magazines such as the *Australasian*, Clarke listened out for and recorded the language of the city, especially its bohemian demi-monde. He dedicated one of his pieces to recording what he called Melbourne's 'language of bohemia', which he described as 'cant, slang, dog latin, thieves' latin, bastard French, mangled Hebrew, and spoiled Egyptian, [and] which forms the secret tongue of our fraternity'.[53] It was a 'hideous barbaric gabble … fast becoming a language peculiar to the city'.[54] Many of the terms included in Clarke's recording of this 'language of bohemia' are attested underworld terms: a thief was a *cracksman* or a *magsman*; to be flogged was to *nap the tease*; to be hanged was to be *topped, tucked up, turned up* or *stretched*; to be honest was to be *on the square*; and a 'turnkey' in a gaol was a *jigger dubber*.[55]

Most of the terms Clarke recorded can be traced in dictionaries of cant and slang, such as those of Francis Grose and James Hardy Vaux. How common these words actually were and how often they were used in 1870s Melbourne are unanswerable questions, as they are rarely recorded. Clarke enjoyed writing sensational stories. Nevertheless, we can assume that at least some slang and cant words were used and in circulation, both as remnants of the earlier flash language brought with the convicts (some of whom would have still been alive in the 1870s) and as words brought to the colonies with the diverse influx of people through the middle of the 19th century.

While the main preoccupation for many Australian writers in this period was the bush, some also depicted life in the city. Writers such as Clarke and crime novelist Fergus Hume, in books such as Hume's popular *The Mystery of a Hansom Cab* (1886), depicted a darker side of urban Australia. A murder mystery set in Melbourne, it made use of bad language, employing euphemisms such as *dashed* and *bloomin'*, and a few disguised swear words such as *G—* and *d—*.[56] It also explored issues around class divides in Melbourne, and showed how bad language could function to mark class identity. While most of the characters in the novel use the occasional curse word, it is one of the working-class, urban and melodramatic characters, Mother Guttersnipe, who is most closely associated with the use of bad language in the book.

The growth of the city, as well as the idea that urban centres bred subcultures of crime, prompted the creation of dictionaries that could record and translate the language of the underworld and its denizens. An interest in chronicling the distinctive language of Australia was also fed by the Australian cultural nationalism being developed through turn-of-the-century literary culture as discussed in the last chapter, as well as scholarly interests. Edward Ellis Morris, a professor of languages at the University of Melbourne, compiled and published *Austral English: A Dictionary of Australasian Words, Phrases and Usages* in 1888, the first serious lexicographical attempt to identify and record the various terms that made up Australian English. It included mostly flora- and fauna-related terms. There were no 'vulgar' words in *Austral English*, and only a very few slang terms. According to one source, the students of the University of Melbourne were so outraged at the absence of *bloody* in Morris's dictionary that they attended a degree ceremony where Morris got his doctorate of letters with one of them dressed in a gown and carrying a tome labelled 'The Great Australian Adjective'.[57]

Several other dictionaries produced in the Australian colonies at the end of the 19th century were focused on slang, much of it the slang of the city. The first Australian slang dictionary to appear in this period was the anonymous *The Sydney Slang Dictionary*, published in 1882. It was followed by Cornelius Crowe's *The Australian Slang Dictionary*, published in Melbourne in 1895. Both of these dictionaries consisted of mainly non-Australian terms, many of them borrowed from British collections of underworld slang. They can be considered as essentially lexicons of crime-related language.[58] Nevertheless, both reinforced a link between 'Australian-ness' and 'slang', as well as helping to shape and promote particular ideas about criminality.

While we don't know who authored *The Sydney Slang Dictionary*, we do know something about Cornelius Crowe. Crowe was born in Ireland in 1853, emigrated to Victoria in the 1870s, and joined the Victorian Police in 1880, where he worked until his retirement in 1897. Echoing his predecessor Vaux, his dictionary was, he claimed, part of his contribution to fighting corruption and crime.[59] By understanding the language of criminals, he believed, they could be better policed and brought to justice. He wrote in his preface to *The Australian Slang Dictionary*: 'My aim in compiling this small Dictionary is to place in the hands of the police and the public a work through which they may become conversant with the slang terms used by the rogue fraternity as a medium of communication with others … I trust the circulation of this work will have the desired effect of preventing criminals, rogues and gamblers from conversing with impunity in the presence of the police and public.'[60]

Both dictionaries of slang included many terms that were lurid, colourful expressions from the criminal underworld. Crowe's dictionary includes entries such as: *bummer* 'a loafer', *eye water* 'gin', *groggy* 'drunk', *Hell and Tommy* 'utter destruction', *knocker face* 'an ugly face', *muck snipe* 'the gambler who loses all he possesses', *off his onion* 'to be crazy, wrong in the head', *sauce box* 'an impertinent young person', *Venus' curse* 'venereal disease', and *yamoo* 'a low and degraded person'. Bad language is alluded to, but not openly included. *The Sydney Slang Dictionary* includes the term *antiscriptural* 'oaths, foul language'. Crowe includes entries for *Billingsgate* 'foul language', *slang* 'unauthorized vulgar language', and *unparliamentary* (or *unscriptural*) *language* 'language unfit for conversation'. Yet the only actual swear word included is *bloody*, which Crowe defines as 'a word used very often inadvertently by the uneducated'.

We can clearly track how such accounts of underworld language used it to stereotype women. This is true of many slang collections – they historically (and even today) include a variety of terms that objectify women or suggest something about a working-class woman's moral status and occupation. Moral judgements are often clearly passed in the included definitions. For example, *The Sydney Slang Dictionary* includes the word *mollisher*, defined as 'a low girl or woman', and adding 'generally a female cohabiting with a man who thieves'. Various terms for women considered to be sex workers or in some way immoral include *Nymphs du Pavé* 'streetwalkers', *troll and trollocks* 'idle women', *Jezebel* 'a loudly-dressed woman of doubtful character', and *cab moll* 'a low woman'. Other terms that were generally sexist include: *hay-bag* 'a common woman', *petticoat government* 'ruled by women', *rantipoll* 'a noisy, rude girl', *White Sergeant* 'a wife who controls her husband', and *drab* 'a vulgar woman'.

One other collection of Australian slang in this period is worth mentioning, gathered by AG Stephens and SE O'Brien. Stephens was born in 1865 in Toowoomba in southern Queensland, and became sub-editor of *The Bulletin* in 1893. He went on to be manager of Bulletin Publications in 1896, leaving that job in 1906 to work full-time on producing his own magazine, the *Bookfellow*. O'Brien was a freelance writer for *The Bulletin* from 1898 to 1907.[61] Both were keen to develop a distinctive national culture, and their compilation of a collection of slang (which they hoped would eventually find publication as a dictionary although it never did) was intended to contribute to this patriotic project. This endeavour was partly a response to the publication of Morris's *Austral English*, which they felt misrepresented what was unique about Australian English. Stephens believed the Australianness of Australian English was most evident in slang and colloquialisms.[62] Interestingly, however, scholarly analysis of their material concludes that while 90 per cent of their material is slang/colloquial, only 52 per cent is uniquely Australian.[63]

While Stephens and O'Brien sought to record an Australian

vocabulary to promote their vision of the Australian character as the typical knockabout bush worker, many of their terms record aspects of urban, as much as rural life. For example, they included terms such as *drum* a brothel, *pushite* 'a rough or larrikin', and *ram* 'a libertine or licentious man'. Reflecting *The Bulletin*'s preoccupation with condemning wowsers, they also include the derogatory *water-bag* for a teetotaller or temperance advocate.

The material collected in Stephens and O'Brien indicates both the general preoccupations of slang, such as the objectification of women, and particular aspects of late 19th-century Australian culture, such as the number of racially inflected slang terms (see below), and the way teetotallers were attacked. Aside from racist, sexist and homophobic terms, probably the most offensive term to appear in the collection is *suck-hole*, a variant of *suck-arse*, and used for someone considered to be a sycophant. Stephens and O'Brien gloss this word in fairly graphic terms: 'Workmen's epithet for a tale-bearer or informer who ingratiates himself with foreman or master by doing informing or other dirty work. "He would suck the boss's hole if he asked him to."'

LANGUAGE AND THE 'OTHER'

Slang dictionaries, as well as the popular culture and public discourse of late 19th- and early 20th-century Australia, provide us with clear evidence for the prevalence of racist and homophobic terms. Such language played an important role in shaping dominant views of those considered 'other' to white, heterosexual Australia. Racist language is a significant feature of the Australian English lexicon generally. But the language of turn-of-the-century Australia was particularly virulent in the way it stereotyped particular groups, boosted by the proliferation of a print culture that perpetuated, reproduced, and even coined a range of racial epithets and slurs. Stereotyping, argues historian Liz Conor, serves to 'generate expectations and beliefs about the characteristics of members of groups, groups designated by types'.[64] These types obscured the reality of the complex lives and identities of their targets, and perpetuated structures of inequality and discrimination.

Language plays a vital role in forming stereotypes that have power over people's lives, and hence it is important to understand the role that slurs and epithets have played historically. These terms are not discussed here to cause offence or trauma; but rather, as Conor argues in her examination of the stereotypes of Indigenous women that circulated in the 19th century and beyond, to provide 'potential to incite a reckoning'.[65] These words should shock and disturb us, at the very least reminding us of the insidious ways that discriminatory and offensive language have operated in the past to impact on people's lived experience.

The evolution of language that demonises the 'other' took place within a broader turn-of-the-century transnational culture that viewed the world through a prism of racial difference. It was also informed by more localised anxieties such as a desire to restrict non-British migration and keep Australia 'for the white man'. Fears of an 'Asian invasion' were particularly strong in Australia around the turn of the century and fostered racial panics.[66] Print played a central role in circulating ideas that stereotyped the racial other, with publications such as *The Bulletin* being particularly influential in this process.

Indigenous people were subjected to racism in many forms throughout this period, from violence (physical, sexual and psychological) to the effects of 'protection' policies that aimed to oversee and control Indigenous lives and that often involved segregation on reserves and missions, as well as the removal of children.[67] The speaking of English was often enforced, with many Indigenous people being unable to use their own languages. The extinction of many languages was one consequence of this. The result was often the loss of Country, traditions, culture and family.

Alongside a system of control and violence, many Indigenous people were the targets of a language that degraded them and reflected the oppression to which they were subject. Between 1880 and 1920, numerous racial slurs came into circulation, adding to a racialised vocabulary already in existence and that persisted well into the 20th century. Popular magazines such as *The Bulletin* played a significant role in both coining and reproducing this vocabulary, popularising racial discourses and understandings that had profound effects on Australian culture, as well as the lived experiences of Indigenous people. *The Bulletin* provides the first recorded evidence in 1906 for *Abo* for an Aboriginal person and is a major source of printed evidence for this word up to the First World War. It was perhaps first brought into usage through a column in the magazine *Aboriginalities* printed from 1887; the word's rapid rise to popularity probably not only reflected the racial prejudices of the period but also fit with the way Australian English was increasingly being understood as informal (and illustrated by the use of abbreviations). Another term commonly used in the 20th century, recorded first in 1914, was *boong*. Its origins are unclear; although some have speculated an origin in an Aboriginal language, there is no evidence to support this.

A variety of terms for an Indigenous woman as the object of a white man's sexual gratification were first recorded in the 1890s. They include *station gin*, *stud gin* and *fancy gin*. The white man in such circumstances could be called a *combo, squaw man, gin-shepherd, gin-banger, gin-boy, gin-masher, gin-stealer* or a *gin-burglar*. Many of these terms can be found in the pages of *The Bulletin*. Indigenous people with mixed parentage were referred to as *half-castes*, but also *piebalds, half-breeds* and *creamies*. These terms are deeply uncomfortable to read today, but they do expose the nature of Australian race relations in this period.

The real, lived impacts of such racist language are evident in the recollections of Muruwari man Jimmie Barker. As a young boy living on Brewarrina mission in the 1910s, he found that once he learned to read, what little reading material he had available was generally racist: 'Now that I was able to read I found that the *Bulletin* and newspapers were full of derogatory stories about blacks and "Jacky Jacky". Some of them were in the form of jokes, but the joke was always on Jacky, who never knew as much as the other fellows.'[68]

Indigenous people were not the only targets of racist and ethnic slurs in this period. Directly linked to perceptions of urban corruption was the proliferation of slurs used about Jewish people that connected them to money-lending. This drew on a much longer history of stereotypes in use in British English. Stephens and O'Brien include an entry in their collection of Australian slang for *Ikey Mo*, 'a nickname applied to the bookmaking/betting fraternity', to which they appended the note that in Australia 'the larger proportion of bookmakers is Jewish'. *Ikey-mo* was commonly used from the 1880s as a derogatory term for a Jewish person, as well as a term for a bookmaker, and probably popularised by a character of that name who appeared in a popular British comic strip featuring Ally Sloper (from 1867). The more general term *yid* was in use in Australia from at least the 1880s and was also recorded in Stephens and O'Brien.

Connected with anxieties about the nature of, and threats to, white Australia was the language used to stereotype the Chinese in Australia, some terms of which had their origins in the gold-rush period. There was a proliferation of terms for a Chinese person, well out of proportion to their actual population numbers. Chinese people in Australia were often depicted in the popular culture of the period as gamblers, drug addicts and sexual deviants.[69] Some of the terms used to stereotype Chinese people were not exclusively Australian, but were in popular use in the colonies to describe a population white colonists regarded as 'other' and culturally mysterious, and who spoke languages that most white Australians could not understand. The term *Celestial* (from *celestial empire* for China), in use in the Australian colonies from the 1830s, was also used in British and American English. *John Chinaman* and *Johnny*, used to describe a person from China, date to the early 1850s. *Mongolian* was first used in the Australian colonies for a person from China in 1857, with the first recorded use specifically likening the arrival of Chinese people in Australia to the Mongolian hordes. *Chinkie* was first recorded in 1872, *Chow* in 1876, and *Chink* in 1885.

Chinaman, a more generic term for a Chinese person in standard English, lent itself to several disparaging Australian phrases, including *Chinaman's trot*, a term for a type of shuffling gait seen as stereotypically Chinese and first recorded in 1867, and *(one) must have killed a Chinaman*, first recorded in 1893 and indicating bad luck. *Ah Cabbage* and *Ah Sin*, used for a Chinese person, were both recorded in *The Bulletin* in the late 19th century. Stephens and O'Brien also include the terms *yellow agony* and *yellow man* in their collection of Australian slang. One of the last of the many anti-Chinese slurs to enter Australian English is *pong*, first recorded in 1910. Probably coming from a conception that 'Pong' was a common Chinese surname, this word was frequently used in publications such as *Truth* and *The Bulletin*, and like the other terms already mentioned, reflected popular discussions around race and anxiety about a potential 'Asian invasion'. A real consequence of this kind of racist discourse – other than the way it reflected and enhanced discrimination towards Asian people on an everyday basis – was to push the newly created federal government towards its official White Australia policy through the introduction of the *Immigration Restriction Act* in 1901, building on various restrictive pieces of colonial legislation that had been introduced in the 1880s.

As Australian masculinity was increasingly coded as white (and ideally 'Anglo'), it was also coded as heterosexual. By the end of the 19th century, some writers were articulating concerns about the effects of homosexuality, not least because 'deviant' sexuality, as it was then constructed, was perceived as a threat to the white race. While many slurs and epithets for gay people would emerge through the 20th century, one of the most prominent within Australian usage was *poofter*. This word dates to at least the 1880s and is formed on the standard English *poof*. Our first recorded evidence is found in 1888 in a court deposition: 'Thompson said he Irvine was a pouffter. Some of them knew what a pouffter is.'[70] The word was in popular usage by the turn of the century as a slur against gay men, but also those perceived to be 'effeminate'. Stephens and O'Brien's manuscript includes an entry for *pouf, or poufter*, which they define as 'a sodomite or effeminate man'. They also record the entry *joey*, defined by them as 'an hermaphrodite or sodomite: applied generally to any foppish or effeminate young man'. *Joey* came up in an 1895 Sydney court case against a clerk accused of indecently assaulting two paperboys, indicating some currency for the term.[71] A few other terms for someone perceived to be effeminate are recorded in the late 19th and early 20th centuries. One of these is *gussie*, probably from the name *Augustus*, seen as stereotypically effeminate. Another is *tinkle-tinkle*, recorded during the First World War.[72] Such terms reveal a preoccupation around this time with threats to virile Australian masculinity, and underpin the formation of a homophobic public discourse that would last for the next century and continues today.

Finally, religious slurs were also a feature of this period of Australian history, although they are fewer in number and don't carry the same weight of prejudice as did the racial and homophobic slurs of the period. There were multiple humorous names for a clergyman in circulation, mostly popularised by *The Bulletin* (and probably not actually used in everyday speech), many of whose writers liked to mock religious authority. These include *doxology dumper*, *hymnslinger* and *scripture-tickler*. The Protestant–Catholic animosity, prevalent in Australia into the 20th century and reflecting middle-class Protestant hostility to working-class Catholicism (which crossed over into anti-Irish sentiment), was reflected in a number of derogatory terms for the respective faiths. In Australia, a Roman Catholic could be called a *tyke*, and a Protestant a *proddy* or *prod*.

BARRACKING AND BAD LANGUAGE

Sport developed apace through the second half of the 19th century, entrenching itself in the lives of many Australians who enthusiastically became both spectators and participants in a variety of sports, including boxing, horseracing, cricket and football (both rugby and Australian Rules football). Sport became an important part of Australian popular culture and social life; as such, bad language was perhaps inevitably associated with at least some sports.

Verbal violence quickly became a noticeable feature of playing and spectating in a number of Australian sports. It's striking that Australian English contains two commonly used terms for this kind of speech: *barracking*, which has been particularly associated with Australian Rules football, and more recently *sledging*, which has been connected to cricket. Australian sports culture reflected class and status divisions – for example, cricket was regarded as middle-class, while sports such as Australian Rules football were associated more with working-class culture.[73] Some sports, especially through the late 19th and early 20th centuries, were also linked to gambling and drinking. Alcohol could cause spectators to become rowdy, and to engage in fighting as well as bad language. Boxing, for example, was especially notorious as part of a distinctively male sub-culture and was seen to promote a culture of gambling and drinking.[74]

In terms of public commentary about bad language, certain sports seemed to attract particular notice. Horseracing attracted occasional criticism for the popularity of swearing by those who were members of the 'horsey fraternity'. In 1914 it was observed that Western Australian jockey Alfred Audas had 'let loose a sewer-like stream of lingual lechery on the surprised stewards'.[75] But the real problem in relation to horseracing in the public mind was linked to gambling, as those who gambled on the outcome of races were likely to swear if they won, but also if they lost. In 1894 the Methodist Church declared its objection to horseracing meetings, arguing that the 'associations of blasphemy, profanity and obscenity, which could not be avoided in the crowds that attended, the gambling in many forms which always took place, and the utter selfishness displayed in the desire to win someone else's money with no equivalent given for it, all tended to make the race carnival a place where no professing Christian or lover of his fellow man should be seen'.[76] One particular horse, Carbern, was noted in 1922 as having 'done nothing since except encourage punters to profanity' after winning his first race at age three.[77]

Australian Rules football seems to be the sport that drew the most commentary for its association with bad language, both on and off the field. *The Bulletin* reported in 1891 that some Ballarat Wesleyans were calling for leading football clubs to 'strike at the root' of the evils of betting and bad language so that Christians could attend football matches in good conscience.[78] A few years later, an account of a Bendigo football match called for the association to 'protect the public who attend the matches by putting down all bad language'. It also called for umpires to be protected, with 'obscene language on the field [being] worse than bodily injury'.[79] Another article complained of bad language at a football match being able to be heard by 'a lady at her fireside 200 yards away'.[80] And – the ultimate comparison – one complaint called bad language at the football 'the bullocking element'.[81] Numerous similar reports attest to complaints about bad language being used on the field – and some players even being disqualified altogether because of how they spoke to umpires.

Off the field, supporters could be just as enthusiastic in their use of robust language. The word *barracker* was first recorded in 1883, and by the end of the 19th century a culture of *barracking* was well entrenched in the colonies. Sports historian Matthew Klugman has traced the culture of barracking through the late 19th century and links it to larrikinism, insofar as both cultures resisted prevailing ideals of respectability.[82] As we can see, the language used to complain of barrackers echoed that used about larrikins: a commentator in 1899, for example, observed that the 'ears of respectable residents are polluted by the bad language and blasphemy which fill the air at Sunday football matches'.[83]

Importantly, Klugman's research also reveals the presence of female barrackers among the spectators. These women were often condemned in popular depictions as violent and cruel.[84] Their presence complicates any easy assumption that the domain of sports was male-only (and so a place where men could swear more freely) – women also operated within the culture of spectatorship and could participate in the use of vigorous language. But women paid a price for this, compromising their femininity and their reputation because of their transgressive behaviour.

By the early 20th century, the culture of the football field was also the subject of humour in publications such as *The Bulletin*.

Frank Henty, a *Bulletin* writer, composed a poem, 'The Blameless Game', about films of matches being shown in Melbourne. These films were of course silent, and so could not capture the soundtrack of a match, making them, in the words of the poet, 'the expurgated football game'. Henty wrote:

> Though dreadful noises blue the air
> When fagged-out, fumbling players catch
> It hot, wild language is not there
> At Melbourne's flicker football match.[85]

It is perhaps unsurprising that by 1910 publications such as *The Bulletin* had started to celebrate the language used in the domain of sport: it supported their vision of the typical Australian man as vigorous, masculine and tough.

Why did Australian Rules develop such a strong association with bad language? It is worth noting that Australian Rules was often identified as 'the Australian game' through the late 19th and into the early 20th century – it is possible that this influenced a perception of it as a sport more prone to bad language than others. There seems to be something of a reality behind this – many commentaries do suggest that Australian Rules involved bad language on and off the field, and this was perhaps prompted by the speed of the game and way it was played. As one commentator observed in 1905, there seemed to be many 'who thought that the frequent use of strong and abusive language was one of the rudiments of the Australian game'.[86] Australian Rules attracted an almost 'tribal' culture of spectating in Victoria – including women and young people – that quickly became entrenched. There was also a class element to this, as it was popular with the working classes. Hence it was seen as not only attracting those who might swear, but was subject to more criticism as a result.

Was the 'sports swearer' an acceptable swearer? Arguably, at this point in Australian history, not quite yet. The worlds of football barracking or horseracing were not generally considered to be respectable enough and they were not yet closely linked to a dominant Australian identity.

@&%$

The end of the 19th century and the first decades of the 20th century were a period of expansion for the Australian English vocabulary, as well as one of cultural creativity. The vocabularies of both swearing and discriminatory language increased, boosted by the growth in print culture. Both the bush swearer and the city swearer were features of Australian culture on the eve of the First World War. The war would bring together the two to create a new white, male Australian swearing type: the digger. As we'll see, the working-class culture of the larrikin would find legitimacy through the exploits of Australian soldiers and, fused with the mythology of the bush, would make bad language a marker of what would become the most celebrated figure of Australian history.

Chapter 5

THE FIRST WORLD WAR DIGGER
AND HIS BAD LANGUAGE

Joseph Beeston, a doctor who served with the Australian Army Medical Corps at Gallipoli, commented in 1916 that '[p]rofanity oozes from [the Australian Tommy] like music from a barrel organ'.[1] *All Abaht It*, a soldier magazine, described the 'Australian language' as having three very marked properties: 'forceful, expressive, and unprintable'.[2] And George Cuttriss, an army chaplain, writing in 1918, said of the Australian soldier's language: 'His language at times is not too choice. It is said that on occasions the outburst has been so hot that the water carts have been consumed in flames.'[3] The diggers of the First World War became renowned for their swearing, something that became an integral part of the way they performed their Australian identity, and a marker of their independence from, and contempt for, the constraints of military authority.

Profanity and coarse language had long been the preserve of the soldier's world, especially the infantry soldier, and was shared by the other English-speaking armies the Australians served alongside. But during the First World War, the Australians laid a particular claim to an informal and even a bad language that blended into their larger celebration of the 'larrikin' digger. The digger brought together the mythological qualities popularly associated with the bushman with those of the ordinary working-class bloke to create a new Australian masculine archetype. He would be celebrated, and his use of bad language – at least of the milder variety – would give it even greater legitimacy as something inherently Australian.

The war also provides us with a trove of sources for tracing everyday attitudes towards and habits of using bad language. If popular culture mythologised the digger who used bad language, soldiers themselves demonstrated their own, personal, and more mixed feelings about its use. The war therefore not only shows us how a mythology of Australian bad language was evolving, but also provides us with an invaluable snapshot of everyday attitudes towards bad language at a critical moment in the development of national identity.

SOLDIERS AND SWEARING

Encountering swearing as a soldier was unavoidable. For the young men who enlisted to serve during the First World War, profanity was an everyday feature of the new life they had been thrown into; it was also something that could bond soldiers together as 'mates'. If some of them hadn't previously indulged in much bad language, they would certainly find reason to swear during a bloody and brutal war.

Historian Peter Stanley describes the First AIF (Australian Imperial Force) as 'a hard, masculine world'.[4] A number of soldiers brought with them the rough language of the bush or the city, but others found such language confronting. Stanley McDowell, on first enlisting and finding himself in the Liverpool training camp in Sydney, described his tent-mates as '"good fellows" [who] swear something cruel and some of them have many other faults but still good fellows'.[5] After the men departed Australia for Egypt, they quickly gained a reputation for drinking, rioting and otherwise causing trouble. Some soldiers were less than impressed with their fellow servicemen. While in Egypt, Burford Sampson wrote in his diary about the Australian soldiers who had arrived before him. They were, he declared, 'booze maddened Australian larrikins' who used the 'most filthy language'. He thought them a disgrace.[6]

Various other comments by soldiers suggest that not all of them were keen on the prevalent swearing. JG Ridley, a religious man who regularly read the Bible and prayed (he would go on to serve as a chaplain in the Second World War), noted the 'filthy talk by chaps in the tent'.[7] He also disapproved of the 'vulgar songs' sung at a concert he attended in March 1919; he thought them 'very common' and 'a poor attempt at humour'.[8] William James Birch similarly complained about what he described as a 'disgusting concert party', saying that Australians 'appreciate clean wit on the stage'.[9] Eric Evans, a sergeant, also disapproved of the language he regularly heard during his service abroad. In his diary, he described walking into the sergeants' mess: 'I'm no prude, but the language in the sergeants' mess is obscene and filthy all the time, and many of the jokes are lewd. It does have its humorous side, though, and I am sometimes forced to laugh against my will. "Bastard" is included in virtually every sentence.'[10]

Yet swearing was a part of life in the army, and it was acknowledged as an unavoidable emotional response to the situation the men found themselves in. Evans described the men as swearing 'very loudly' in the trenches when everyone got wet in the rain, and again when they were forced to go on an eight-mile march with no break for the first five miles – 'the language and grumbling was shocking'.[11] Archie Barwick, when spending a freezing night on the Western Front in October 1916, wrote in his diary: 'You should have heard the language, but all the swearing never stopped the frost or cold so we just had to grin and bear it.'[12] In January

1917, he wrote again: 'I would not like to write what the boys said about the Hun, France and things in general unprintable. I know my own language was not of the best.'[13] William (Bill) Naughton wrote home after Bullecourt expressing that he wanted nothing more than to go home, feeling that he had done enough fighting: 'I don't think I'm exactly a squib but frig 'em I've done enough for the two of us'.[14]

While few of the accounts written by nurses make much mention of their feelings about bad language (or, indeed, their own use of it), there was definitely an awareness that 'strong language' was something that many of the men they cared for indulged in. One British nurse commented that 'strong language is often – in fact, nearly always, a strong man's outlet in times of severe pain, yet never once have I heard an oath from a suffering soldier … when a sister is present soldiers behave accordingly'. She went on to recount how one British soldier had been charged with using profane language in front of one of the nursing sisters.[15] This story suggests that while soldiers certainly used bad language, they recognised that social constraints remained and that they risked punishment for using bad language in the wrong context, and so censored themselves accordingly.

Soldiers undoubtedly also self-censored their own accounts, and their attempts at censoring their own bad language suggests some discomfort in admitting openly to the extent to which they used profanity. Even in the privacy of their diaries, soldiers sometimes disguised swear words. For example, Douglas Bruce Searle, travelling on the *Orsova* in September 1915, complained of a British soldier on board: 'One Tommy on board was actually trying to sell a pair of pyjamas he stole from the Hospital. This is a good example of a British soldier. They are b— rotters and I detest them.'[16] Letters home were more likely to avoid using bad language, because men were often writing to family, including mothers and sisters, or wives and girlfriends. Occasionally, though, soldiers did feel that it was acceptable to include a few profanities in a letter home, especially if writing to another man. In his description of fighting on Gallipoli, Captain Ted Fethers included both the words *bloody* and *bastard* in a letter home to his girlfriend's father. At the end of the letter, he instructed the father, 'don't read this letter to [the father's wife or daughter] as I have used a little language'.[17] Unusually, Sapper Gilbert Perry was prepared to at least reference bad language in a letter to his mother. In recounting a close call for a fellow soldier, he wrote: 'I bent over him, the better to see, and also to hear his profane language. I didn't mind the language, I enjoyed the very sound of life indicating words. The — got me.' (Perry's comrade was only grazed.)[18]

Bad language was considered something that distinguished the Australian men from the other troops, especially the British, and several soldiers commented on the bad language of the Australians without judgement, and even with some pride. Australian soldier Private Eion Campbell, discussing his experiences of Gallipoli, attested to the reputation of the Australians for their profanity, which he described as 'something to be remembered'. He recounted: 'The different attitudes of men towards shell fire was aptly described by an Indian soldier who explained that "shell came, Englishman duck down, Australian stand up, shake fist and say You b— b—".'[19] Another account of fighting on Gallipoli similarly marked out the Australians' distinctive use of bad language, again seen to be a marker of their fighting spirit. Sergeant Lawrence wrote in his diary: 'When the Turks charge they usually cry "Allah! Allah!" And our boys reply, "come on, you bastards, we'll give you Allah", and from the frequent use of this word the poor old Turk wants to know if "bastard" is one of our gods.'[20]

SWEARING AND SOLDIERS' OWN CULTURE

Soldiers took with them to war a popular culture made up of various elements including music hall song as well as a familiarity with the books and poetry of the bush. They read magazines such as *The Bulletin*, and popular novels by writers as varied as Nat Gould, who wrote about horseracing and boxing, and Marie Corelli, a British writer of sentimental, if slightly racy, romances. They were influenced by the bush poets, and later by writers popular during the war, such as CJ Dennis. Digger culture, expressed in songs and in magazines produced on troopships and in trenches, blended the popular culture of both bush and city to create something with its own distinctive Australian flavour.

Soldiers created a variety of rough and ready publications during the war, ranging from one-page hand-written sheets to more sophisticated magazines run off printing presses. They featured contributions by soldiers, some of whom were experienced writers, artists and journalists, and some of whom were amateurs. These magazines played an important role for the troops. Their purpose was 'to amuse, divert, and generally entertain their readers'.[21] They helped to cement bonds between soldiers, provided an outlet for the expression of minor grievances, and promoted the 'manly virtues and rugged independence of the citizen soldier'.[22] A sense of Australian identity was also cultivated through these publications, including Australian soldiers' tendency to express contempt for authority.[23] Folklore scholar Graham Seal describes trench culture as 'profoundly masculine, single-minded in the imperative to survive, violent, vulgar and savagely satirical. But it could also be sentimental, nostalgic and even "soft" or emotional.'[24] Troopship and trench magazines reflected – and refracted – these qualities.

Although swearing has been seen as 'integral to the oral discourse of the trenches', serious swearing doesn't appear in troopship and trench magazines.[25] Soldiers' magazines were often sent home to family and friends, and it was recognised that strong language would not be considered acceptable to appear in print or to be used outside of the closed world of the military. Yet we can trace the use of some disguised bad language through these publications. Some of the most common disguises to be found include *blanky*, *b—y*, *my b—y oath* and *bally*. All attest to soldiers' ubiquitous use of *bloody*. *Bastard*, usually just with letters excised rather than disguised through euphemism, is also frequently found. A piece of dialogue in the trench magazine *Aussie: The Australian Soldiers' Magazine*, produced on the Western Front in 1918, is typical: "'Ain't you the b[astard],' he said, 'that stole my b[lood]y dog up in Winton ten b[lood]y years ago?'"[26]

The *Kia Ora Coo-ee*, produced in the Middle East in 1918, also made use of a variety of euphemistic bad language. Such language most frequently appears within soldiers' dialogue, and included words such as *blazes*, *blooming*, *Gor' struth*, *damned*, *cripes* and *cow*. Written in 1918, the poem 'Going Home' captures the style of language often employed in these trench magazines:

What's that yer say? We're goin' home?
    What skitin' stunt's on now?
What blighter's puttin' that around? Some
    dirty, lyin' cow!
Yer say it's dinkum, Bill, ole boy, it's in the
    'Gyppo Mail'
Hi! walid, iggery, talaheen! I'll read this
    bloomin' tale!
Mafeesh faloush. Yer've got no chance of
    Malish! 'Ere! Sling yer 'ook.
It's worth a deener if it's tru, and Cripes!
    It is, Bill. Look!

They're sendin' all us old 'uns 'ome, if new
    'uns come or not!
Let's get inside the bivvy, Bill, the sun's
    too blindin' 'ot.[27]

Profanity could be used to illustrate and promote the soldiers' distinctive Australianness and masculinity. For example, bad language could be linked to their reputation as superior fighters. In the November 1915 edition of troopship magazine the *Expeditionary*, one amateur poet declared:

So just watch the blanky wires
And you'll find there's something doing when we get across
    the sea
We're the coots you've picked Australyer
And, strewth, we will not fail yer.[28]

Disguised bad language was most commonly used within humorous anecdotes and jokes. Humour was absolutely essential in the face of the horrors of war, and even in just coping with the daily difficulties of military life. It was 'one of the most powerful instruments of psychological and political resistance on the battlefield and on the home front'.[29] There are many examples of bad language used to humorous effect in trench and troopship magazines.

The Dardanelles Driveller, produced at Gallipoli, in a poem about 'Y' Beach included the lines: 'To call this thing a beach is stiff, / It's nothing but a b[loody] cliff. / Why beach?'[30] Some of this kind of verse echoed the style of *The Bulletin*, and even earlier popular depictions of cursing. In the *Kia Ora Coo-ee*, one poem about camels included the verse:

You splaw-footed cow,
You humpty backed freak!
Listen here now,
You lop-sided streak!!![31]

Although not actual profanity, this style of creative insult echoes Ned Kelly's Jerilderie Letter as well as the style of some bush anecdotes. Many humorous stories featured the voluble Australian soldier using bad language in response to his situation. For example, a story in *Aussie* featured a transport driver, negotiating a wet and slippery road one night, when a woman appears in the road before him. 'He stopped just in time to avoid running the woman down. When he got back his breath, he vomited three mouthfuls of the great Australian slanguage over the figure on the road.' There is no response, so he throws 'another collection of variegated slanguage over her'. There is still no response. It turns out it's a stone angel, put there by some of his mates.[32] Jokes often played on the Aussie soldier's distinctive attitude, expressed through their use of language:

Polite Frenchman: Bon soir, monsieur?
Aussie (misunderstanding): Bonza war, be blowed! It's the worst blanky war I've ever been to.[33]

Soldiers' songs provide us with further insight into the way bad language formed an essential part of their culture. Songs were central to soldier culture during the First World War, and many of them make reference to topics such as sex and alcohol, or were complaints about military life and hierarchy. They often had their origin in music hall, but variations of these, with obscene lyrics, proliferated during the war.[34]

Graham Seal suggests that most printed versions of soldiers' songs from the First World War were bowdlerised, with *bloody* being replaced with *ruddy*, *bally* or *blinking*, and *arse* with *grass*. While *fuck* and *cunt* were words undoubtedly used by soldiers, they were rarely alluded to in printed versions of songs, he argues; the relevant verses would be left out altogether or completely rewritten.[35] But it is possible to find some songs with such language, if excised, such as the famous 'Mademoiselle from Armentières'. In the version recorded in John Brophy and Eric Partridge's *Songs and Slang of the British Soldier 1914–1918*, they include the verse:

> Mademoiselle from Armenteers,
> > Parley-vous!
> Mademoiselle from Armenteers,
> > She hasn't been — for forty years,
> > Inky-pinky parley-vous.[36]

The missing word is clearly *fucked*. The song had enormous popularity across the English-speaking armies. Brophy and Partridge's version only includes one verse, and they include an editorial note explaining that there are many 'differing and vague collections of verses with the poor woman described as experiencing many vulgar mishaps, but we do not propose to print them here'.[37] Nevertheless, the songs they record in their collections, although censored, make clear that words such as *fuck*, *shit*, *balls*, *pissed* and *arse* were frequently a feature.

Few soldiers mention such songs in their letters or diaries, although there is the occasional reference. Arthur James Russell Davison records the following verse from 'a few of the ditties the boys sing in the trenches' in a 1916 letter home:

We are a ragtag Army
The ANZACs
We cannot shoot, we don't salute
What — use are we.[38]

This particular song captures not just the soldiers' use of profanity (the missing word could be *bloody* or *fucking*), but also the celebration, if ironic, of the Australian soldiers and their notorious lack of discipline within army culture.

MYTHOLOGISING THE DIGGER AND HIS BAD LANGUAGE

Soldiers' own culture helped to mythologise the digger's experience of the war, but so did the more officially produced accounts of the First AIF's exploits, especially those telling the story of the men who fought at Gallipoli. They were the original Anzacs and were turned into legendary warriors through the writing of men like CEW Bean, reporter and later official historian of the Australian contribution to the First World War.

Bean's *The Anzac Book* (1916) has been called 'the first real unveiling of the "official" literary portrait of the Digger'.[39] It was a bestseller, and had an enormous impact on the popular imagination.[40] Bean compiled it from contributions he received from soldiers at Gallipoli. He selected those that conveyed the more noble virtues of the soldiers and ignored some of the less valorous activities they engaged in. But he did include items that referred to soldiers' use of language, suggesting that mild swearing could potentially fit with the heroic, stoic image he wanted to create. Bad language (or its disguised forms) especially appeared in contributions that were humorous and those that drew on the style and tone of *The Bulletin*. For example, one entitled 'Anzac Dialogues' included words such as *blime* and *fair cow*, and another entitled 'The Dag' included *bloomin'*, *strike me* and *strike me pink*. Other contributions included disguised instances of *damn* and *bloody*. Another explicitly linked the soldier back to the now-mythic bullock-driver: 'Bang! Bang! Went a couple of bombs, followed by cries and shouts from Abdul, and above it all we were certain we heard fragments of language, of the category known in Australia as "bullocky".' Bean clearly did not feel that this kind of relatively tame bad language would tarnish his vision of an Anzac/digger identity – indeed, it could enhance it, although he was cautious in this, especially as time went on. His later writing often preferred to enhance the more ideal, proper 'Anzac' over the coarser 'digger'.

Oliver Hogue was a journalist before the war who enlisted and served at Gallipoli. He wrote numerous articles for the *Sydney Morning Herald* under the name 'Trooper Bluegum', that were then published in book form. His *Trooper Bluegum at the Dardanelles* (1916) also worked to elevate the Australian soldier into mythic status. While the book did not include explicit bad language, there were several allusions to the reputation of Australian soldiers as swearers. He noted that they were known as 'The Linguists', and '[s]ome of the British Tommies used to stand in awe when they heard an Australian bullock driver give vent to his feelings. I have even heard it said that a reputable Australian curate who went to the front in the ranks used the most disreputable language in charging a Turkish trench.'[41]

The work of CJ Dennis played a significant role in the ongoing evolution of the 'larrikin' digger. Dennis's *The Songs of a Sentimental Bloke* was published in 1915, sold 67 000 copies in its first year of publication,[42] and was even published in a special 'trench' edition with a cover that suggested that it could be sent to a soldier overseas. *Sentimental Bloke* does not deal with the war, but is the story of Bill, a larrikin, who seeks to win the heart of Doreen.

Dennis's biographer Philip Butterss argues that the Bloke brought into the city 'much of the ethos of the nineteenth-century bush legend, [and] values such as egalitarianism, mateship and anti-authoritarianism'.[43] The story of Bill proved to be enormously popular when it was published in 1915, the love story appealing in a period of wartime anxiety.[44] *Sentimental Bloke*'s appeal was also in part, Butterss argues, because the story downplayed divisions in Australian society – it acknowledged that class, sectarian and urban–rural divisions existed, but glossed over them in favour of a picture of unity.[45]

Sentimental Bloke is full of slang and depicts speech in the popular 'Cockney' style – for example, dropping 'g's, using *sez* for 'says', *bin* for 'been', and *fer* for 'for'. Dennis's book also included a glossary, a fact that suggests he did not expect all (or even most) of his readers to be familiar with all of the slang he used.* Examples include *gorspil-cove* for a minister, *book* for nose, *bit of fluff* for a woman, and *head over turkey* for head over heels, alongside more traditional Australianisms such as *cobber* and *bonzer*. There is little in Dennis's work that is actual profanity, but the ubiquity of slang was regarded as somewhat vulgar and uneducated in some quarters: some Australians recall that the working-class speech depicted by Dennis was not completely embraced in all middle-class households.[46] Important, however, was the way this style of language was nevertheless identified as uniquely and poetically Australian.

Sentimental Bloke turned the larrikin into a mythic figure, and with the successful sequel *The Moods of Ginger Mick* (1916) that took Bill's mate Mick to war, the digger was connected to a

---

* Arguably the fact of the glossary was intended to distance the reader from those he depicted – they were 'other' to the reader, thus suggesting the typical reader was not a user of that language, merely an observer.

powerful Australian cultural mythology. *Moods* was well received not only by the people at home in Australia, but also by the diggers, who were more than happy with the way Dennis depicted them.[47] As already mentioned, their own cultural productions called on his style, and *Aussie: The Australian Soldiers' Magazine* devoted several pages to a discussion of his work in 1918.

Throughout the war, numerous stories appeared in the press celebrating the Australian soldier, and they often included a character who made liberal use of profanity. Through such stories and jokes, the swearing larrikin digger became an entrenched cultural figure for Australian readers. In 1916, Brisbane newspaper *The Queenslander* reprinted a comic anecdote from *On the Anzac Trail* (a book authored by 'Anzac') that described soldiers at a Gallipoli concert party. A bomb was thrown by the Turkish forces that caused the music to stop, '[f]ollowed [by a] customary volley of blasphemy in backblocks Australian'. One of the diggers, described as a 'very profane Australian', was discovered at the bottom of a trench with one of his mates declaring that the unfortunate digger was 'full up of gramophone needles, if we only had a — record we could play a — tune on him!'[48]

Many of these stories, jokes and anecdotes played on the style of speech found in the work of writers such as CJ Dennis and made it that of the typical digger. The digger often used swearing to mock authority, as in the following humorous sketch that depicted a conversation, as overheard on a train, between 'an Anzac' and a 'pious patriot', quoted at length here. The Anzac merrily uses bad language, shocking the wowserish 'pious patriot':

> Anzac: We chased the — Boches outer the — village, an'
> gave the — pertickler 'ell before they 'ad time to —

Pious Patriot (severely): I – I really must protest against such terrible language being used in a public railway carriage.

Anzac (astonished): Eh? 'Terrible langwidge'? 'Oo's using terrible langwidge? I on'y said we chased the — Boches outer the — village, an' gave the — pertickler 'ell. There ain't nothink in that, is there, mate? (appealing to working man friend).

Friend: 'Corse there ain't nothink in it. Mild, I calls it.

Pious Patriot: It is shocking to find that you do not realise the horrible character of the words you use.

Anzac: Wot you don't seem ter realise, mister, is that I'm torkin' about the 'Uns. If you know a better name than '— Boches' for the 'Uns, I should like to 'ear it. An' if you'd ever seen a village wot theyd bin drove out of, I'd like to know wot you could call it but a — village.

Pious Patriot: But such epithets sound shocking and appalling to ears attuned to pure words and expression.

Anzac (impatiently): 'Ow can you use pure words and expressions w'en you're torkin' about the 'Uns? If you'd seen wot they've done, like wot I 'ave, you wouldn't be able to find swear words 'ot an' strong enough for 'em! P'raps you would 'ave liked me to say 'We drove the luvly Boches outer the charmin village an' put it across them proper.'

Pious Patriot: Oh, well, there may be some excuse for using vigorous language when speaking of our enemies and their atrocious deeds, but I'm sorry to say the use of bad language on all occasions is becoming characteristic of the Australian soldier.

Anzac: It ain't surprisin' – is it? Look wot 'e 'as to go through. A bit of 'ard swearin' now an' then is a sorter safety valve wot 'e lets orf steam with. 'E don't mean no 'arm by it. At 'ome or abroad, the soljer 'as to put up with wot would make a six-cylinder saint swear.[49]

The anecdote concludes with the Anzac mounting a common defence of swearing – that it is about letting off steam in the difficult and traumatic context of war. Readers at the time were encouraged to identify with the soldier, not the censorious critic.

JUSTIFYING THE DIGGERS' BAD LANGUAGE

The humour of Dennis, as well as that of many soldier magazines, and anecdotes, poems and jokes in the mainstream press of the period, all helped in shifting popular attitudes towards swearing and, more generally, slang. But while we can see the general acceptance if not celebration of the digger's larrikin style and language, there were also complaints made from some quarters about soldiers' bad language. The war stirred up vigorous discussion about soldiers' language. For example, one Adelaide newspaper complained in early 1918 about the 'foul, polluted, abominable and degrading language' of the training camps; interestingly, the language they complained of was that considered 'worse' than *bloody* and *damn*, which they believed to be acceptable.[50] But it was far more common for there to be at least some guarded defence of why soldiers needed to swear.

Chaplains tried to provide what they called 'wholesome entertainments' to distract soldiers from pursuing sex, drink and other problematic activities.[51] They often commented on the troops' bad language. Reverend Stacy Waddy, an army chaplain, after conducting a church service at the Liverpool training camp in Sydney, reported that he had preached to the men about their language, asking them whether they believed it was 'worthy of them'. If they thought it absolutely necessary, he told them, they should 'swear sensibly'. He complained of the narrowness of their profanity – they used only three swear words that were in his opinion 'meaningless, monotonous, and dirty' (he doesn't identify the words). They would, he suggested, be better off engaging in 'a bit of sound, intelligible, clean swearing'.[52] Indeed, the men should consider being more creative and original. 'Your Anglo-Saxon forefathers', he chastised them, 'would blush with shame at you trying to be angry spluttering out half a dozen words over and over again.' He even suggested a competition to find new words that would not be the 'language of the latrine' or 'degrading to the female sex'.[53]

Those who defended swearing argued that while the language of the soldiers might be bad, it was, as another chaplain argued, 'without offence or meaning'. A British collection of soldier songs and slang edited by John Brophy and Eric Partridge appeared in 1930. Partridge, a New Zealander, served in the First AIF, and was undoubtedly aware of bad language – he went on to become the foremost slang lexicographer of his day – but the 1930 edition, appearing at a time when print censorship was still active, shied away from including anything too explicitly offensive. Nevertheless, the editors provided a lengthy discussion of soldiers' bad language in their introduction. They argued that the conversation of soldiers 'was technically obscene in almost every sentence' but such words were 'mere intensives'. 'Ninety-nine times out of a hundred there was no thought in the soldier's mind of the literal and obscene meaning of the word upon his lips.' They acknowledged 'three very ugly words' around which 'almost all Army obscenity revolved' – these were *fuck*, *cunt* and *bugger*. The words are not printed, but there is enough information provided to identify them. The use of such swear words by soldiers, Brophy and Partridge argued, was related to 'the emotionalism, the danger of war, and the enforced absence of women's society'. Their discussion therefore vacillated between defending the use of bad language because of the context in which soldiers found themselves, and it therefore having no real intent, and a condemnation of it as 'ugly' and tending to 'coarsen and degrade'. They reflected further that if the war had 'slacken[ed] the inhibitions of speech', this was due to the 'degrading and brutalizing effects' of the war itself.[54]

While Brophy and Partridge wrote a sophisticated reflection on the nature of bad language in wartime well after the fact, many others provided variants of the same arguments during the war itself. Lieutenant H Bowden Fletcher, writing on the topic of war and religion for the *Methodist*, a religious newspaper published in Sydney, acknowledged the vices of soldiers including drinking, swearing and gambling, but also argued that this didn't mean they 'were doomed to everlasting torment as children of the devil'. He wasn't going to justify their behaviour, 'but would point out in passing that Billjim's swearing is not blasphemy, but purely a safety-valve, a rough one no doubt, but the conditions are certainly rough'.[55] He went on to lavishly praise the character of the fighting soldiers, thereby assuring readers of the soldiers' virtues. Another writer, who praised many of the qualities of 'Billzac', argued that his 'generous use of slang and "langwidge" is really due to ... [a] dislike of showing his true feelings'.[56]

RECORDING THE LANGUAGE OF THE DIGGERS

Two lexicons of Australian digger language appeared soon after the war and, unlike Brophy and Partridge's somewhat sanitised glossary of war words published in 1930 in Britain, they include a number of more explicit entries. WH Downing's *Digger Dialects* was published in 1919, and AG Pretty's 'Glossary of Slang and Peculiar Terms in Use in the AIF' was collected and compiled between 1921 and 1924 by the library staff at the Australian War Museum (now Australian War Memorial).[57] Both of these slang collections attest to the fact that not only was slang part of the soldiers' regular vocabulary but so was swearing.

Downing (1893–1965) served in the First AIF on the Western Front. When he returned to Australia, he wrote a memoir of his experience, but struggled to get it published. His prospective publisher, the Melbourne-based Lothian, not yet prepared to invest in his memoir, instead asked him if he would be willing to compile a glossary of AIF slang. Downing complied, completing it supposedly over a weekend. It was published in 1919. The collection was intended to be a collaborative affair. Lothian initially put out a call for returned men to assist Downing with the collection: 'All phrases and terms will be printed in their naked beauty. No attempt to suppress or to discriminate is being made. It is felt that "Digger Dialects" should be made as complete as possible. Those who don't like it can therefore leave it alone.'[58] Whether or not Downing in fact received contributions from fellow returned soldiers is unfortunately not revealed in the extant archival material.

Downing's introduction stated that the glossary was the product of a 'new national type' with a 'keen and vigorous mentality'. For him, the language of the soldiers showed Australian soldiers' inherent virility and strength. *Digger Dialects* includes the first recorded evidence for the abbreviated form of *bullshit*, *bullsh*, which he defines as '(1) insincerity; (2) an incorrect or insincere thing; (3) flattery; (4) praise'. He also includes a number of *fuck*-related terms: *f.a.* is defined as '(1) "Field artillery"; (2) "Fanny Adams", or "Sweet Fanny Adams" – nothing; vacuity'. Both *f.a.* and *Fanny Adams* are well-attested euphemisms for *fuck all*. Also included are *blow-to-fook*, defined as 'shatter to fragments', and *fooker* for 'an English private'. Another word that would have fallen well out of the bounds of acceptable language is *carksucker* (*cocksucker**) defined as 'an American soldier'. All of these terms played on pronunciation as a type of euphemism.

The *Sydney Morning Herald*'s review of *Digger Dialects* noted that the soldier 'has come home full of strange oaths and curious terms of speech. However, Mr Downing has taken pity on the civilian's ignorance, and compiled *Digger Dialects*.'[59] Contemporary reviews did not object to the inclusion of strong language, and one reviewer even suggested that the collection did not, despite its relative frankness, go as far as it could have. A review in *The Bayonet* (Melbourne) – a returned soldiers' magazine – from January 1919 commented that some of the terms in the collection 'have had to be toned down in order to allow them to appear in print, but the explanations given are near enough to the mark to refresh the memories of any of the Diggers who, having settled down to the humdrum methods of civilian life, may be forgetting some of the expressive phrases of the soldiering days'.[60]

AG Pretty's collection was compiled for the Australian War Museum around 1920–1921 – possibly it was intended to accompany Bean's *Official History* or simply as part of the Australian War

---

*   This word is first recorded in the *OED* in the 1880s in both the literal sense, 'a person who performs fellatio', and as a term for 'a stupid or obnoxious person'.

Museum's efforts to preserve what it could of the First AIF's wartime experience. It was never published.[61] Pretty's lexicon replicates a number of Downing's entries, including the ones just described. In a few instances, he elaborates on or varies the Downing gloss: for example, Downing includes *f.f.f.*, which he defines as 'completely miserable' and an abbreviation for 'forlorn, famished and far from home'; Pretty defines it as 'completely miserable; frigged, fucked, and far from home; forlorn, famished and far from home'. Downing includes *p.o.q.* defined as 'push off quick; go away', but Pretty's gloss for this entry clarifies that *p.o.q.* was an abbreviation of *piss off quickly*. Pretty also records the terms *f.o.q.* for *fuck off quickly* and *get well fucked*. The latter he defines as 'an exclamation expressing disgust and suggesting an unpleasant course of action to the person in question or a poor opinion of him'.

AFTER THE WAR

In 1919, a newspaper article headed 'Digger Yabber' talked about the way language had been affected by the war. The Australian soldier's speech had been transformed into a 'weird and wonderful thing', not just through the adoption of slang, but also because of the 'really well-done blasphemy' that coloured his speech.[62] The positive qualities associated with the digger had ensured that bad language (of the milder variety at least) shifted into the realms of acceptability. Language of the informal, colloquial and even profane sort could now be regarded as in some way quintessentially Australian.

The experience of war had justified the use of at least some profanity by soldiers. But despite the celebration of the larrikin digger, returned soldiers were not expected to continue using such language. The Australian press, for example, complained of a 'flood' of bad language after the war's end, and no longer believed that the 'safety-valve for the emotions' argument held up. 'The period of emotionalism has passed, and in the comparative calm which has succeeded it, men still employ the words which they used in the passions of war,' argued one newspaper. It had now, argued this writer, become a habit.[63] The main returned soldiers' organisation, the Returned Sailors and Soldiers Imperial League of Australia, rejected the notion that returned soldiers were in any way responsible for 'the present prevalence of obscenity, profanity and bad language'.[64] The issue was clearly contentious. Would bad language be considered acceptable if published in the books written about the war?

The interwar period saw a definite reaction against bad language, especially of the sexual and obscene kind, as we'll see in the next chapter. Censorship increased, and soldiers' writing would come to be censored, even as bad language was seen to be an authentic marker of the war experience. Literary novels written about the war thus provide us with some interesting perspectives on how soldiers' bad language was dealt with in the interwar period. A close examination of one novel about the First World War, Frederic Manning's *The Middle Parts of Fortune*, published in 1930 under the title *Her Privates We* in expurgated form, illustrates a kind of artistry in the work of disguising (and not disguising) the language of soldiers at war. In the expurgated edition, bad language is still conveyed as an essential feature of war but is dealt with carefully, in keeping with the censorship of the period.

Frederic Manning was Australian born, growing up in Sydney, but he lived most of his adult life in Britain. He joined the British Army late in 1915 (he was in his 30s at the time). He enlisted as a private but subsequently applied for officer training, eventually getting a commission. But he spent most of his time in the military in disgrace, due to excessive drinking. In 1916, Manning saw action at the front, fighting at the Somme.[65] He resigned his commission in January 1918 as a result of his infractions, and left the army.

Peter Davies, a British publisher who had served in the war, encouraged Manning to write *The Middle Parts of Fortune*.[66] *Her Privates We*, the expurgated version, was published under the pseudonym 'Private 19022' and the identity of the author kept secret. The mystery around who the author was helped to boost interest in the book, which appeared in the midst of the 'war books boom' that saw the publication of works such as Robert Graves' *Goodbye to All That* (1929), Erich Maria Remarque's *All Quiet on the Western Front* (1929), and Siegfried Sassoon's *Memoirs of an Infantry Officer* (1930).[67] While it was a fictional account of army life and fighting at the Somme, it was based very much on Manning's own experiences. The expurgated edition was a great success, and many critics felt that it was the 'first book to tell the truth from the common soldier's point of view'. By April 1930, over 15 000 copies had been sold.[68] An unexpurgated edition, published under the *Middle Parts* title, was available by private subscription in Britain.

Manning's book captures the language of soldiers, but a close comparison of the two editions can give us insight into the way expurgation functioned to obscure – but also to highlight – such language. Whoever attended to the editing of the expurgated version (and it's unclear if this was Manning himself, or, more likely, Peter Davies*) did so thoughtfully, with deliberate choices made in replacing 'bad' words.

Manning made liberal use of *fuck* and *fucking* in the unexpurgated *Middle Parts*. In the expurgated *Her Privates We*, some of

---

*   There is no clear evidence on this. The person responsible for replacing profanity (if not the author) remains, in literary history, obscure.

the *fucking*s are changed to *bloody*, and others to *blasted* or *bleedin'*. But most are changed to *mucking*. This disguise is a very thin one – while the use of *bloody*, *blasted* and *bleeding* were curses in their own right (and there were also original examples of the use of the word *bloody*), *muck* and *mucking* are not 'real' curses, but rather thinly veiled *fuck*s and *fucking*s. Replacements are carefully chosen: on the whole, it is more common for *muck* and *mucking* to be used in instances of greater importance – such as in the context of battle. Here the reader is to understand that combat requires strong language. In other contexts, it matters much less, and so *blasted* or *bloody* – which the reader would not easily identify as being changed without consulting the unexpurgated edition – can suffice.

Another commonly replaced word is *bugger* (used for a person), changed to *beggar* and occasionally *bleeder*. In British English, *bugger* was a strong word of abuse – by comparison, the word *bastard* is notably not replaced for the expurgated edition. Overall, only a few words are completely disguised by asterisks or a dash in the expurgated edition. One is *buggery* (for example, used in the phrase 'He told me to go to buggery, sir'), perhaps considered too hard to replace, and the other is a word in a sexual joke about a girl. The word deleted in *Her Privates We* is 'tight', not in itself offensive, but if it had remained, the joke would have been sexually suggestive.*

Despite the expurgation, *Her Privates We* still suggests much about the language of soldiers and while it is not as powerful as the unexpurgated edition, it makes the language of soldiers vivid and real to the reader. Indeed, explicit language can be considered vital

---

* The joke involved telling a tale of a girl who had gone to the outhouses with a man called Johnson. She asks Johnson to send for a doctor because she had had a fit; one of the other men says: 'a bloody tight fit, I suppose'. 'Tight' is deleted in *Her Privates We* and included in full in *Middle Parts*.

to the power of conveying not only the nature of life as a soldier but also to express the fear and horror of trench warfare. In this sense, it can be seen as not just about lending an air of authenticity to the war novel (because in fact not all soldiers would necessarily have spoken like this), but also functioning as an essential marker of the aesthetic of war writing in the 1930s and beyond.

We also see much bad language in use in Leonard Mann's *Flesh in Armour*. Privately published by Mann in Melbourne in 1932, this fictional account of a battalion's experiences through 1917 and 1918 on the Western Front and in London is often considered one of the finest of Australia's war novels. He enlisted in 1917 and saw service on the Western Front. Despite his powerful literary depiction of the war, Mann didn't find a publisher, hence why it was privately published, and despite positive reviews from a number of notable Australian critics, *Flesh in Armour* failed to gain much of a readership.

The book seeks to convey the full experience of war, including its coarseness and brutality. This included its language. As one reviewer, himself a veteran, commented, the book gets it right: 'idioms, jokes, prejudices, aspirations, brutalities – the very names and nicknames are racy of Australia'. But others found the book far too accurate in its depiction of the coarseness of army life, especially when it came to its frank depictions of sex.[69]

Mann's book undoubtedly gives us insight into the language of soldiers. Words such as *bloody, bastard* and *damn* are spelled out, and are shown to be commonly part of soldiers' speech. Yet a number of other words are excised, with the most likely 'missing' word in many instances being *fuck* or *fucking*. For example, when the men are told not to forget some shovels, they respond with '— the shovels', and in another instance, one soldier exclaims 'Orders! Orders! — the bloody — orders!' When two men argue, one says 'You, — you, you bastard!'[70] Bad language is not a source of humour in *Flesh in Armour*, rather, it is used to punctuate the realities and brutalities of war.

Not everyone was happy with this so-called 'realistic' depiction of soldiers in the publications of the 'war books boom'. The secretary of the Victorian RSL, for example, agreed with the criticism against these books levelled by British writer Ian Hay (author of war novel *The First Hundred Thousand*). He asserted that the diggers were 'just like anybody else – decent fellows in most cases', but the books depicted the men as 'degraded'.[71] Another critic argued that such books 'want us to believe that the average soldier was bestial, and devoid of all common sense', but he argued that the returned soldiers 'protested vigorously against this parody and libel of the average soldier'. '[T]his type of novel' needed to be 'finished'. 'The theme has been overworked, and we are tired of hearing only this side of the war.'[72]

$#@*

The work of Frederic Manning and Leonard Mann indicates an attempt in both Britain and Australia in the interwar period to use bad – and especially frank – language to depict the realities of war. It was used as a marker of authenticity. But stripped of its humour and having moved into a stronger category of profanity that reflected sexual and bodily functions, it became far less acceptable than the humorous *bloody* of the wartime digger. *Bloody* was now mostly legitimate, if not entirely respectable, and authentically Australian, a sign of the diggers thumbing their nose at authority, but *fuck*, if beginning to become visible in print, was still to be censored as much as possible. If the First World War saw the creation of the digger as a new and acceptable form of the Australian larrikin, the dark underside of that character still lurked not that far beneath the surface. The swearing digger's legitimacy had its limits, and the interwar period in Australia would be marked by a growing obsession with censoring the obscene.

PART THREE

CENSORING AND LIBERATING
BAD LANGUAGE, 1920–1980

6

CENSORSHIP, CONTROL AND BAD LANGUAGE

In 1948, an Adelaide newspaper commented on the importance of the state in controlling the 'poison [that] comes chiefly through the ears and the eyes'. This should be done through 'repress[ing] and punish[ing] obscene and filthy talk', and prohibiting 'indecent behavior, indecent pictures, indecent books and papers'. This was, the writer argued, a 'Pure Food Act for what ear and eye consume, lest individuals be destroyed by septic sights and septic words whether spoken or written'.[1]

The tradition around bad language concerned with respectability and propriety morphed in the period following the First World War into a preoccupation with the obscene, shared with Britain and the USA but stronger in Australia. From a concern with swear words that were largely derived from religious taboos (*bloody* and *damn*), the new bad language that came under scrutiny was that of bodily functions (*fuck* and *shit*). Historians identify what they call a 'quarantined culture' that evolved through these years.[2] Australians were kept culturally isolated through both censorship and a more general rejection of cultural, social and political influences (often regarded as 'foreign') that might corrupt them. Modernist culture especially inspired misgivings, and print was a prime target in all of this, viewed with particular suspicion because people tended to enjoy it in private. Obscenity – particularly anything sexual and including obscene language – was seen as a threat.

As a consequence, a regime of censorship would last until the end of the 1960s.

The other tradition around bad language, the one that celebrated its use as a source of humour, manliness and Australianness, did not disappear through these decades. Mild swear words such as *bloody* continued to be normalised, and to be even more closely linked to what it meant to be Australian. Indeed, so powerful was this idea of Australianness that the so-called 'New Australians' – postwar European migrants – would be required to become familiar with the swear words and colloquialisms of Australia if they wished to belong.

Australia's reputation as a swearing nation – at least when it came to mild swear words – was still secure, despite the state's attempt to stamp out the obscene, as suggested by a 1964 case in which a Coffs Harbour magistrate fined a man for using the word *bloody* in a public place. By the mid-1960s the notion that *bloody* could really be offensive was not very credible, and so the incident garnered international commentary. Eric Partridge, by then the world's foremost English slang lexicographer, declared the magistrate to be 'out of date linguistically'. *Bloody* was, he said dismissively, a 'second-rate swearword' and 'certainly no longer an indecent word'. A British peer, Lord Boothby, also weighed in on the case: 'They'll never stop swearing in Australia – they swear like hell.'[3]

KEEPING OBSCENE WORDS OUT

Prior to the 1920s, there was little formal censorship of print in Australia. State Customs seized some imported books – authors targeted included French writers Émile Zola and Guy de Maupassant – in the 1880s. Their books, such as Zola's *Thérèse Raquin* and Maupassant's *A Woman's Life*, were considered lewd, indecent and immoral.[4] Such literature was characterised in the press as the 'deadly infection of French literary vice'.[5] There was also a range of colonial obscenity laws in place that gave the police power to enter premises suspected of housing indecent literature and to seize it.[6] But censorship was intermittent, and there was no clear understanding of what exactly constituted the 'obscene'.

The 20th century brought with it a new preoccupation with objectionable literature and the construction of a much more elaborate censorship regime, starting in the interwar period. Literary scholar Nicole Moore, who has written extensively about Australian literary censorship, suggests that Australia was one of the strongest censors in the Western world.[7]

Most reading material came into Australia from overseas, and Customs had the greatest power to seize material and so prohibit its circulation. But there were other mechanisms that prevented certain printed material from circulating within Australia, including police powers, postal regulation, and the use of legislation such as the Public Health Acts, and Theatre and Public Halls Acts. A Literary Censorship Board was established in 1933, with representatives from both the literary and legal worlds sitting on it, that provided advice to Customs and to government as to what should and should not be banned.[8]

Much of this censorship was concerned with sex, religion, and to a lesser extent, political subversion (especially Bolshevism and communism), and censorship was often framed around the need to protect Australia's 'purity'.[9] Anxiety over issues such as abortion, homosexuality, promiscuity and atheism, among others, inspired censorship as a possible solution to the threat they posed. Customs defined 'indecency' as '(a) offensive to common propriety or adjudged to be subversive of morality; offending modesty or delicacy; unfit to be seen or heard; immodest; grossly obscene; (b) contrary to what is fit and proper; unbecoming'.[10] But defining what was, for example, offensive to 'modesty or delicacy' was clearly open to interpretation, and many things could be considered indecent.

As Moore argues, the real aim of censorship was to maintain certain political or religious interests, and reinforce particular social divisions and hierarchies.[11] In other words, censorship was all about those in power making decisions about what was or was not acceptable to them, and preventing anything considered to be critical and/or subversive of their power. Such censorship had real impacts: it could severely limit the knowledge that people had access to, for example, around sexuality and birth control.

By the 1920s, Australians were consuming about 3.5 million imported books annually.[12] But many titles were prevented from circulating in Australia as a result of increasing censorship regulation. A lot of them were censored for their depictions of sexuality. Banned books included Radclyffe Hall's *The Well of Loneliness* (1928), a novel with a lesbian theme and banned in Australia in 1929; James Joyce's *Ulysses* (1922); Ernest Hemingway's *A Farewell to Arms* (1929); and DH Lawrence's notorious *Lady Chatterley's Lover* (1928). Some Australian writers published by overseas publishers found their works excluded from their own country by being stopped from import. For example, Norman Lindsay's *Redheap* (1930) was banned from Australia, with one critic arguing that the book, which dealt with a young man's sexuality and included an abortion scene, 'wallow[ed] in dirt'.[13]

Profanity was sometimes a significant part of the reasoning behind a book's suppression, but usually when other objectionable elements also existed. For example, British author Norah James's book, *Sleeveless Errand* (1929), contained over 30 instances of the word *bloody* and over 60 of *damn*. But it also included references to homosexuality, and so was banned in both Britain and Australia (although not in the USA, where the language was modified).[14]

Blasphemy, in the sense of disrespecting God and/or religion, was of some concern in all this. Aldous Huxley's *Brave New World* (1932) was banned in Australia from 1932 until 1937, with a particular objection being the use of 'Ford' as a deity (and hence a substitute for 'Lord'). Religious organisations called for authorities to ban the book, arguing that the novel depicted contempt for God, as well as promoting promiscuity.[15]

The interwar decades thus saw a great deal of important modern literature prevented from circulating in Australia (some of these books could still be obtained through various means, but it was generally very difficult to do so). Such censorship imposed a kind of cultural quarantine on Australia, impoverishing the artistic and cultural landscape as a result. While language was only one element of what exercised censors, it was clearly closely intertwined with the concerns that so often threatened authority: 'aberrant' sexuality, radical politics, hostility to religion, and contempt for what was considered to be respectable.

WAR, LANGUAGE AND CENSORSHIP

The Second World War brought a new generation of Australians into the services and revived the idea of the swearing soldier. In a culture of censorship, how much of his real language would be permitted?

Swearing was to be expected in the services to at least some extent, and, as in the First World War, such language was a source of humour. In 1941 a poem written by John Barr was printed in a Sydney newspaper under the title 'The Eloquent AIF'. It mocked the fact that the Chief Secretary of New South Wales, Alwyn Tonking, had railed against the use of bad language by the Second AIF:

Boy, when you're in the fighting force,
On campaigns as they've planned 'em,
Pray, leave behind expressions coarse,
For Mister Tonking's banned 'em –

...

Still, there are times when slips are made
By cooks (who're weak and flaccid).
They curse and swear at things mislaid
In diction far from placid.
Thus, one used langwidge awful sour;

...

Beware such lapses, worthy son;
In AIF they are not done.[16]

The Second World War years also saw some discussion of bad language in the press. When in 1943 *Salt*, the regular magazine of the Australian Army Education Service, quoted a Ninth Division corporal saying that he wanted a 'chance to get stuck into these Jap bastards', another digger wrote to the magazine to object to the use of the word *bastard*. He argued that: 'We all use it at battle stations. That is unavoidable. When we come down here on leave or to our families we try to get away from it. There is a difference between the spoken and the printed word. A dash would have conveyed to us just as well what the Ninth Division corporal meant.'[17] But this opinion was not taken to represent that of the average fighting man. *Salt* replied that the magazine was printed for the services, and that this was what the man had actually said and so they made no apology for using the word. There was similarly quite a bit of discussion in the Australian press over the incident, but mostly the use of the word received reasonable sanction. Perhaps this was because it was directed at the Japanese: *Salt* censored *bastard* in a subsequent issue when it was used in a poem and did not refer to the enemy.[18]

Yet public debate could hardly convey the realities of swearing in the services that, as in the First World War, was robust and obscene. The war's official historian Gavin Long compiled a collection of war words, assisted by Major Alec Hill, who served in both North Africa and New Guinea (and later became a military historian and biographer). Included in their wordlists are several uses of *fuck*. Although disguised with dashes in their manuscript, there is a lengthy entry explaining that the word is 'used frequently, almost invariably in the adjectival form' and recording the personal observation '[t]he other day I heard "Come and get it!", the cry of the company cook, converted to "Come and f[uck]in' get it!"' They also included *fuck all*, *fuck off*, *fuck about* and *fucked* in their lists. Other terms in the collection with varying levels of vulgarity include *browned off*, *balls*, *bore it up them* and *rooted*.[19]

Services culture revelled in the sexual and obscene, as revealed in *Mess Songs and Rhymes of the RAAF 1939–45*, a privately published collection produced in New Guinea in September 1945. The bawdy ditties that appear in this collection attest to both the obscene language and the preoccupation with sex that undoubtedly featured strongly in the lives of many servicemen. One stanza of the song 'Poor Blind Nell' conveys the strength of the obscenity:

He shagged her till his prick was sore,
And balls as black as charcoal,
And did he marry poor blind Nell?
He did, Pig's Fucking Arsehole![20]

Post–Second World War novels about the war made much use of disguised strong language, both as a reflection of life in the services, as well as to convey the experience of war and battle. American novels led the way here. James Jones's *From Here to Eternity* (1951) contained 50 disguised instances of *fuck*; Norman Mailer's *The*

Naked and the Dead (1948) substituted the thinly disguised *fug* for *fuck*, and included *mother-fuggin'*. Such books continued a trend for the word *fuck* to be seen in print, even if in barely disguised fashion. A variety of substitute *fuck*s came into greater currency as a result, including *fog* and the more popular *frig*.

But obscene language, even in the context of war, was still subject to censure in Australia, indicating that acceptance of bad language was fitful rather than progressive. Lawson Glassop's war novel *We Were the Rats* was published by Australian publisher Angus and Robertson in 1944. It sold 11 000 copies before being banned in 1946, when the author and publisher were put on trial for obscenity. Unlike many of the books then banned, which were imported and often by overseas authors, Glassop's account of a soldier's experience in the Second AIF and during the siege of Tobruk laid claim to being authentically 'Australian'.[21] The novel follows the story of a young man, Mick, who enlists to fight, falls in love, experiences military service, and sees action in North Africa.

Glassop's novel uses both Australian slang and strong language to convey something of the 'Australianness' of the soldiers and to convey an authenticity about military life. While explicit language in *We Were the Rats* is disguised, it is easy to decode. The men are depicted as regular swearers. Written in the first person from Mick's perspective, he describes what he hears on his first night in the barracks:

> I have never heard such sustained abuse. 'Go and get —, you bastard!' 'You rotten old —, go back to — bed!', 'The old codger's mad', 'Get —, it's the middle of the — night', 'You're not still workin' in the — mine', and 'You might've won the M.M. and D.C.M. in the last — war, but by Christ, you won't live to get to this bloody one'.[22]

Bastard and *bugger* are liberally used throughout the book in full – disguised words include *fuck*, *fucking*, and *fucked*, as well as in a few instances *shit*, *piss* and *balls*.

Glassop uses language to make his depiction of army life authentic, but the story also suggests that Mick, while not exactly shocked by the bad language he hears, recognises the coarsening effect of military life. For example, in another passage in the novel, Mick and his mates encounter a sex worker in Cairo:

> '—?', she asked, with devastating candour. It was the old word again, the word C.O.s had tried to stamp out in Australia, Palestine and Tobruk. It was the ugliest word in the world. I recoiled, for I had never heard a woman say it before. '—?', she asked again. 'No? Well — off' and she laughed a wild, high-pitched laugh. Most of the soldiers laughed. We soon learned that it was one of their stock jokes, like their use of an Arabic expression which ordered you to do something physically impossible.[23]

During the obscenity trial, the prosecution used several passages as evidence, including several stanzas from the poem 'The Bastard from the Bush' that appeared in the book. This poem, a folk version of 'Captain of the Push' (discussed in chapter 3), liberally uses words such as *fuck*. The other material the prosecution used to argue obscenity is a short chapter describing the men reading 'perv books', with one of them reading out erotic passages to the others.

The trial found against the book, provoking outrage in some quarters. The acting president of the New South Wales RSL called the decision against the novel the 'height of absurdity'.[24] Indeed, the kind of language Glassop used was, as we've seen in the collection of soldiers' vocabulary by Gavin Long and in the collection of *Mess Songs*, reflective of the way the services spoke.

We Were the Rats was prosecuted just before New South Wales laws changed to allow for such cases to be defended on the grounds of literary and artistic merit. This change in the law would shape, to at least some extent, the way censorship and obscenity trials operated. As for Glassop's novel, it was published in an expurgated version in 1961 that deleted some of the language and omitted the chapter about the perv books altogether.[25]

In the post–Second World War period, expletives such as *fuck* continued to offend, despite their increased visibility. As was clear from literary censorship both before and during the Second World War, there was a significant anxiety around representations of sexuality, especially homosexuality or explicit heterosexuality, for fear of its corrupting effect. These anxieties continued to prompt efforts to suppress books until the censorship regime crumbled at the end of the 1960s.

If one word defines the contested literary culture of swearing through the middle decades of the 20th century then, it would be *fuck*. Nicole Moore writes that '[n]o Australian novel had been able to use the word fucking before 1946, when Robert Close's *Love Me Sailor* set out to use the word "rutting" as a meaningful euphemism'. As Close himself admitted of *rutting*: 'I did use it as a substitute for "fuck" and thought it a good one as you know it means fucking between animals.'[26] Other obscenities used in his novel include *bastard*, *bitch*, *bloody*, *goddamn*, *Jesus Christ*, and vulgar slang such as *split-whisker**. But the main concern for authorities, who charged the author with obscenity, was the realistic depiction of sex, and

---

* A term for a woman as a sexual object; the slang *to part the whiskers* 'of a man, to have sexual intercourse' is recorded in *Green's Dictionary of Slang*. *Whiskers* is American slang for pubic hair.

the working-class masculine sexuality it represented.[27] Moore contends that Close's trial and subsequent imprisonment (he was initially sentenced to three months but this was later reduced to ten days) had a 'significant impact on the representation of sexuality in Australian culture', repressing any link between explicit sex and Australian national identity.[28]

The theatre was another site of controversy for language in the period immediately following the Second World War. One of the most interesting examples is the Sumner Locke Elliott play *Rusty Bugles*, first produced in 1948 in Sydney. It was initially banned from production, but the ban was lifted 'conditional on the elimination of certain phrases and swear words'.[29] The play, set at an Ordnance Depot in the Northern Territory in 1944, reflects some of Elliott's own experiences as an ordnance clerk during the war, and the language he heard in the service. In the published version of the play, Elliott asks his audience to 'forgive and tolerate' the bad language, because 'I, too, was shocked at first, until the constant repetition drove all obscenity from the words and rendered them harmless'.[30]* It includes expressions such as *get ripped, perv, bastard, bitch, friggin'* and *the tom-tits* (rhyming slang for *the shits*). The play also makes much use of Australian colloquial speech, foreshadowing the wave of plays in the post–Second World War decades that used a rich Australian vernacular: for example, the use of *gig ape* 'a fool', *pratt* 'backside', *galah* and *drongo. Rusty Bugles* proved to be popular with audiences: it ran for five months in Sydney and six months in Melbourne.[31]

---

*   It is interesting to note that Frederic Manning's (see Chapter 5), Glassop's, and Elliott's main characters (somewhat autobiographical in all three cases) all purport to be shocked by bad language, and to some extent distance themselves from it. It is unclear if this reflected their own beliefs or was more about telling the reader that such language was not 'theirs' but about the world in which they found themselves in wartime.

CONTROLLING INDIGENOUS LIVES AND LANGUAGE

If literary censorship represented one attempt to control and police the norms and boundaries of Australian society and culture, the assimilation policies of the post–Second World War decades that affected Indigenous people represented another. While the assimilation policies that shaped Indigenous lives in the 1940s, 50s and 60s were multifarious in their nature and effect, language played a small but significant role – both in the attempt to make Indigenous people stop speaking their own languages and in punishing individuals who used profanity.

Between Federation and the Second World War, an apparatus of 'protection' was created to control Indigenous lives. The state could remove Indigenous children, they were forced to live on missions, and they were subject to all sorts of control on their movement, education and employment.[32] Racism and discrimination affected lives profoundly. Indigenous activism grew in response to this, with a significant moment of protest being the Day of Mourning held on 26 January 1938, the 150th anniversary of the arrival of the First Fleet.

After the war, with overt racism seen as somewhat less palatable in the aftermath of Nazism and the Holocaust, a shift towards policies of 'assimilation' predicated on cultural and social change took place. Within this paradigm, Indigenous people were expected to take up the cultural and social practices and norms of Anglo-Australians.[33] A key aim of assimilation was that of national 'belonging', as a racial idea of citizenship changed to one based on particular civic virtues and values that everyone was expected to conform to.

Many Indigenous people in this period lived on missions and reserves. They were often given new names, forced to speak English, punished for speaking their own languages, and torn away from family, culture and Country. Many recount how they were made to speak English and punished if they spoke their own language, Muruwari man Jimmie Barker, born in 1900 in Cunnamulla, was moved with his mother to a station called Milroy, 40 miles from Brewarrina, when he was eight years old.[34] In 1912, his family was moved to 'the Mission'. On his first day at school, Jimmie was confronted with 'how unacceptable Aborigines are to other people'. The teacher, Keogh, made it clear to him that Aboriginal people were 'just "nothing"'. He said to the children that 'he never wanted to hear a word of any Aboriginal language: they were all too dirty'.[35] Jimmie blamed white people for the loss of Indigenous languages: 'I have noticed that when people were talking to one another in Muruwari or Ngema the white man who heard them would immediately jeer at "old Jacky-Jacky speaking in his dirty lingo". On many occasions I have noticed that the dark people would just stop talking when a white person approached, as they did not want to appear foolish.'[36] Jimmie Barker played an important role in the 1970s in the recording and preservation of the Muruwari language.

Wangkumara woman Lorna Dixon recounts how, after being removed to a mission station at Brewarrina in 1938, her family were told by the mission manager that '[y]our Aboriginal language is dirty and English must be spoken at all times. I don't want to hear any of your filthy lingo and if I do, you'll suffer.' As biographer and collaborator Janet Mathews writes: 'Thus young people were brought up to scorn their native language. This was why so few people knew that Lorna's Wonggumara [Wangkumara] was locked away until I appeared with my tape recorder.'[37] Like Jimmie Barker, Lorna Dixon was vital to the project of recording the language and history of her community.

Many similar stories can be found. Arthur Malcolm, who lived at the Yarrabah mission in Queensland, recalls that up to the 1940s, missionaries told Indigenous people to 'cut out your language and all speak English'. He reflects: 'It was very sad – so it goes back to the mid 1920s that we all can't speak our own language. Just a few words that you pick up like in some of the languages.'[38] Doug Abbott, who was raised on the Hermannsburg mission and worked in the pastoral industry, was not allowed to speak his language in front of white people, or he would be flogged.[39] Suzanne Nurra, who grew up at the Daly River mission school in the Northern Territory, similarly recalls: 'In those days we weren't allowed to speak in language or in Kriol. If I did, then I had to be punished for not speaking English.'[40]

Alongside the admonition not to speak in language, Indigenous people were expected not to swear. Ted Mitchell, who lived on the Woorabinda Aboriginal settlement in Queensland, recalled that they 'weren't allowed to swear or throw rubbish around'.[41] Agnes Page, who grew up at the Daly River mission in the Northern Territory, remembered punishment for swearing.[42] Anthropologist David S Trigger records the following story from a man on the Doomadgee settlement in Queensland. When he was a young man:

> I didn't know nothing about Christian people, [I was] meeting me old mates, swearing away [in the presence of the white manager] and everybody looking guilty y'know, they been tell me: 'These fellas don't swear, this the mission and all this and that …' I was 'shamed too; see I was so used to all the *Mandagi* [Whites outside Doomadgee] y'know.[43]

A number of Indigenous people observed that the worst language was in fact that used by white people. Lorna Dixon recalls that before arriving at the mission at Brewarrina, 'none of us – not even Dad – knew anything about swearing or drinking. From that first night onwards we had to listen to people using shocking language and fighting between themselves.'[44]

Swearing was also used as a means of calling an Indigenous person's morality into question, especially if they were female. In a Darwin court case that involved the sexual assault of young girls (described as 'half-caste') at the North Australian Division of the Methodist Overseas Mission by a man named Kelvin Hopkins Grainger-Smith, the testimony of a witness (also a young girl) was challenged by questioning her character. She admitted, it was reported in the press, to having 'a bad character for swearing and untidiness'.[45] This was seen to discredit her other testimony.

Swearing in an Indigenous language could however offer an opportunity to poke fun at authority. In one account of the Goulburn Island mission in the 1940s, some girls working in the mission house 'had fun teaching the missionary's children some Maung "swear words" that they thought would shock him and his wife. They encouraged the children to try these out while they giggled in the background. The parents suspected the words were "naughty" but did not understand them.'[46]

A popular story about the use of language as a joke at white people's expense is the story of *moomba*. When a name was being discussed for a new Melbourne festival in 1954, Wiradjuri man Bill Onus, a unionist and Indigenous activist, suggested *moomba* as a joke; *moomba* in several Victorian Aboriginal languages could be loosely translated as *up your bum*. Linguist Piers Kelly has tried to untangle the truth of this story, and while the 'bum' story cannot be completely ruled out, it is probably the case that Onus suggested the name having taken it from a Queensland wordlist and drawing from the idea of a celebration (possibly from a translation of 'out of the dark').[47] Nevertheless, both this story and that of the mission girls attests to the subversive potential of bad language for Indigenous Australians.

THE NEW AUSTRALIANS

Postwar Australia saw significant demographic change, as more than two million migrants arrived in Australia between 1947 and the end of the 1960s. These migrants were mostly British, but many came from various European countries, including Greece, Italy and Yugoslavia. People were starting to challenge the White Australia policy that to this point excluded nearly all but Western European migrants through expanding who was considered to be a 'suitable' migrant. Australia would be changed forever by this migration, with a new diversity of culture and languages within the cultural landscape. New arrivals were expected to conform – 'assimilate' – to what was often referred to as the 'Australian way of life'. Exactly what this constituted was somewhat unclear,[48] but one of the cultural norms that migrants *were* expected to adhere to was the speaking of English, and for some the adoption of bad language (at least words such as *bloody*) were seen as essential to becoming truly Australian.

The federal government established a number of policies and programs to help new arrivals assimilate. The Chifley government launched Good Neighbour Councils in 1950 to involve the community in helping migrants to settle. Such programs aimed not just to help migrants, but were also about educating 'old' Australians and making them more accepting of new arrivals.[49] Learning English was flagged as one priority, and programs were set up to encourage this. For example, there was a 'Learn English' drive in 1959, in which volunteer groups such as the Country Women's Association played an important role.[50]

Migrants were expected to 'become Australian' and were advised that they should not persist in speaking their own language, especially in public. This was because many 'old' Australians were uncomfortable with their presence, and particularly disliked hearing foreign languages. Historian Joy Damousi writes that '[m]igrants saw this as a particularly insidious and oppressive aspect of assimilation, and one which they recall as especially punishing'.[51] Damousi's interviews with Greek migrants reveal that some recall the disapproval they experienced when speaking Greek in public, as well as their struggles with the pressure of learning English.[52] Anthropologist and sociologist Gillian Bottomley similarly notes that even second-generation Greek-Australians in the late 1960s and early 1970s 'spoke about their embarrassment and isolation in relentlessly Anglophone environments'.[53]

Migrants also faced discrimination in the form of slurs and epithets aimed at them, and which reinforced their relative lack of power. Such insults added to the already well-entrenched racist Australian vocabulary. Those who came to Australia during and after the war as refugees were referred to by disparaging terms such as *reffo*, *balt* and *nuts and balts*. The term *DP* ('displaced person') also came to have negative connotations. The government tried to change the language around new arrivals by calling for them to be known as 'New Australians' in all official communication.[54] The term *New Australian* quickly became entrenched in the Australian English vocabulary, sometimes abbreviated to *Naussie* or *Newstralian*. But slurs did not disappear from popular use. Migrants from countries such as Italy and Greece were commonly called *wog* and *dago* (Italians were also *Eyeties* or *Eyetos*), and many migrants recall the racism that they endured.[55]

Wog is probably the most well-known term for migrants used as a slur in post–Second World War Australia. It came from a more general use in British English as an offensive term for a foreigner and was in particular use during the Second World War in North Africa, where the English-speaking armies often referred to Arabs as *wogs*. The soldiers of the Second AIF used the term, and undoubtedly brought it back with them, but the first evidence in the Australian printed record, as applied to a migrant, is fairly late (1966). It is possible it was only as southern European culture came to have a real impact on Australian culture in the 1960s and 70s that the word was taken up in a major way (displacing earlier commonly heard terms such as *dago*); as we'll see in a later chapter, migrants later came to reclaim it, especially the Greek and Italian communities.

Various other derogatory terms entered the vocabulary in relation to the presence of new migrant groups: *grill* (especially applied to a Greek migrant); *Jew chum*, a pun on *new chum* and applied to Jewish refugees from Europe; *reffo* initially referring to a 'refugee' but then applied to any European migrant to Australia, especially one from southern Europe; *rice and sago*, rhyming slang for *dago*; and *Yugo* for an immigrant from what was then Yugoslavia. Later recorded rhyming slang terms for *wog* include *Dapto dog* and *chocolate frog*, and *bubble and squeak* for *Greek*.*

The issue of language as a barrier to, yet a means for, assimilation is captured in one of the best-selling books of the 1950s: Nino Culotta's comic novel *They're a Weird Mob* (1957). While published under the name (and written from the imagined perspective) of an Italian migrant to Australia, the book was in fact written by Anglo-Australian John O'Grady. It was an immediate bestseller and remained at or near the top of the Australian bestseller lists for nearly two years.[56] When it was revealed that O'Grady was the real author, he became a local celebrity – and the book remained popular. O'Grady wrote under a number of pseudonyms, but his assumption of an Italian identity made this work one of cultural appropriation that underlined the dominance of ideas of cultural assimilation at the time of its publication.

---

*   Evidence for such rhyming slang terms is often limited to collections of rhyming slang, and it's unclear just how common such terms were in everyday usage.

They're a Weird Mob uses the mysteries of Australian English as a significant source of humour. Nino, who has just arrived in Australia, tells us that he speaks 'good' English, and that Australians speak some whole other language. He observes: 'Most Australians speak English like I speak Hindustani, which I don't. In general, they use English words, but in a way that makes no sense to anyone else.'[57] A number of comic episodes in the book involve misunderstandings based on this.

Australians' propensity for the word *bloody* is particularly played on for humour. When he first arrives, Nino gets taken to, as the taxi driver calls it, 'King's bloody Cross', and Nino thinks this is its actual name. Later, in an encounter with a policeman, he repeats 'King's bloody Cross' only to be warned to '[l]eave the bloody out. That's a swear word in this country.'[58] In fact, the Australian characters (especially the builders' labourers who Nino comes to work with) use *bloody*, *bastard* and *bugger* all the time, attesting to not only the normality of the words, but also the way they are seen as intrinsic to Australian English and, by extension, Australian identity and character.

Nino does experience racism, with one character calling an Italian family (who are speaking Italian on a train) 'bloody dago spies', 'bloody dagoes' and 'pinheads'.[59] But the racist is quickly discredited, and his attitude is presented in the book as unacceptable. Ultimately, Nino makes friends with 'old Australians' who welcome him, and marries an Australian girl, Kay.

O'Grady uses Nino's character and perspective to make several lengthy observations on the nature of Australian behaviour and language, clearly connecting the two. The typical Australian, according to O'Grady:

> works hard, with much cursing and swearing, and is most unhappy when he has no work to do. He loves beer and

tobacco, and impassioned argument. He is kind and generous and abusive. He will swear at you, and call you insulting names, and love you like a brother. He is without malice. He will fight you with skill and ferocity, and buy you a beer immediately afterwards.[60]

And:

There is no better way of life in the world than that of the Australian. I firmly believe this. The grumbling, growling, cursing, profane, laughing, beer drinking, abusive, loyal-to-his-mates Australian is one of the few free men left on this earth. He fears no one, crawls to no one, bludges on no one, and acknowledges no master. Learn his way. Learn his language.[61]

The film of the book was released in 1966 with Italian movie star Walter Chiari starring as Nino. It changes the story somewhat, both to show the glories of Sydney as a tourist and/or migrant destination and of Walter Chiari's physique, and to create a more dramatic romance with Kay. There are fewer instances of swearing in the movie than the book, reflecting that film was still conservative when it came to such things – there is a shorter, tamer version of the 'King's bloody Cross' scene, some use of *bloody* and *bastard*, and a single instance of 'don't give me the *tom tits*'.

Notably, the film version ends with Nino, introducing the more middle-class and affluent Kay to his working-class mates, yelling 'bring out the bloody beer'; Kay responds, to the delight of the mates, with 'That's a bloody good idea'. Everyone takes off their jackets, relaxes, and starts drinking copious amounts of beer, accompanied by the soundtrack song 'It's a man's, man's country, sweetheart'. Both book and movie underline the notion of swearing and drinking as core to Australian values. These values are male, but should be embraced, or at least sanctioned, by women. The popularity of *Weird Mob* attested to the elevation of what might be considered Australian working-class values, behaviour and language to universally Australian status – a process no doubt aided by the presence of migrants as the new 'other'.

Both book and film of *Weird Mob* were extremely popular, and they aimed to reassure 'old Australians' that 'new Australians' could not only assimilate but come to understand, enjoy and share in Australian cultural values (drinking beer, swearing, joking around). Few scholars have pointed to the specific role swearing plays for O'Grady in what he conceived of as (primarily male) 'Australianness'. But undoubtedly swearing was important as a signifier of a certain type of Australianness that new arrivals were being urged to embrace. Swearing, done correctly and in the right context, was essential to establishing relationships and for showing yourself to be the right sort of bloke, the right sort of mate, and the right sort of Australian.

An indication, perhaps, of the influence of *Weird Mob*'s vision of Australianness as connected to swearing is revealed in the following story from 1966. A builder's labourer had been fired from his job at a council building project for swearing; the man argued that he had just been swearing 'about some building material' and not at the foreman. His fellow workers walked off the job and went on strike in solidarity. The company agreed to employ him on another job, but the union called for the man to be reinstated. The union secretary argued that the industry was 'well known as a swearing industry, and the company's action had been too drastic'. When picketing the building site, the strikers told the foreman he should go and see the popular movie *They're a Weird Mob*.[62]

Books such as *Weird Mob* attest, and perhaps even contributed, to the ongoing amelioration of words such as *bugger, bloody* and *bastard*. By the middle of the 20th century, *bugger* had become normalised in Australian English, even if it was still considered a coarse colloquialism. Expressions such as *buggerise around*, *I'm buggered*, *bugger all* and *bugger it* are all first recorded in Australian English through the middle of the 20th century and feature strongly in Australian English to the present day.

O'Grady followed up *Weird Mob* with the publication of *Aussie English* (1965). This comic glossary was prefaced with the comments: 'Australians respect a man for what he is, not for what he represents. Most of them have no respect for constituted authority, very little for tradition, and none at all for the English language.' He acknowledged some of the language as 'vulgar' but only insofar as 'vulgar' was that 'pertaining to the common people'.[63] In this book, O'Grady defines *bastard* as 'an extremely useful noun, as valuable to Australians as the coconut is to Polynesians', but warned the reader to refrain from using it until 'you become familiar with all the shades of meaning'. He warned against using *bugger* or any of the *four-letter words* in the presence of women. He also warned Americans in particular about the use of the word *root* because its Australian meaning – 'a fundamental, biological, extremely vulgar application' – was very different from the US sense of the word.

Root entered Australian English in the 1940s and quickly established itself in the lexicon. While our first recorded evidence is for the transferred sense of *rooted* meaning 'to be finished, ruined, exhausted', it almost certainly comes from the more literal sense of *root* meaning sexual intercourse (noun and verb both first recorded in 1958). According to the *Australian National Dictionary*, the origin of the term probably comes from *root* 'penis'. By the 1950s, popular culture was using *get rooted* in the sense of *get stuffed* or *get fucked*, as well as *rooted* in the sense of 'exhausted, fucked'. The rhyming slang *Wellington boot* is recorded in 1977, but it was undoubtedly around before then as the first evidence for it is in a shortened form – *wellington*, first recorded in 1970. Later expressions elaborating on *root* include *root ute* (a vehicle, usually a panel van, furnished with a mattress on which to have sex) and *root rat* (a sexually promiscuous man). Unlike some other Australianisms, *root* has remained a peculiarly Australian term, and not one easily understood by outsiders.

BODGIES, WIDGIES AND POPULAR CULTURE

Popular culture could reinforce the link between Australian values and swearing, as we've just seen with *Weird Mob*, but it could also present threats. A whole range of anxieties around imported popular culture were expressed from the 1920s right through to the 1960s and beyond – we've seen this already with the censorship of imported books. In the years between the world wars, some critics also feared the effect of imported, especially American, popular culture, including jazz music, crooning, comic books and films.

While bad language in the sense of swearing was not associated with this particular paranoia about Americanisation (after all, the Americans pioneered the Hays Code to ensure that Hollywood films would be free of bad language and any hint of immorality or sex), critics periodically feared that American slang would displace not only educated speech but also good Aussie slang. In 1937, a humorous poem lamented that Australian speech was being lost: 'For the grand Australian language, which was ours in days of old, / Has been k.o.'d by the Yankees and is laid out flat and cold'.[64] This fear only escalated during the Second World War and was conflated with the anxieties caused by the presence of so many American servicemen – referred to as *septic tanks* (also known as *septics* or *seppos*, rhyming slang for 'Yanks').

After the Second World War ended, fears over the dire

influence of American culture persisted. In particular, a great anxiety revolved around the fact that young people were developing their own, American-influenced, youth culture. Australian teenagers were undoubtedly influenced by American popular culture, and then, as now, this included adopting imported slang. Historian Catherine Fisher has studied the increase in the use of American slang in Australian magazines for teenage girls in the 1950s. She argues that American forms of slang were attractive to young people, not least because they represented all that was considered modern, youthful and international.[65]

In particular, a 'moral panic' developed over bodgies and widgies (a youth subculture where young people dressed in distinctive ways and listened to rock 'n' roll music; 'bodgies' were male and 'widgies' were female) in the 1950s. This was not only about fear of the Americanisation of youth – it extended the kinds of concerns expressed about young people with too much time on their hands and a determination to shape their own cultural practices. Discussion of the 'problem' of the bodgie echoed the kinds of concerns expressed about the larrikin.

Bodgies were, as larrikins were before them, known and condemned for swearing, which was often alleged to accompany a propensity to violence. The press of the day frequently commented on this. In South Australia in 1952, for example, a young man named Albert Henry Hollingsworth was arrested outside a dance hall for swearing. The prosecuting sergeant asked the court to 'take a serious view of this. It is typical bodgie behaviour.'[66] In 1954, a Liberal politician from Queensland asked for the police to raid hamburger joints 'featuring juke boxes and bodgies and widgies' because of the 'language, rowdyism and other noise' that these 'groups of hooligans' caused.[67] The latter complaint neatly connected the bodgie to the quintessentially 'American' phenomena of hamburger joints and jukeboxes.

The popularity of rock 'n' roll music within youth culture, with its sexual and racial overtones, also fed the anxieties of the older generation. Local rockers such as Col Joye and Johnny O'Keefe became notorious for their bad behaviour, including drinking, but they were also working-class heroes, helping to shape a new home-grown popular music and fashion culture that drew on American inspirations.

While bodgies likely used the usual range of swear words (a documentary on the bodgies broadcast on ABC radio in 1952 included use of the word *bloody* and was met with much outrage from some quarters[68]), they also employed a range of slang, some of which was imported from the USA. In 1951, *Pix* magazine included an article on bodgies – who were suspicious of the *squares* (those who were not 'cool') – that included a guide to some of this slang. According to *Pix*, drinking a milkshake was *guzzling foam*, a steady girlfriend was *the royal smooth*, someone who didn't understand something was described as *his plates don't beat*, and applying lipstick was *etching the edges*.[69] As with most youth slang, language marked a community that excluded the older generation; also, as with youth slang in other times and places, it was a source of some disapproval and concern from that generation. Coupled with concerns about swearing and violence, slang made bodgie culture something for the older generation to be anxious about but something many young people embraced.

LANGUAGE OF THE PRISON

The culture of the bodgies and widgies, including its slang and swearing, marked off a youthful subculture. Despite the fears of some, there was not much threat to all this, although it foreshadowed the more significant changes that would come in the 1960s and 70s. But what of the criminal underworld? As it had done in the previous century, there was a continuing tradition of language from this world and from prison – which included a great deal of sexual language – that defined an identity oppositional to the norms of 'respectable' Australia, and remained a 'secret' language not in the public domain.

The question of whether Australian crime figures used bad language is perhaps one with an obvious answer. But it is worth noting that in at least the early decades of the 20th century, some female crime figures, such as Kate Leigh, who built her criminal empire on the sex trade, illegal alcohol and gambling, embraced respectability in terms of personal behaviour, at least in avoiding drinking and swearing in public.[70] For Leigh, outward respectability was important. That bad language was otherwise a fairly ordinary feature of the lives of those in criminal circles is pretty clear. For example, the book *Sydney Noir: The Golden Years* (2017), which chronicles the 'golden years' of sleazy and corrupt Sydney in the 1950s, notes the use of the word *cunt* as a common term of address within underworld circles.[71]

More interesting for us, perhaps, is the 'secret' language of prisons. Prison and underworld language is a phenomenon that can be found everywhere, but we are fortunate in having some record of Australian (male) prison language. While much prison language before this period is lost, two prison glossaries, one from 1944 and another from 1950, record some of the words used. These give us insight into a closed world in which language was a means of inclusion and exclusion, and of describing a brutal and difficult existence.

The first Australian prison glossary was compiled in 1944 by Ted Hartley, who was imprisoned for being a conscientious objector during the war. Kylie Tennant, author of books such as *The Battlers* (1941) and *Ride on Stranger* (1943), asked Hartley to compile a list of underworld and prison slang that she could use for a book she was planning to write (it appeared in 1953 as *The Joyful Condemned**). Hartley assisted her by compiling a detailed word list. The second glossary, 'The Argot', was compiled by a long-term prisoner known only as 'Thirty-Five'.[72]

The two glossaries, which have been extensively examined by lexicographer Gary Simes, contain many words that fall into the 'vulgar slang' category. There are a number of words relating to sex or that describe the genitals: the penis could be called a *bat, blue vein, kerb, lunch, mutton gun, slug* or *zoobrick*. A male sexual partner was known as a *cat, horse's hoof* (rhyming slang for *poof*), *honey bum* or *quean*. There are various terms for intercourse (for example, *juicy fruit*, rhyming slang for *root*), cunnilingus (for example, *to go downstairs for breakfast*), and masturbation (for example, *flip oneself off*). The word *cunt* appears in several entries – *cold as a nun's cunt, cunt-starver* – but interestingly enough, despite the general subject matter of the glossary, Simes suggests that 'Thirty-Five' asked for the entry *cold as a nun's cunt* to be deleted, as well as another entry, *Jesus Alchrist Bloody Mighty*. Whether this was because of the religious connection in both these glossary entries is unknown – but it does indicate a certain squeamishness about particular words and terms not otherwise expressed in the collection.

Such glossaries give us an insight into the world of prisons and suggest that language in these contexts could be brutal and vulgar, and also indicated sex between men. This language was largely hidden from view but circulated in closed communities.

---

*   The novel has a lot of slang, but not much swearing. However, for the 1950s, there is some blunt language: for example, the use of the word *bastard*, and one woman is referred to as a *lying little bitch*.

AN AUSTRALIAN TRADITION?

Bad language undoubtedly continued to shore up ideas of Australian identity through the post–Second World War decades. We've seen already that calling for migrants and Indigenous people to speak English (and condemning their own languages as 'bad') was integral to the ideas of Australianness promoted from the 1940s through to the 1960s. Yet bad language in the form of swearing continued to be part of an Australian tradition of humour and larrikinism, especially underpinning a masculine (and white and heterosexual) idea of Australian identity.

The 1950s and 60s saw a resurgence of general interest in 'Australiana', as well as critical reflections on what being an Australian meant. This interest built on similar attempts by Australian literary writers through the 1930s, but more explicitly sought inspiration from what writers and intellectuals saw as an Australian radical tradition of the past, rather than drawing inspiration from Australia's present. For example, Vance Palmer's *The Legend of the Nineties* (1954) and Russel Ward's *The Australian Legend* (1958) rediscovered and celebrated the Australian bush tradition and its chroniclers. Ward's book in particular was influential in seeking to find inspiration in a radical folk tradition to inform the Australian present. Journals such as *Overland*, which nurtured writing that celebrated working-class and folk culture, began publication.[73] Collections of folklore, bush ballads and traditional stories also appeared in this period.

There was a surge of interest in Australian English, most notably with the publication of Sidney Baker's study of the Australian accent and colloquial speech in his book *The Australian Language* (1945; second edition 1966). Baker was a New Zealander by birth. He came to Australia in 1935 and worked as a journalist. He became Australia's foremost recorder of the Australian lexicon in the middle decades of the 20th century, partly inspired by a trip to London just before the Second World War that brought his attention to the many Australian and New Zealand colloquialisms that the British did not understand.[74] One of his goals in writing *The Australian Language*, other than recording a vocabulary that might otherwise be lost, was to provide the 'stuff' that could inspire authentic Australian literature. Baker was a great cultural nationalist and wanted Australians to write about themselves and their country. But he faced something of a personal challenge in recording the vulgarities of the Australian idiom, as he also wanted to argue against an association of Australian English with such vulgarity. While he acknowledged 'profanity [had] provided an accompaniment, or at least an undertone, to our social growth', he asserted that 'not more than 1% of Australia's slang inventions are vulgarisms or near-vulgarisms'.[75] Yet he couldn't avoid talking about profanity. By the time he wrote his study, it was clear that words such as *bastard* and *bugger* were entrenched in the Australian vernacular and were rarely considered as words to get too upset about. Nevertheless, he warned against excessive profanity, especially in Australian writing: 'These efforts represent attempts to intensify and to colour, but they tend to become wearisome and have little to recommend them.'[76]

Bad language as part of an Australian folk tradition was less ambivalently embraced by those who vigorously challenged censorship, including the bohemian Sydney Push and Melbourne Drift. The Sydney Push, a group active in the 1950s who shared a libertarian perspective and who saw themselves as sexually liberated intellectual anarchists, laid the groundwork for some of the cultural changes of the late 1960s and 1970s. Centred initially around University of Sydney philosopher John Anderson, the Push included figures such as Roelof Smilde, Harry Hooton, Lillian Roxon and Darcy Waters. A core libertarian cause was free speech and opposition to censorship.[77] The Melbourne Drift included figures such as Barry Humphries and Germaine Greer (Greer was later also a part of the Sydney Push). It was from this bohemian milieu that some of the challenges to censorship emerged, and revelling in the use of bad, especially sexual, language was central to this. For example, in the early 1950s, Barry Humphries created Dadaist-inspired performances that included yelling swear words such as *shit* and *bugger* as part of his efforts to offend and provoke audiences.[78]

Bad language including the obscene was also seen to be an important part of the Australian 'folk tradition', and the intellectuals and cultural figures of groups such as the Push embraced the bawdy folk tradition that had a long history in Australia. This tradition undoubtedly came to Australia with the convicts, and a number of bawdy folk songs and poems are attributed to the 1890s, such as 'The Bastard from the Bush'. The two world wars added to the stock of such verse. Much of this used bad language, especially sexual language, but also often reflected criticisms of authority. This folk tradition was thus also co-opted into a radical leftist politics that challenged the staid conservatism of Australia in the 1950s and 60s. The radical and subversive potential of bad language was well recognised.

One of the most notable collections of this type is a mimeographed collection of songs and ballads, published in 1962, entitled *Snatches and Lays* and attributed to 'Sebastian Hogbotel' and 'Simon Ffuckes'. The original publication was produced, according to the compilers, 'as a pill to purge puritanism'.[79] It was purportedly a collection of songs 'as sung by sailors, soldiers, airmen, students and the like in and around Australia between the years, say 1940 and 1960'.[80] Only two of the songs were given any authorship attribution – one was written by poet AD Hope ('The Ballad of Dan Homer') and another by critic and writer RF Brissenden ('The Canberra Blues').

The compilers – true names Stephen Murray-Smith, an academic who was also one of the founders of *Overland*, and Ken Gott, a journalist – were both communists and active on the political left. They declared in their introduction to the collection that '[f]ucking made all of us, and one of the reasons we are publishing this collection is because we think it is time to say so, not in mealy-mouthed euphemisms, but in the language that people use'. They objected to the fact that society allowed an execution by hanging to be referred to, but not a fuck. 'Why must such a centrally important group of human activities such as fucking, shitting and pissing be ignored?', they asked. 'Why must our vocabulary and our perception of experience be impoverished by taboos which strike at such fundamental activities?' Words were only 'dirty', they argued, because they were hidden in the dark. They concluded:

> These songs are an affirmation of faith in people and of
> contempt for wowsers. It is a curious fact that so much which
> goes to make up Australia cannot be defined positively,
> but only in terms of opposition to the wowser, the eternal
> grey nark, born without balls, guts or gullet, slimy and
> sanctimonious, a figure to be pitied and pilloried.[81]

The fondness for 'dirty ditties' was shared by the Push, where such songs were, according to their historian, 'a staple'.[82] The songs hold little back in terms of language, as well as frank sexual imagery and lewdness. The song 'Heigh Ho Says Rowley', for example, includes language typical of the collection:

> C is for cunt all slimy with piss,
> D is the drunkard who gave it a kiss …
> W is the whore who thought fucking a farce,
> And X, Y and Z you can shove up your arse.[83]

Some of the songs played on popular culture of the period, such as the racy 'Pull Me Dungarees Down', sung to the tune of 'Tie Me Kangaroo Down'. Others reflected the more political aims of the compilers in mocking religion and the church, such as 'Ecclesiastical':

> There was a young lady called Alice
> Who pissed in the Archbishop's chalice,
> It wasn't for need
> She committed the deed
> But simply sectarian malice.[84]

*%$#

Snatches and Lays provides a bridge from the wartime years, when songs such as these might have been enthusiastically sung by those in the services, to the Libertarian Push and other bohemian groups, and through to the decline of censorship and the embrace of sex and swearing that marked the counterculture of the late 1960s and 1970s. While the main aim of such collections was to challenge censorship and the sexual mores of the period, they also suggested the centrality of a bad language that included rather than excluded the obscene to an Australian popular tradition that mocked authority. This tradition was perhaps at least in part a construction – it sought to connect to ideas about the 'radical' working class and was used to challenge the prevailing stuffiness and hypocrisy of the Menzies era and its attempts to control people's behaviour – but it was powerful, if still on the margins. The bad language tradition was also still overwhelmingly male dominated. Although women had a presence – Kay's 'bloody good idea' in the movie of *They're a Weird Mob*, the embrace of slang by the widgie, and the women of bohemia singing bawdy songs – like New Australians and Indigenous Australians, their relationship to bad language remained complex and ambiguous.

As we'll see in the next chapter, bad language would be more than enthusiastically embraced as a marker of the counterculture challenging and satirising the 'respectable' norms of middle-class Australian society, and women would more openly claim a right to use bad language as a sign of their liberation. While the visibility and ubiquity of bad language was undoubtedly a marker of the counterculture, publications such as *Snatches and Lays* remind us of a longer Australian tradition of using bad language to shock and subvert.

7

LIBERATING BAD LANGUAGE

In 1961, poet Gwen Harwood published an acrostic sonnet in *The Bulletin*. Unbeknownst to the magazine's editors, the first letter of each line, taken together, spelled out 'Fuck all editors'. Several thousand copies that had already been printed were subsequently withdrawn.[1] These kinds of challenges to censorship intensified throughout the 1960s as an array of voices called for the end of the regime. Young people especially took up the task of challenging authority; testing censorship was just one way to draw attention to the new cultural expressions they were forging.

The 1970s saw the collapse of the old censorship regime in Australia and the emergence of a counterculture that embraced bad language as a means to shock and to challenge authority. Culture, especially film and theatre, embraced four-letter words to illustrate a bold new era of frankness. Groups who were marginalised in Australian society also used language, including profanity but also challenges to discriminatory language, as a means of mobilising political resistance and shaping new identities for themselves. By the end of the decade, the bad language landscape had changed in fundamental, perhaps irreversible, ways. As the personal became political, language once only heard in private (or not at all) was now far more likely to be heard defiantly and loudly in public.

CHALLENGING CENSORSHIP IN PRINT

As I discussed at the end of the last chapter, when the first edition of *Snatches and Lays* was published, it only circulated privately as a mimeographed collection. By 1973, it was published by Sun Books and sold in bookshops, albeit with a warning on the front cover that read: 'Suggested for sale to mature readers only'. Between 1964 and 1971, writes Nicole Moore, Australia's literary censorship regime was undone.[2] The last novel to be charged with obscenity was Philip Roth's *Portnoy's Complaint* (1969); the publisher, Penguin Australia, deliberately sought to use the publication of Roth's novel as an opportunity to challenge the censorship system, with trials taking place across the country. The book included graphic sexuality, especially scenes of masturbation, as well as the use of words such as *cunt, prick* and *fuck*. Many witnesses argued in favour of the book's literary merit, including novelist Patrick White, who at the Victorian trial testified that he had no problem with the language and indeed used it himself. While the outcomes of the trials were mixed (for example, in New South Wales the bookseller Angus and Robertson was tried twice, with no verdicts reached in either case), the state was increasingly finding it harder to justify its actions in keeping books such as these, clearly of literary value, from being sold in Australia. *Portnoy's Complaint* was taken off the banned list in 1972.[3] This represented the culmination of efforts that had been going on for at least a decade before.

Through the 1960s, a new generation of writers, artists and activists, many of whom were first published in underground magazines and student publications, challenged the prevailing censorship regime as well as changing the broader culture through these years. Their publications became the voice of those coming of age, who sought to change what could be expressed in public. Students across countries such as the USA, Britain and Australia, as well as European nations, played an important role in shaping popular culture, and in debating and challenging political, cultural and social norms. They demanded freedom of speech and freedom from censorship. Using bad language was just one way of challenging the norms that they were rebelling against – but it wasn't only about using swear words such as *fuck*. As cultural historians Robin Gerster and Jan Bassett argue, the counterculture saw concepts such as 'authority', 'capitalism', 'the Establishment', 'sexism' and 'Vietnam' as the true 'dirty words'.[4]

Historian Sally Percival Wood's study of the Australian student press in the 1960s demonstrates how important swearing and the obscene was for the students who were seeking to challenge authority and censorship.[5] Magazines such as the University of New South Wales' (UNSW) *Tharunka*, the University of Melbourne's *Farrago*, the University of Sydney's *Honi Soit*, and the Australian National University's *Woroni* became important forums for expressing political ideas and creativity. The production of these kinds of magazines, as well as feminist and other underground publications, was facilitated by important technological advances that allowed relatively cheap but good-quality offset printing.

One of the first and most notorious publications to test prevailing censorship was *Oz*. Launched in April 1963, it became a countercultural legend. Early editions were edited by Richard Neville and Richard Walsh, and featured the artwork of Martin Sharp. Satire and humour were a mainstay of the magazine, and figures and institutions of authority and power were regular targets. They also attacked censorship and Australian insularity. By 1964, *Oz* had a circulation in Sydney of 10 000, and when it went national in 1965, it sold up to 40 000 copies.[6]

But *Oz* was quickly targeted by authorities. The fourth edition attracted obscenity charges, and the editors were fined £20 each.[7] The sixth edition also incurred obscenity charges, but this time the editors ran an 'artistic and literary merit' defence in which numerous academics and experts testified on their behalf. The editors were still found guilty and sentenced to six months' hard labour. They were successful in their appeal, but the experience prompted Neville and Sharp to depart for London, where they went on to publish a popular British edition of *Oz*. The Australian version continued to be published up until February 1969.

Bad language was clearly a part, although not all, of what was believed to be the obscene nature of *Oz* (both Australian and British editions), but reading copies today, the language is tame in comparison with the satire and social commentary, which still packs a punch. Australian *Oz* did occasionally play with, as well as make use of, profanity, although there is in fact surprisingly little (in comparison to, for example, nudity and discussions of sex). Swearing was still mostly alluded to rather than explicitly used, in keeping with the ever-present threat of prosecution. The editors and contributors employed some creative disguises for swearing: for example, in the sixth edition, Martin Sharp drew a cartoon of popular folk singer Joan Baez with the caption 'get folked'. In another edition, the word *shit* was used; there was also a discussion about the death of comedian Lenny Bruce – himself controversial for swearing prolifically in his comedy. *Oz*'s obituary thanks Bruce for the fact that 'novelists didn't have to say "frig" anymore'.[8]

Underground publications such as *Troll, High Times, Super Plague, Cane Toad Times, Ubu News* and *Eyeball* were inspired by, and followed the path of, *Oz*.[9] *High Times* discussed topics such as ecology, music, popular culture, sex and drugs. Like *Oz*, there is not much actual swearing, although there is some use of *shit*.[10] One word many of these radical papers occasionally used was *fucking* (in the sense of sex):[11] this reflected both the liberation of using a taboo word such as *fuck*, as well as changing attitudes to sex that made the act less about romance and more about pleasure and self-expression.[12]

The *Kings Cross Whisper*, a satirical newspaper modelled on the British magazine *Private Eye*, and whose contributors included actor Max Cullen, used a lot of sexual innuendo and some bad language. It mocked authority, politicians and wowsers, and satirised current affairs. In 1967, it provided the 'Whisper All Aussie Dictionary', which included terms such as *Donald Duck* (rhyming slang for *fuck*). It also made use of a variety of vulgar Australianisms such as *pissorf*, *upya dinger*, *bulldust* and *acre* (a euphemism for *arse*). It also alluded to swearing through humorous word play, as in this mock response to a letter of complaint from 'Offended': 'I'm sure the sailor was not being crude when he said "frigate" in your presence.'[13] The aim of the satire was, Cullen mused later, specifically Australian: 'having a go at the bastards by laughing at 'em'.[14]

The UNSW student magazine *Tharunka* attracted the greatest notoriety of the university newspapers when it was taken to trial. On 23 June 1970, *Tharunka* printed the poem 'Cunt Is a Christian Word', and the editors were subsequently charged with obscenity. Demonstrations were held to protest against the trial. Wendy Bacon, *Tharunka*'s editor and a member of the UNSW student group Kensington Libertarians, protested wearing a nun's habit, adorned with a sign saying 'I have been fucked by God's steel prick' – a reference to the poem, which criticises Christianity's repression of sex and women ('For everyone knows Jesus has a special reward / For cunts untouched by masculine hands'[15]). Her protest in turn led her to be charged for 'wearing an obscene publication'. In March 1971 Bacon was summonsed to appear in the Magistrates' Court on 11 charges of obscenity.[16] During the trial, supporters painted slogans outside magistrate Judge Hicks' home, including *Hix Sux Dix* and *Fux Verdix*. Bacon was sentenced to eight days in prison.

The British version of *Oz*, published from 1967 to 1973, was an example of Australian humour and obscenity exported – but it also reflected a broader transnational counterculture shared by Australia and Britain that sought to reshape what could be written about in this period. *Oz* proved no more acceptable to British authorities than the Australian editions had been at home. In 1971, the editors of British *Oz* were put on trial for obscenity. There was considerable discussion during the trial about the language *Oz* used, especially the words *cunt* and *bollocks*. One expert who appeared for the defence, social commentator George Melly, was memorably challenged by the prosecutor: 'So you would call your little daughter a cunt, would you?' Melly replied, 'No, I don't think she is one. But I might apply it to a politician.'[17] The editors were found guilty of publishing an obscene magazine, but the trial and the judgement were targets of considerable general ridicule and criticism.

The floodgates of bad language were opening. Student and underground publications challenged what could be put into print, chipping away at the absurdities of the censorship regime. *Portnoy's Complaint* and its trials showed that the regime was full of contradictions about when and why something should be censored and proved it to be ultimately foolish. But it was the stage and the movie screen that would forever transform the profanity that could be heard in public.

SWEARING ON THE STAGE

The Australian stage assumed considerable importance in the cultural shifts of the 1960s and 70s. Playwrights explored and critiqued Australian values and character, creating authentically Australian voices for the stage. But they also looked to use bad language as part of their critique of Australian values, and to expose the darker side of Australian society.

Alan Seymour's *The One Day of the Year* took a critical look at the role of Anzac Day in Australian society and culture. Written in 1958, it was first performed in 1960. The script was published by Angus and Robertson in 1962, and was followed by a novel based on the play. At the time of writing, Anzac Day was not the sacred day for Australia that it later became; veterans who marched did not attract much of an audience or public appreciation. In his play, Seymour conveys the contempt the younger generation felt for their veteran fathers, while also probing what this relationship and conflict between the generations might mean. Like other plays of the period, it attempts to capture something of the Australian vernacular. Seymour himself commented on this: 'selectivity, compression and absolute accuracy to the *emotional* truth behind the speech can produce something quintessential which reveals far more than the way a nation speaks: it somehow catches, isolates, illumines the way its people think and feel'.[18]

Seymour's play delivers the Australian vernacular through the characters of Alf, a Second World War veteran, and his mate Wacka, a First World War veteran. Alf is the prototypical 'ocker' – prejudiced, rough, and fond of swearing and drinking. The language in *The One Day of the Year* is nothing like that of plays from later in the decade, but it liberally makes use of words such as *bloody*. Indeed, as Alf's wife comments in the play, 'Alf. It's bloody this and bloody that every two seconds. I know how much you've had when you get to this bloody stage.'[19] The play focuses on the tensions between Alf and his son Hughie. Hughie's contempt for his father and his generation is clearly expressed through strong language. At one point, he declares, 'Oh, frig the old diggers'; later he says that the Gallipoli campaign meant 'Bugger all'.[20]

Seymour, along with playwrights such as Ray Lawler in his *Summer of the Seventeenth Doll* (1955), were beginning to put Australian accents and vernacular, as well as a rougher form of language, on the stage. This trend continued as the 1960s went on. Alex Buzo was one of the most important Australian playwrights of the later 1960s, and he made extensive use of the Australian vernacular. But he also used offensive language, often quite deliberately, to shock his audience. Perhaps the most controversial of his plays at the time was *Norm and Ahmed*, another play to feature a Second World War veteran presented as a prejudiced, insular character.

Norm and Ahmed was first performed at the Old Tote Theatre in Sydney in 1968. It depicts an encounter between Norm, an Australian, and Ahmed, who is from Pakistan. Norm was one of the Rats of Tobruk (and his father a Gallipoli veteran). He encounters Ahmed, and they engage in a conversation that forms the main guts of the play. Norm clearly suffers from war trauma – at one point when recounting his war experiences, he grabs Ahmed by the throat. Norm advises Ahmed that he should settle down in Australia, find a wife ('something more than just a weekend root'), and raise a family. At the end of the play, Norm holds his hand out for Ahmed to shake, and it appears to be a moment of an 'old Australian' accepting a 'new Australian' and offering him friendship. Instead, Norm punches him, bashes his head against a post, and flings Ahmed's body over a guardrail. He utters just two words that conclude the play: 'Fuckin' boong.' The ending is shocking – both in its physical violence, and in the violence of the language used.[21]

The 1969 Melbourne La Mama Theatre production of *Norm and Ahmed* resulted in police action. Producer Graeme Blundell and lead actor Lindsay Smith were charged and found guilty for 'using or aiding and abetting the use of obscene words'. When the play was performed in Brisbane, Norman Staines, the actor playing Norm, was also arrested and charged with obscene language. What was found objectionable in all this, of course, was not the racism of *boong*, but the use of the word *fucking*.[22]

Other plays similarly incurred charges of obscenity – usually for *fuck* – in the late 1960s, but audiences increasingly intervened to protest against such actions. In 1968 New South Wales Chief Secretary Eric Willis ordered police action against the one-act play *Motel* (part of the play *American Hurrah*) because the actors wrote *fuck* and other obscenities on the wall of the set. Although the play proceeded without the banned segment, a special one-off performance of the original play took place; the police attempted to arrest the actors but the audience obstructed them and tore up the set to destroy the evidence.[23] Nine actors from the Australian Performing Group were arrested for obscene language during the Melbourne performance of anti-censorship satire *Whatever Happened to Realism*, a play by John Romeril. In response to the arrests, the audience booed and began chanting *fuck* to the accompaniment of a rhythm and blues band.[24]

In 1969, John Krummel and Charles Little, actors from the Playbox Theatre, were charged with obscene language when using the word *fuck* in the Melbourne production of the controversial *The Boys in the Band* (it was permitted in the Sydney production).[25] The Melbourne co-producer of the play, which was groundbreaking in its depiction of gay life, defended it to the press, arguing that all advertising for the play had warned that it was 'Suitable only for adults'.[26] The magistrate initially dismissed the charges, but the Vice Squad insisted on a review. The review subsequently led to the actors being fined. Producer Harry M Miller called the convictions 'ludicrous', commenting: 'The law as it stands means that the script can be bought and read but one mustn't move their lips when reading it.'[27]

By the 1970s plays were using profanity without much controversy, as well as making liberal use of the Australian vernacular. Alex Buzo's play *Rooted*, first performed in 1969, used terms such as *piss off, chunder-guts, bull-artist* and, of course, *root*.[28] David

Williamson's play *The Removalists* (1971) explored Australian power, masculinity and violence. In the play, the abusive husband, Kenny, says things to his sister-in-law, who is helping his wife leave him, such as 'If roots were hamburgers, you could feed a bloody army', and accuses her of being a 'bloody trollop'. After the police arrive to deal with Kenny, he calls them 'cunt' and 'fuckwit' before one of them beats him to death.[29] This reminds us that bad language was not just used in these plays to shock or titillate the audience. As with *Norm and Ahmed*, profanity highlighted, even amplified, the dark, violent underside of Australian society and masculinity that Buzo and Williamson explored.

Playwrights of the late 1960s and 70s thus became notorious for their use of bad language. In 1973, the *Sydney Morning Herald* reported that police were going to be asked to take stronger action against people who swore in public places after an alderman reported that 'he had received complaints of people at Kings Cross using four-letter words "so voluble and profane that one would think they were attending a modern play at the theatre"'.[30]

THE RISE OF THE OCKER

The plays and films of the 1970s facilitated the development of a new Australian character: the 'ocker'. The ocker was a man with a broad Australian accent, who used vulgar and sometimes profane language, drank beer, and loved to mock authority. Its origin is in a nickname for a character named Oscar (played by Ron Frazer) in the popular Australian television program *The Mavis Bramston Show* that ran from 1964 to 1968. *Ocker* (or *Okker*) was a common form of Oscar in use in Australia from the early 20th century, but its application to the character in the program saw it become a generic term used for a person regarded as boorish, uncultivated and aggressive in their Australianness. The ocker would be both celebrated and condemned. He was brought to life most memorably in the character of Barry McKenzie, but he was also examined through various characters in the plays of David Williamson, and later in characters played by Paul Hogan. The ocker reflected an evolution of Australian masculinity and nationalism – especially the idea of the larrikin – in the 1970s.

Barry Humphries (born 1934) is an influential and distinctive figure in the story of Australian English. More than just about any other single cultural figure, Humphries introduced a variety of new words and idioms into the language. Some of these were words he coined; others found their way into print for the first time through publications Humphries penned, or through their use in the McKenzie films. Many of the terms were what we might call 'vulgar colloquialisms'. His use of language was inventive and original – he didn't resort to shocking through the use of standard swear words such as *fuck* or *shit*, as much as he did through wickedly evocative images. For example, female pubic hair was *the map of Tasmania* and to urinate was *to syphon the python* or *point Percy at the porcelain*. Humphries also created iconic Australian characters who shaped perceptions of Australian nationalism and culture. Barry McKenzie was the most important vehicle for Humphries' linguistic innovations.

McKenzie first appeared in 1964 in a comic strip drawn by Nicholas Garland and with text by Humphries, and was published in the satirical British magazine *Private Eye*. The strip became a cult hit in the UK but was banned in Australia.[31] Humphries and his creation, even more so than *Oz* magazine, provide a good example of how Australian bad language was being exported for consumption abroad, even as it was being restricted at home.

The first of the Barry McKenzie films, *The Adventures of Barry McKenzie*, was released in 1972, just as formal censorship was ending. It was directed and written by Bruce Beresford, and produced by Phillip Adams. It begins with Barry (aka Bazza, played by Barry Crocker) and his aunt Edna (Barry Humphries doing an early incarnation of his famous character Edna Everage) heading off to the mother country. The film consists of a series of sketches in which Bazza, the hapless innocent abroad, encounters a variety of characters including a snobby British couple and a hippie band, and he appears on a television arts program. We also meet one of his Australian friends, Leslie, a woman who has, after a failed marriage, taken up with a female partner named Claude. In the film's climactic scene, Bazza, who has been invited on to the arts program as a representative Aussie expatriate, mocks the 'serious' intellectual questions with his answers, and ultimately pulls his pants down and flashes his *donger* (a term first recorded in Australian English in 1962 and popularised by Humphries). A detective, who has been chasing him for some time, wants to arrest him for public indecency and obscene language, but he is knocked out by Bazza's mates before he can do so. In a subsequent scene, they set fire to the program's set and try to put it out by drinking copious amounts of beer and urinating on it. The film mocks pretensions of all kinds, from those of traditional elites and intellectuals to those of the counterculture.

Barry loves beer, and likes to boast of his imagined sexual conquests (although he never actually succeeds in these endeavours). An ocker confused by the 'Poms', he is often clad in a T-shirt that says 'Pommy Bastard'. There is a surreal, absurdist quality to the film, but one of the great sources of humour is Bazza's language and his miscommunication with the 'Poms' who often have no idea what he is talking about. His language relates to a fairly narrow set of topics, all of which reflect his great preoccupations: drinking beer and rooting. So we encounter many new expressions for sex, vomiting, urination and the penis. Here are some of the words and idioms used in the McKenzie films:

Vomiting: *chunder, yodel, park the tiger, technicolour yawn, the big spit, park the pea soup, liquid laugh*

Sexual intercourse: *bang like an outhouse door, spear the bearded clam, date with a fur doughnut, sink the sausage*

Cunnilingus: *coo-ee up the old snake gully, dining at the Y, yodel up the valley*

Penis: *one-eyed trouser snake, pyjama python, beef bayonet, beef bugle, mutton dagger, old fella*

Urinating: *splash your boots, go where the big knobs hang out, shake hands with the wife's best friend, syphon the python, unbutton the mutton, point Percy at the porcelain, shake hands with the unemployed, wring the rattlesnake*

Masturbating/masturbator: *jerkin' the gherkin, flog the lizard, twang the wire, Mrs Palm and her five daughters, rod walloper.*

Through the McKenzie character, Humphries also uses a number of Australian idioms that he coined or helped to give new life to in connecting them to the Australian ocker, including: *dry as a dead dingo's donger, stone the crows, don't come the raw prawn, strike me pink, hope all your chooks turn into emus and kick your dunny down,* and *fair suck of the sauce bottle.* While much of this language is certainly vulgar, and in some cases sexually explicit, the McKenzie movies do not include much actual swearing. There are some abusive terms directed at various characters. For example, Barry calls the Customs officer who confiscates his suitcase full of Foster's beer a *bastard.* He calls his friend Curly (in jest) a *hippie poof* and a *silly dag.* The British are often referred to or addressed as *pom poofs, pom pervs* or *pommy drongos.*

In the sequel *Barry McKenzie Holds His Own,* released in 1974, Edna is kidnapped by Count Plasma from Transylvania, and Bazza and his mates save her. Compared to the first instalment, the language is somewhat more explicit, reflecting the increasing acceptance of four-letter words as the 1970s went on. There is still a limited amount of swearing, but there are words such as *shit*, *arsehole* and *prickface* that didn't feature in the first film. A typical joke in this movie goes along these lines: a female student says to Barry, 'I'm studying Kant'; he replies 'So am I'.[32]

Where did Humphries find Bazza's language? Cultural historian Tony Moore provides an extensive commentary on its origins:

> Some of Bazza's vernacular was authentic, picked up by
> Humphries from his builder father's labourers, in the school
> playground and in the pubs of Melbourne and Sydney. 'It
> was marvellously liberating,' Humphries recalled, 'to lift
> slang from C.J. Dennis, Geelong Grammar, Bluey and
> Curly, the mural felicities of divers memorable dunnies …'
> He particularly recalled from childhood a hefty tradesman
> informing his mates he was 'off to strain the potatoes'. But no
> actual Australian could surpass Barry McKenzie. Humphries
> happily admitted topping up 'our seemingly inexhaustible
> reservoirs of slang' for bodily functions by coining 'quaintly
> indecent neologisms … so that the whole thing became
> an intriguing verbal pastiche of the real and grotesque
> imaginary.' Phrases like 'busy as a one-armed Sydney cab
> driver with crabs' and 'point Percy at the porcelain' were
> Humphries originals. Nevertheless, Barry McKenzie's
> four letter words never get worse than 'shit'. Why use
> unimaginative words like 'fuck' when you can say 'in up to
> the apricots and off like a grenade'?[33]

Moore writes that Humphries' comedy 'revels in parodying the prejudices and ignorant certainties of old white Australia'.[34] He adds that there was a strong anti-establishment element to Barry, reflecting the 'larrikin libertarianism' of the Melbourne bohemian subculture of which Humphries had been a part.[35] Arguably, the McKenzie films fall into a longer tradition of self-mocking Australian humour, identified by actor and producer John McCallum. As McCallum writes, 'the most successful popular comedy in Australia … exploited feelings of inadequacy which are a very real part of the way in which Australians see themselves'.[36]

What should we make of Humphries' ubiquitous use of terms like *poof* and *poofter*? In 1972, scholar and gay rights activist Dennis Altman criticised *The Adventures of Barry McKenzie* as 'the most vicious anti-homosexual film of all time'.[37] But other commentators have pointed out that Humphries' writing emerged from a libertarian, surrealist tradition, and elements of gender subversion are present in the first film – for example, when Barry dresses as a woman while Leslie (the bisexual character) wears trousers. It can also be argued, however, that the ocker character, whatever the satirical intent, helped to entrench certain unsavoury characteristics into a particular version of Australian masculinity. The homophobic, sexist, beer-drinking, vulgar ocker was not always taken as ironically as perhaps it was meant to be, but rather he was celebrated, and even internalised.

How did contemporary critics respond to Barry McKenzie? The first film, according to film critic Sandra Hall, was 'one-note humour all the way', and its sentiments were little more than 'updated Dad 'n' Dave'. To her, 'Bazza isn't much more than a verbal compost heap'.[38] Many saw the film as ghastly and vulgar.[39] Yet Barry Humphries, Bazza and Edna were on their way to becoming Australian legends.

The ocker was a cultural figure much discussed in the 1970s, often critically. In 1974 *The Australian* newspaper noted that: 'The new Australian boorishness is known as Ockerism, from a slob-like character called Ocker in a television series, the embodiment of selfish, blinkered self-satisfaction.'[40] Writers for *The Bulletin*

argued in 1977 that the ocker had become an 'Australian tyranni-
cal myth'.[41] Yet they propagated the ongoing development of this
ocker myth even as they condemned it. The idea of a process of
ockerisation, something being *ockerised*, or being *ockerish* all became
cause for comment or concern through the 1970s. And by 1978
Australia was even dubbed *Ocker-land*. Much of all this discussion
reflected an anxiety about just what Australian nationalism might
be after the country turned away from England as a source of identity. For some it perhaps also revealed too starkly the darker side of
the idealised Australian male culture.

Critical examination of the ocker was also present in the work
of playwright and screenwriter David Williamson, especially in
Don's Party. The story explores Australian masculinity and subur-
ban disillusionment. Williamson argued that it was 'a satirical play
emphasising the worst aspects of Australian suburbia in 1969'.[42]
Both play (1973) and film (1976) make liberal use of bad language
and Australian vernacular to underline the nature of the (notably
middle-class) characters depicted. In both, the character of Don,
who is holding an election-night party in 1969 (the election that
Gough Whitlam lost), is greeted by his mate Cooley with 'G'day
cunt-features', and there are instances of words such as *bullshit,
ratshit, arse, stuffed, screw, bugger me, fuck, fuck off, bullshit artist,
shit* and *shitting*. Both men and women swear, although all the
fucks and *cunts* are spoken only by male characters, reflecting an
ongoing gendered stereotype of bad language use. Bad language is
also used as a source of humorous wordplay in *Don's Party*, notably
in the dialogue when Cooley, who enjoys sleeping around, says,
'I used to say "fuck" but I get more fucks when I say "screw" [to
women]'.[43] Another striking feature of the film is the enormous
amount of alcohol the men consume – drink continued to be central to Australian male culture, and linked to the worst aspects of
male behaviour.

So, language played an essential role in the making of the Australian ocker. Whether the ocker was to be taken as a celebration or a cause for criticism, he helped to establish a 'national language' of what writer Lisa Jacobson calls 'Colloquial-Ockerism', 'a medley of urban curses and outback mateship punctuated by swills of beer'.[44] Importantly, works such as *Don's Party* made this a language owned not just by the working classes, but also increasingly by the middle classes; it was perhaps also something that brought together the old Australia with a newer, more modern Australia. Bad language became essentially 'Australian' and therefore imagined as beyond class, although it was still very much male.[45]

By the time the ocker was imagined in the characters of Paul Hogan (first in *The Paul Hogan Show* on television and then in the 1980s in the larrikin character of *Crocodile Dundee*), he was much tamer, even sentimental – Hogan's use of Australian slang words such as *galah* was almost nostalgic, as were many of the characters he played. Perhaps because it was aimed at television and, with *Dundee*, US movie audiences, Hogan avoided any significant profanity, the strongest word in the film being *shit*. Tellingly, perhaps, the first *Crocodile Dundee* movie (1986) includes two scenes where Dundee, a character who could be seen as one that blends the bushman, the larrikin and the ocker, punching a man for using bad language in front of women.

TELEVISION, FILM, AND THE SHOCK OF BAD LANGUAGE

Swearing in film was commonplace by the 1970s. Bad language in American films quickly increased from the end of the 1960s, with groundbreaking films such as *Easy Rider* (1969) and *Midnight Cowboy* (1969) paving the way. American films of the 1970s included the full range of swear words, including *shit* and *fuck*.

Films also engaged in increased levels of violence, as well as frank depictions, and sometimes discussions, of sex. Replacing older systems of censorship, ratings systems were introduced as a way to manage the level of profanity, violence and sex – if a broader audience was sought for a film, such things had to be limited or left out altogether.

Australian films of the 1970s enthusiastically embraced depictions of sex, nudity and swearing. The film version of *Don's Party*, for example, includes full frontal nudity (male and female), and sex scenes as well as discussions of sex. It retained much of the play's language, including the use of *fuck* and *cunt*. But arguably the film is more preoccupied with sex than the play, and this reflects a definite trend seen in the movies of the 1970s. With the demise of censorship, film could push the boundaries of what could be depicted on screen. The 1970s thus saw the production of numerous Australian films – some of which are now known as *Ozploitation* films – that depicted nudity and sex on screen. Ozploitation movies included *Stork* (1971), *Alvin Purple* (1973) and *Petersen* (1974). Yet while these films undoubtedly unsettle even the modern viewer with full frontal nudity and graphic depictions of sex, as well as their sexism and misogyny, swearing was somewhat peripheral to the way these films sought to shock their audiences.

Adapting a book for the screen in the 1970s could offer opportunities to include stronger language and more sex. *Helga's Web*, a 1970 novel by Australian crime writer Jon Cleary, was adapted into a 1975 movie, *Scobie Malone*, starring Jack Thompson. The film spends a lot of time showing women's breasts and having Scobie (a police detective) bed various women all while solving the murder of high-class mistress and sex worker Helga. Language is tame compared to the nudity and sex. There are several uses of *bloody* and *bastard*, as well as *bitch*, and these match the level of language in the novel. But there are also a few uses of stronger words – mostly when Scobie is particularly frustrated by being thwarted from arresting the culprit (a government minister who was sleeping with Helga and whom she was blackmailing). He uses both *fuck it* and *shit!* These do not appear in the novel, perhaps reflecting the difference that just a few years made (1970 to 1975) in terms of language.

Swearing could also be used to emphasise a particular type of Australian masculinity, enhancing the Australian bad language mythology. This was clear in the figure of the ocker but could also be seen in masculine figures such as the police detective (Scobie Malone) as well as 'classic' Australian characters. These include the shearers of *Sunday Too Far Away* (1975), a film set in an out-back sheep station just before the 1956 shearers' strike over a cut to wages and again starring Jack Thompson. Although historical, the film uses bad language and Australian vernacular to underline the masculinity and Australianness of the shearers. Expressions such as *giving me the shits*, *balltearer of a day*, *pig's arse* and *fair cow*, along with *buggered* and *bastard*, are used.

Television changed much more slowly than film, reflecting the role of the medium within the family home. Yet it too began to test what was acceptable. In Britain, *fuck* was first uttered on television by critic Kenneth Tynan in 1965.[46] The incident merited press coverage in Australia, and links back to the story of *Oz*. When Richard Neville took on the job of movie reviewer for the *Sydney Morning Herald* in the mid-1960s, Martin Sharp drew a cartoon in response to the outrage of Tynan saying *fuck* on television, featuring a yob shouting 'Get Tynanned'. The paper however refused to print it.[47] *Get Tynanned* enjoyed a brief vogue as a euphemism for *get fucked*.

Graham Kennedy is a notable figure in the Australian story of bad language on television, although he is preceded by newsreader Kevin Crease, who accidentally said *fucking hell* on Adelaide television in 1969. Kennedy made his name on the show *In Melbourne*

Tonight, which ran from 1957 until 1970, followed by *The Graham Kennedy Show*, which began broadcasting in 1972. He tested the Australian Broadcasting Control Board through the use of phrases such as 'that's a horse's arse'. But where he really pushed boundaries on television was with his infamous 'crow call' *faarrrkkk* in 1975. As a result, the board told Kennedy he was contravening public standards and had to stop. After this warning, his show had to be pre-recorded.[48] The pre-recording subsequently allowed the network to edit out a critical statement he made about an Australian senator; as a result, Kennedy resigned.

Comedy shows were particularly important vehicles in shifting attitudes around language, often through innuendo and double entendres. Kennedy returned to television to host the game/comedy show *Blankety Blanks* in 1976 (it ran until 1978).[49] *Blankety Blanks* allowed Kennedy to revel in suggestive language.[50] The show, which asked celebrities to guess missing words in a sentence, had plenty of scope for people at home (and on stage) to imagine a rude word. For example, in one segment Kennedy described a man who got so drunk that he mistook his wife for a turkey and tried to [blank] her. The celebrity guests on the stage then tried to guess the 'blanked' word, selecting words such as 'pluck' and 'stuff'.[51]

Various comedy shows in the 1970s engaged with bad language, if still somewhat tamely, as part of a general challenge to the kinds of television shows previously broadcast. For example, *The Aunty Jack Show* (1972–73), a surrealist comedy program with outrageous characters and bizarre humour, made some use of profanity, although it was very mild. Its main character was Aunty Jack, played by Grahame Bond in drag, who frequently threatened to 'rip yer bloody arms off'. The show was popular with younger viewers, although many people complained about it. *The Naked Vicar Show* (1977–78) included a segment lampooning gardening advice programs called 'Getting Rooted'.[52] By the late 1970s, television was shifting only slowly; bad language on television would continue to be a source of controversy and subject to various forms of regulation well into the next century.

FOUR-LETTER WORDS

The 1960s and 70s saw the rise of the 'four-letter word' – most commonly this was *fuck*, but could also be *shit* or *cunt*. The expression *four-letter word* became a common usage and a topic of conversation in its own right. A 1969 editorial in the *Canberra Times*, for example, noted that 'four-letter words and the detail of sexual experiences are proliferating across the pages of the Western world', but defended its decision not to publish the actual 'four-letter word meaning sexual intercourse' (in relation to a recently published novel), on the basis of freedom of choice. 'It is true', they argued, 'that a printed word is merely a grouping of letters and cannot be inherently obscene, but it is a fact, too, that many people object to some words.' As the newspaper was read by 'wives and children', the editorial concluded, it was better not to print the word.[53]

The *Canberra Times* finally printed the controversial four-letter word – *fuck* – two years later, as part of a report on a Liberal MP who had used a different four-letter word (*arse*) to make a point about changing standards and censorship.[54] The word did not appear in more general contexts, however, until the 1980s. The courts also discussed the 'problem' of four-letter words as standards began to shift in these years. In 1972, for example, the Adelaide Supreme Court ruled that the 'use of four-letter words was not necessarily indecent'. Context increasingly came to matter in how such language was regarded.[55]

If federal parliament is anything to go by, *bloody*, *bugger* and *bastard* had all become relatively normalised by the end of the 1960s, although they could still lead to a charge of unparliamentary, disorderly language. Four-letter words were spoken in parliament in the 1970s (and no doubt had been spoken privately by politicians for a long time before that). The first *shit* appeared in a literal sense in Hansard in 1971, and in a figurative one in 1979. A mention of *fuck* was made in parliament in 1971 also, when the member for Prospect, Dick Klugman, talked about censorship, and quoted from a former censor to query why *fuck* continued to be banned, when *bugger*, 'used even in quite frivolous contexts', was permissible.[56] A year later, there was a lengthy debate in the Senate as to whether the word *fuck* should be recorded in Hansard. A Tasmanian senator challenged the power of the president of the Senate to have the word removed from Hansard. Australian Labor Party Senator Justin O'Byrne decried such a power, arguing that *fuck* was now an 'accepted word'. Challenged by Senator Jack Little to go out and say it on a street corner in Canberra because he would find himself arrested, O'Byrne retorted: 'What rubbish. You have been using it yourself for years.' (A charge Little denied.)[57]

What about broadcast media? In 1975, it was noted that the ABC would allow the 'use of four-letter words on its radio programs in some circumstances', according to its chair, Richard Downing. He argued that '[t]he ABC should record society for society and not necessarily protect it ... Social standards are changing rapidly and I would like the ABC staff to have maximum freedom to discuss topics of controversy and delicacy as long as they do it responsibly.' While it wouldn't suggest that these words would be used normally, '[i]t is accepted, however, that on rare occasions the subject matter and form of discussions or presentation, while acceptable, may require and justify the use of these words and expressions'.[58] Radio programming, like print media, continues even today to exercise considerable caution when it comes to four-letter words.

Let's examine some of these contentious and controversial four-letter words in more detail. We've seen that *fuck* is iconic to the 1960s and 70s. *Fuck* can be used in many different ways and is a highly versatile swear word. Its origin is Germanic, possibly with an Indo-European root meaning 'strike'. It came into English, as a verb meaning 'sexual intercourse', in the early 16th century. As an exclamation – *fuck!* – it can express a whole range of emotions from anger to dismay to disappointment to surprise. It can be used as a term of abuse – for example, *you dumb fuck* – and it can be used to refer directly to the act of copulation. It can be used in expressions such as *what the fuck?*, *fuck you!* and *fuck all*. *Fuck* is also widely used as an intensifier in adjectival form – *fucking* (also *fuckin'* and, more recently in Australia, often written as *fucken* in order to represent a broad Australian pronunciation of *fucking*).

Fuck also combines with other words to create new words – usually insults and derogatory terms. *Fuckface*, *fucktard*, *fuckbag*, *fuckless wonder*, *fuckmuppet*, *fuckknuckle* and *fuckpig* are just a sample of these. None of these are exclusively Australian, but we do lay claim to *fuckwit*. *Fuckwit* is an Australianism, first recorded in Alex Buzo's play *The Front Room Boys* (1969); it is also recorded in plays from the early 1970s. It has subsequently been exported to the world, although it remains more widely used (or at least found in print) in Australia. And although dating from the 1980s, we also lay claim to the expression *no wuckers* (from *no wucking furries*, a transposition of *no fucking worries*). *Fuck* has thus proven to be a lexically productive feature of Australian English.

Another ubiquitous four-letter word is *shit*, which has developed from Old English *scitte* 'diarrhoea' and is probably of Germanic origin. As a term of abuse for someone, the evidence dates to the 16th century, but it isn't until the 19th century that its use is recorded as an exclamation. While *shit* was widely used across English-speaking countries, many *shit*-related words and expressions appear to be more commonly or originally Australian. Many first find their way into print in the 1960s, often through the playwrights and cultural figures already discussed, although they were no doubt around long before in spoken usage. The verb form *to shit someone* (to annoy someone, as in 'he shits me') is Australian, first recorded in 1965. The exclamation *shit a brick* has much early Australian evidence, and was used in the Barry McKenzie comic strip. *Deadshit* is first recorded in the Alex Buzo play *Macquarie* (1971). The rhyming slang *Edgar Britt* is also first recorded in a Buzo play, *The Front Room Boys* (1969), but the earlier rhyming slang form *Jimmy Britts* (also *Jim-brit*) is recorded in the 1950s.* *Packing shit* is first recorded in 1971. *Cunning as a shithouse rat* is recorded in 1962. *Ratshit* is first recorded in the underground magazine *Kings Cross Whisper* in 1970; the noun use is also found elsewhere, but the adjectival form (for example, 'you look ratshit') is Australian. *Shitkicker*, first recorded as prison slang, is Australian. Another Australianism is *shitcan* 'to denigrate', first recorded in 1974. *Shitty*, an Australian term meaning bad-tempered, is first recorded in 1971, and *stiff shit* is first recorded in 1969. *Bang like a shithouse door* is another Humphries-ism, first recorded in 1968. Writer and children's folklore specialist June Factor, in her dictionary of Australian *Kidspeak*, also records *dickshit*, *shitbag* and *shitface*, all insults used of a person.[59]

The last of the four-letter words, *cunt*, is a word with a long history. *Cunt* is found in Middle English, and possibly has a much longer history with an origin in classical Latin. It's found in place names in the 13th century and does not appear to be particularly

---

*   Edgar Britt was a jockey and Jimmy Britt a boxer. Celebrity and sports names often feature in rhyming slang.

taboo until the obscene (the sexual and the excretory) began to overtake religious oaths as the most reviled bad language. Its first use as a term meaning 'a promiscuous woman' dates to the 17th century; from the 1860s, it is recorded as a term of abuse for a man. But it was the most taboo term of all through much of the 20th century. It is little wonder that the counterculture and radicals of the 1970s took ownership of the word, as did popular culture; as we'll see, Germaine Greer claimed it as part of the counterculture and as feminist politics, and 1970s Australian films did not shy away from using it, although only sparingly. Nevertheless, it is not until recently that the word really seems to be moving towards mainstream acceptability and usage.

THE LANGUAGE OF LIBERATION: WOMEN

Historian Michelle Arrow has noted the 1970s as a period in which widespread beliefs about what should be private or public shifted. Activism around women's rights, gay rights, and Indigenous rights all served to bring the personal to bear on the political.[60] For women, changing language was an important tool in transforming the structures that oppressed them. In addition, bad language became a means of liberating women from the straitjacket of 'respectable' female behaviour. Neither battle was won easily – nor are these battles complete even today.

Despite the radical rhetoric taken up by student newspapers – and the role of women such as Wendy Bacon in challenging censorship and obscenity charges – student newspapers reflected a more general ongoing sexism that was all too apparent in the counterculture. As late as the early 1970s, many radical publications featured material that was sexist and degrading to women.[61] And while popular culture might have reflected sexual liberation, it didn't necessarily make much progress in expressing greater respect for women or furthering their rights.

One thing feminists wanted to draw attention to was the use of language, including sexist and stereotyped portrayals of women in the media and popular culture.[62] The feminist campaign against sexist language was a deliberate effort to try and change language use and to make people more aware of the way language could have discriminatory effects. The category of 'bad language' was shifting to include language that discriminates. The major effects of this campaign would be felt in the 1980s and beyond, as government and media became more conscious of the language they used and began to move towards somewhat more gender-neutral language (for example, replacing the use of *chairman* with *chair* or *chairperson*). In the 1970s, feminists campaigned against sexist aspects of common language use, such as the generic *man* just mentioned and the *-ess* suffix used in occupation descriptions (for example *conductress*). They also campaigned for the adoption of the title *Ms* to replace *Miss* and *Mrs*, as the latter two defined women by their marital status, something *Mr* does not do for men.[63]

Feminists also claimed the use of 'traditional' bad language – swearing and the obscene – as a way to shock, and thus as a means of female empowerment. The respectable woman, as we've seen throughout this book, was not supposed to swear or use bad language. And, indeed, Australian writer Nancy Keesing's study of 'sheilaspeak', compiled in the 1980s using the evidence of female correspondents talking about the lives of their mothers and grandmothers, attests to the 'respectable' household as one in which profanity was rarely, if ever, used. 'A polite fiction prevailed', she writes, 'that women would not know the meaning of many a terrible word even if they did hear it.' At worst, women used expressions such as *good gravy* or *muddy great bucket of pitch*, records Keesing.[64] The ideal of the respectable woman exerted a powerful hold and shaped social expectations. Some feminists challenged and sought to destroy these kinds of stereotypes; in addition, they marked a generational rebellion in the use of language. Using bad language (as well as franker language around bodily functions) could be seen as a powerful way to put into action and express their agenda.

Germaine Greer is an important figure in the way feminists turned bad language into a weapon, not only nationally but also internationally. While arguably Greer's actions were motivated as much by her position as a countercultural figure as her feminist politics, language was central to her presentation of herself. Born in 1939 in Melbourne, she attended convent school. When arriving at the University of Melbourne, her friend, author and feminist Beatrice Faust, observed of her: 'She had the full convent syndrome: fucking like crazy, swearing, without being fully formed … The way she talked about sex was morbid. She could swear about it, but not talk about it.' At university, Faust noted that Greer 'specialised in swearing in public, audibly across restaurants'.[65] This behaviour inspired some: Louise Ferrier, who went on to a relationship with *Oz* magazine editor Richard Neville and was an influential cultural figure, remembers that she had been impressed by the fact that Greer was 'the first woman she had known to say "fuck" in public'.[66]

In 1959, Greer went to the University of Sydney, where she became part of the Sydney Push; she then headed to England to go to the University of Cambridge, receiving her PhD in 1968. Greer established herself as a prominent figure within the British counterculture, and she became associated with the Australians of *Oz* magazine. She contributed to *Oz*, writing boundary-pushing articles such as 'The Universal Tonguebath: A Groupie's Vision' which explored the 'group fuck'.[67] Greer also contributed to Amsterdam-based magazine *Suck*, a radical publication that included graphic descriptions of bestiality, incest and paedophilia – nothing was considered off limits.[68] In 1970, her most famous book *The Female Eunuch* was published, making her an international celebrity. She also edited an edition of (British) *Oz* called 'Cunt Power Oz', which had, according to Richard Neville, 'some of our most provocative erotica ever'.[69] To this end, the use of profanity was only one aspect of the way writers like Greer pushed the boundaries of obscenity – and it was hardly the most offensive or shocking.

Greer's challenge to public language came not only through print. In 1972, on a tour of New Zealand, she made a public speech in which she used the words *fuck* and *bullshit*, for which she was charged by police. When Greer appeared before the Auckland Magistrate's Court, people protested outside, many chanting the offensive words, and throwing things at the police.[70] Twenty protestors were arrested.[71] Greer was subsequently acquitted for saying *bullshit*, but *was* found guilty of saying *fuck*. She was given a NZD$40 fine, but never paid it.[72] The *Australian Women's Weekly* reported on Greer's 1972 tour of the Antipodes and quoted her on four-letter words. These she claimed to have learned at convent school: 'I use them now where I think they're appropriate. One in particular [probably *cunt*] … I'd like to take all the steam and violence out of that word. It's a factual word and it should be a gentle one.'[73]

Women's use of bad language also connected to the desire to make what had previously been seen as private into matters for public discussion. This included issues such as women's health, sex and reproduction. The year 1975 was International Women's Year, and an increase in money in the federal arts budget led to support for feminist creative initiatives. One of these initiatives was the poetry anthology *Mother, I'm Rooted*, edited by feminist and activist Kate Jennings.[74] This anthology of poems sought to reflect the breadth of women's experiences and aimed to be a 'highly provocative, political statement'. Many bookshops refused to stock it, and some newspapers refused to review it.[75]

Jennings commented in the preface to the book that she was 'rooted … sad, tired, spooked and gone a slight bit loopy' from dealing with the criticism and disparaging comments from men who dismissed her project.[76] The anthology had 152 contributors and 300 contributions. Jennings looked for contributions that artic-ulated what she considered to be an 'authentic' female experience, including those that addressed motherhood, menstruation, house-work and social conditioning. It sold over 10 000 copies, attracting readers beyond those who would normally read poetry.[77] In terms of objectionable language – as opposed to the radical impact of poems dealing with topics such as rape, sexuality, and menstrua-tion – there is not a great deal. However, Colleen Allen's poem, which opens the anthology, captures the way in which feminists could make use of blunt language as a political statement about the objectification of women:

> They think I'm a hole to fuck,
> They think I'm clay to mould, finger and shape,
> …
> But,
> cunt or me?
> I've yet to see.[78]

Australian women also took advantage of new printing technolo-gies to produce their own print culture, including launching femi-nist newspapers and publications through the first half of the 1970s such as *Mejane, Vashti's Voice, Refractory Girl, Womanspeak, Hecate, Scarlet Woman* and *Fin*.[79] *Mejane* was published in the early 1970s, and tackled topics such as abortion, women in the workplace, the Vietnam War, and women's bodies. Swearing is not much used, but it was clearly a topic of concern to women. In one *Mejane* contribution, a woman named Vera relates how a man had instructed her that feminists might gain more respect by not using four-letter words: 'Be feminine ladies, prove your middleclass dignity to men, and then they might consider making you equal!' This was something many feminists rejected, as did radicals generally. As Vera pointed out after being arrested for saying *fuck* at a Vietnam War protest, 'it became terribly clear that some people are more concerned about a middleclass girl swearing than with a child being napalmed'.[80]

THE LANGUAGE OF LIBERATION: INDIGENOUS AUSTRALIANS

The 1960s also saw various efforts to fight discrimination against Indigenous people, both formal and informal. The Australian Freedom Ride of 1965 drew attention to and protested against segregation practices in rural towns. Most memorably, in 1967, a referendum was held to delete two discriminatory references to Aboriginal people in the Australian Constitution. Although voting rights had already been granted, this referendum became a way of mobilising Australians to publicly support Indigenous acceptance and equality. As historian Russell McGregor writes, the 'overarching [referendum] campaign theme was the need to bring Aboriginal people into the fellowship of the nation'.[81] Legal scholar and Eualeyai/Gamillaroi woman Larissa Behrendt notes that despite this nation-building aim, the referendum did not succeed in overcoming the 'us and them' mentality nor 'herald in an era of non-discrimination'.[82]

An important factor that transformed the nature and tone of Indigenous activism in this period was the shift of Indigenous populations from rural to urban contexts, as Indigenous people gained greater control over their own movement, and with the closing of missions and reserves. The Sydney Indigenous community, for example, went from approximately 2000 people in 1967 (not including the reserve at La Perouse) to 35000 in 1969.[83] Many activists were disillusioned about government handling of Indigenous affairs, and rejected the agenda and ideologies of assimilation. Activists such as Kevin Gilbert, a Wiradjuri man, called attention to the ongoing psychological impacts of the historical experiences of Indigenous people: 'Aboriginal Australia underwent a rape of the soul so profound that the blight continues in the minds of most blacks today', he wrote in 1977.[84]

Inspired in part by the evolution of African-American politics – especially Black Power – activists demanded that Indigenous voices be heard and respected. From the 1970s the term 'self-determination' gained currency in relation to Indigenous policy and activism.[85] Protests such as the Aboriginal Tent Embassy in Canberra and the Gurindji workers' strike at Wave Hill Station increasingly put the focus on Indigenous sovereignty, and land rights began to emerge as a prominent part of the Indigenous political agenda.[86]

Through the 1960s, language became an important focus for asserting Indigenous rights and identity. In 1963, the Yolngu people sent their Bark Petitions signed by clan leaders and elders, written in Yolngu Matha, to federal parliament. It was highly significant that they used their own language – it was tangible evidence of their culture and their survival as a people.[87] The use of Indigenous languages was increasingly asserted as a right by activists in this period, even though, as Steve Mam, a Queenslander of Torres Strait Islander descent, declared in the 1970s, letting his children speak English was the 'only way that I can beat the fucking white man'.[88]

Terminology also mattered. From the early 1960s, Ian Spalding, founder of the lobby group Aboriginal Affairs, began to challenge the way government policies manifested a 'lack of respect' for Indigenous people through the language and terminology used to refer to them. Spalding wrote to Prime Minister Menzies in 1961 asking for the word *Aboriginal* and its derivatives to be capitalised, as well as requesting that government stop using the word *native* to refer to Indigenous people. The activist publication *Smoke Signals* also took up this argument about terminology and naming, publishing an article in March 1962 that called for the capitalised form *Aborigine* to become standard usage.[89] After the 1963 Native Welfare Conference, the federal Department of Territories adopted the capitalised form and agreed to drop the use of *native*, with some other Commonwealth departments following suit.[90] From this point on, the capitalised form began to be established as standard usage.

Racist language also came under increasing scrutiny in this period. In 1964, Barry Christophers, a doctor and a prominent white activist who fought for Indigenous rights, wrote an article for *Smoke Signals* under the heading 'Terminology is Important' in which he listed racist words for Aboriginal people that were highly objectionable and offensive, including *gin*, *abo*, *nigger* and *native*. He rejected use of the word *black*, despite its popularity in the period, because of the negative connotations attached to the colour.[91] Indigenous people did, however, begin to reclaim *Black* as a term of some empowerment. By the 1990s the variant spelling *Blak* (perhaps coined in 1991[92]) was in common use, rejecting the negative colonialist and colour implications of the *Black* spelling.

Black Power had a significant impact on Indigenous activism. The Black Panther Party of Australia was established by Denis Walker in 1971.[93] Some Indigenous activists found inspiration in the ideas and actions of African-American political figures such as Stokely Carmichael (later Kwame Ture) and Malcolm X, and self-determination was a fundamental principle within Aboriginal organisations.[94] Historian Kathy Lothian writes that Black Power offered 'extraordinary visual and rhetorical power', and was an overt rejection of the powerlessness that many Aboriginal people experienced.[95] Indigenous Black Power activists specifically fought against police intimidation, harassment and surveillance in urban areas. For example, activists in Sydney's Redfern carried notebooks and pencils with them to collect evidence of police mistreatment.[96]

As a consequence of the influence of Black Power and its culture, African-American language found its way into Indigenous activist language, seen for example in the use of *honky* and *the man* to describe white oppressors, and *Uncle Tom* to describe those regarded as being in collusion with 'the man'. Victorian activist and political leader Bruce McGuinness, records Lothian, said in 1972 that the 'old book of rules was out', and the 'new book's title' was 'Black is beautiful, right on brothers and sisters, and screw you whitey'.[97] Swearing could also play a role in the language of dissent, as one small glimpse into the protest soundscape reveals. A newspaper report on a National Aborigines' Day march in 1972 recorded that numerous protesters had been heard using 'unseemly words'. It recorded that '[t]he Aboriginal [who was arrested], a leader of the so-called black power group, had been shouting a four-letter word over a loudspeaker at police and advocating the end of pacifism by Aborigines'.[98]

Indigenous activism also focused on the importance of culture as a means of recovering and developing Indigenous voices and identity. Indigenous cultural productions worked to overcome a culture of silence and disempowerment.[99] Activist, actor and playwright Bob Maza attended a Black Power conference in the USA in September 1970 and discovered Amiri Baraka's National Black Theatre in Harlem; this inspired him to establish a National Black Theatre in Redfern in 1972. The Black Theatre was a consciously political undertaking, both as protest and as an attempt to explore what constituted Aboriginality.[100] As Maza argued, 'Black Theatre is geared to communicate with people, not just to entertain'.[101] Prior to the theatre productions of the 1970s, most Indigenous theatre was considered by white Australians to consist only of traditional Aboriginal dance performances, and that tended to get what funding was available.[102] This began to change in the 1970s, with important plays such as *Jack Charles Is Up and Fighting* and *The Cherry Pickers*.

One of the first plays produced by the National Black Theatre company was the satirical revue *Basically Black* (1972). Its cast included Aileen Corpus, Zac Martin, Gary Foley, Bob Maza and Bindi Williams. *Basically Black* satirised a variety of subjects including the Tent Embassy, Evonne Cawley (Goolagong), Neville Bonner, Bennelong and Lord Vestey.[103] Indigenous studies scholar Karen Austin writes that the sketches were at the time considered to be quite shocking, noting the subversive effect of Indigenous actors playing roles that mocked and mimicked themselves.[104] This was probably the first time many white Sydney theatre audiences saw Indigenous artists on the stage.[105] *Basically Black* was popular with audiences, with over 2000 people attending the production at the Nimrod Theatre in Sydney.[106] When it went on tour in Queensland, there was concern over the way it showed Indigenous people 'talking up', and people on the Yarrabah mission were told by the local authorities to stay away from the show; they attended anyway.[107]

One of the most memorable of *Basically Black*'s sketches was 'Super Boong', performed by actor Zac Martin, playing 'Lionel Mouse', a parody of boxer Lionel Rose. Austin notes the reclamation of offensive words such as *boong* through productions such as these: 'Such humour, with its self-styled superiority and indifference to historical racist images and language, deliberately attempts to shock audiences.'[108] The character of 'Super Boong' aimed to use humour to provoke audiences to think about the issues around racism; it also reclaimed racist language. Media studies scholar Alan McKee notes of the use of the offensive word *boong*, '[f]or an Aboriginal person to take up the term "boong" is a necessarily aggressive act, but a very different one to white use of the word'.[109] Humour, Austin further suggests, also served as a vehicle to communicate issues where other forms of more direct or confronting political commentary may have angered audience members.[110] There was also a short-lived attempt in 1973 to create a television show based on the revue – while only a pilot episode was filmed, one of the sketches included was 'Super Boong'.[111]

Indigenous theatre scholar Maryrose Casey's careful analysis of the criticism of Indigenous plays of this period considers the way that plays about contemporary urban Indigenous life were often dismissed as 'political', notwithstanding that they addressed and gave expression to the real experiences of Indigenous people.[112] Critics (who were invariably white) had mixed responses to the show and Casey notes how the use of profanity was understood as a lack of professionalism (something not said of white playwrights who used profanity), rather than as inherent to the articulation of anger. The show was also criticised as 'derivative' and the cast seen to be in need of 'discipline'.[113] One critic, Susie Eisenhuth, writing for the *Sunday Telegraph*, also criticised the amount of swearing, commenting that it would only shock non-Aboriginal people but 'if you're black you'll love it'.[114] White responses to language are also seen, Casey argues, in Donald Horne's comments in his 1980 account of the preceding decade and a half, *Time of Hope*. In the book, Horne praises the use of four-letter words by student protesters as a 'weapon of protest and demystification', but dismisses *Basically Black* with the comment 'the blacks did little more than rant and swear'.[115] Racist attitudes clearly structured these critical responses to the Indigenous use of a bad language of rebellion and resistance.

FIGHTING HOMOPHOBIC LANGUAGE

The 1960s and 70s saw battles for liberation being fought on many fronts. In the Second World War period and the years that followed, homophobic slurs had increasingly featured in the Australian vernacular. Many are first recorded or became more widely used in the 1940s and 50s: *poof*, *poofter*, the rhyming slang *horse's hoof*, *poonce*, *tonk*, *triss* and *wonk*. *Tootsie* and *leso*, meaning 'a lesbian', are also first recorded around this time. A number of these terms were either Australianisms or have a great deal of evidence for their use in Australia.

Terms for a gay man, such as *poonce*, *tonk*, *wonk* and *triss* conveyed a sense of effeminacy and could be used to question the masculinity of a heterosexual man. While homophobic slurs are not in any way exclusive to Australia, homophobic language (extending to concerns over effeminacy) figures quite prominently, revealing a particular anxiety around masculinity that has a long history in Australian culture. Perhaps the 1940s and 50s (the Second World War, which awoke Australian fears about an 'invasion' of American servicemen who would be attractive to Australian women, and the Cold War with its fear of 'deviance') made masculinity and homosexuality of particular concern. What is clear is that such language formed an essential part of the structure of prejudice and discrimination that profoundly affected people's lives.

Discrimination shaped the daily existence of people whose sexualities were different from the dominant, heterosexual, norm of the period.[116] Historian Graham Willett labels the 1950s the 'darkest decade' for same-sex-attracted people in Australia, noting the increase in the number of people charged and convicted in Australia's courts for 'unnatural offences'.[117] Through the 1960s, offensive homophobic language continued to evolve with new items entering the lexicon. The term *shirt-lifter* is first recorded in 1966, *freckle puncher* in 1968, and *bum puncher* in 1977. All of these were Australianisms. The lifting of censorship did mean that homosexuality could be dealt with in print or on film, gradually beginning a shift in community attitudes.

Much of the prevailing 'ocker' culture was based on an exaggerated if ultimately insecure masculinity, as we've already seen. If Barry McKenzie's homophobia was satirical, it nonetheless echoed male anxieties around the topic. The increased focus on sexual liberation did mean, however, that a range of sexual practices and identities began to be depicted, if still in ambivalent ways.

LGBTIQ people began to campaign to change discriminatory laws and to decriminalise their sexual practices; this also meant fighting homophobic language and attitudes and changing the kind of language used to discuss their sexuality. In 1970 CAMP – Campaign Against Moral Persecution – was established to campaign for the rights of LGBTIQ people.[118] By the early 1970s, gays and lesbians in particular were insisting on greater social and legal visibility.[119] Homosexuality began to be decriminalised from the middle of the 1970s, with South Australia being the first state to do so.[120]

Changing language around sexuality was complex, especially when homophobic language was entrenched in the Australian vernacular. The word *gay* did not come into widespread use until the 1970s. A sampling of CAMP's magazine, *Camp Ink*, reveals that there was a shift from early issues in 1970 where the word *homosexual* dominates, to the use of *gay* by 1972, seemingly influenced by the trend from the USA. Overall, the use of the terms *gay* and *lesbian* increased in the 1970s, but Reynolds and Robinson note that many Australian men continued to use terms such as *camp*.[121] This reflected the development of a distinct identity, and an increasing confidence in being 'out' and, for many, 'out and proud'.

*%$!

By the end of the 1970s, Australia's bad language landscape had changed profoundly. Censorship had ended, although there were restrictions on, for example, pornography, and classification systems were introduced for film and television. There was a new freedom to swear. Swearing continued to be tied to an Australian (male) identity – sometimes a source of humour and sometimes revealing the darker underside of Australian society. It was also tied to the re-visioning of Australian national identity in the 1970s, as Australian nationalism was redefined for an age after the end of the British Empire. Bad language could also be claimed by feminists and Indigenous people, among others, as a tool of subversion and empowerment, although still risking punishment and attempts to silence them. The push by activists to draw attention to sexist, racist and homophobic language was an important step in changing understandings of what constituted bad language in Australia. This project would continue into the 1980s and beyond.

PART FOUR

BAD LANGUAGE EVERYWHERE,
1980s–PRESENT

8

C U IN THE NT: BAD LANGUAGE IN MODERN AUSTRALIA

In August 2019, a meme appeared on my Facebook feed. The picture was of a blackboard with the following text written on it: 'A long time ago we had empires run by emperors, then we had kingdoms run by kings, and now we have countries ...' This amusing meme was not particularly shocking in and of itself, but what surprised me was that it had been 'shared' to my feed by my mother-in-law, a woman of fairly conservative views and just about the last person I would expect to share something like this. (She washed my husband's mouth out with soap – literally! – for saying *shit* when he was a child.) As it turned out, she had no idea what the meme meant – she had thought the missing word was 'democracy'. She hastily apologised to all her Facebook friends.

The 'c-word', of all swear words, remains taboo for some, but as we'll see, it's rapidly becoming an 'everyday' swear word for many of the younger generation, if perhaps still used more by men talking to other men than by women. Since the 1970s, Australia has embraced swearing with relatively few reservations in most contexts. Yet there have been, and are, contentious areas that raise the question of who can swear without censure and who can't: some people have called for hip hop songs with confrontational swearing to be banned from the radio, while reality television shows broadcast 'bleeped' words, to much promotional fanfare; we have enjoyed watching 'sweary' dramas such as *The Sopranos*, while politicians called for inquiries into the corrupting effects of the swearing on a Gordon Ramsay show, *Ramsay's Kitchen Nightmares.*

This chapter considers some aspects of swearing in the past 40 or so years. In particular, I'll look at: the ways in which boundaries have been pushed back on swearing yet still remain; how it's acceptable for some people to swear in some contexts but not others; and, most importantly, the shift to a new taboo language – that of discriminatory language, slurs and epithets, and the pushback from those who say that 'political correctness' is stifling 'free speech'. Bad language has arguably become more globalised, notably through the effect of social media. But at the same time, our attitudes towards swearing, and our particular preoccupations and discussions around bad language reveal important aspects of our society as it is now.

COMEDY PUSHING BOUNDARIES

Since the 1980s, comedy has made use and helped to push the boundaries of swearing, as it often has in previous decades. While what we find funny has certainly changed over time, swearing, word play and innuendo have all remained central features of Australian humour.

The 1980s were a decade of change in bad language in Australian comedy. It saw the emergence of 'blue comics' such as Col Elliott, Kevin Bloody Wilson and Rodney Rude into the 'mainstream'.* These comedians were popular with an audience who

---

* Comedians like Rodney Rude have since been rejected by some for racist and homophobic comedy. See James Weir 'Were these Australian Comedians Ever Funny?', News.com.au, <www.news.com.au/entertainment/celebrity-life/were-these-australian-comedians-ever-funny/news-story/b23647cd1ef3fccb2ca75844ff2f919e>.

loved the prolific swearing (the word *fuck* appeared often) and jokes about 'tits and arses'.[1] This kind of comedy began in small local clubs in the 1970s, but very much came into its own in the 1980s. Rude was arrested for obscenity in both Queensland and Western Australia during the 1980s, but when one of his cases went to the Supreme Court, he won. The victory made it easier to perform his kind of act.[2]

Comedians of the 1980s thus came to revel in the opportunity to swear, perhaps sometimes just because of the fact that they were uttering words that for so long had been subject to prosecution or censorship. The comedy act 'The Twelfth Man' is a good example of this kind of humour based on prolific swearing. As part of the act, comedian Billy Birmingham impersonated popular cricket commentators such as Richie Benaud. The Benaud character 'swear[s] his arse off', something the real Benaud would never do, as he commentates on the cricket.[3] The mock commentary uses a lot of *fuck* and *piss off*, as well as insults such as *wanker*.[4]

Comedy performers have also used profanity as a way to attack institutions that hold political, social and cultural power. For example, in 2010 comedian and musician Tim Minchin wrote and performed *The Pope Song*, which included many repetitions of *motherfucker* and *motherfucking*, and the line 'fuck the motherfucking Pope' as a pointed criticism of the Catholic Church's failure to deal with child abuse scandals. In the song, Minchin observes that if people are more offended by the song than by the revelations about institutional child abuse, then they are the problem, so 'fuck you'.[5]

Women have been important in the story of bad language and humour, especially in recent decades. Firstly, they have taken ownership of swearing to subvert the stereotype that women don't use such language. This has helped make women more confident in rejecting expectations around their behaviour and speech.

Secondly, some women have used profanity to challenge institutional power.

Swearing is integral to the comedy of many female Australian comedians. One example is the humour of Jane Turner and Gina Riley. In their sitcom *Kath and Kim*, which they write and perform in, Turner and Riley use swearing and clever word play for humour, and to send up stereotypes around class. One memorable scene in the show has Kim Craig (played by Riley), who is typically depicted as a not-very-bright bogan, saying to several people that she is still waiting for her 'cardonnay'. She insists that the 'ch' in chardonnay is pronounced as a hard 'c', because it is French. When she continues to be corrected by the others, who are laughing at her, she angrily retorts 'oh, all right, chardonnay, chardonnay, you pack of chunts'.[6]

Indigenous women have also used humour, as anthropologist Megan McCullough suggests, to create 'a space wherein Murri[*] people can talk to each other and fight against non-indigenous understandings and perceptions of Murri life'.[7] Swearing is used within this humour in powerful ways. McCullough discusses in detail a particular joke from Northern Queensland that makes a powerful commentary on intimate violence, as well as the racially charged and sexist nature of the justice system that Indigenous women typically experience. In the joke, a Cape York woman describes how her husband beat her and kicked her 'in the cunt'. The husband is taken to court, and the woman is instructed by her solicitor that she must use the word 'vagina' when describing the incident to the court. On the stand, she turns to her solicitor and asks: 'What that flash … word for cunt?'[8]

The Cape York woman in the joke uses the word *cunt*, a word considered 'too riotous and rebellious' for the courtroom, thus

---

*   A name for Indigenous people of Queensland and north-west New South Wales.

subverting the power structures that attempt to control her and her body. McCullough writes that the use of *cunt* in this joke can be considered significant on several levels:

> 'Cunt' can be interpreted as a reference to the fact that policemen and white authority figures are often referred to as 'cunts' during moments of anger and humour made to express anger at whiteness and at authority. Whiteness and authority are often thought of synonymously in the Murri world. By bringing 'cunt' into the courtroom, the woman in the joke reminds the Murri audience that law enforcement can be 'cunts', so to speak.

Given the lengthy history of Indigenous people being charged with public swearing, the joke's use of *cunt* in the courtroom can be viewed, as McCullough argues, as a 'delicious irony and a way to further mock white justice'.[9] Here, humour not only entertains but also profoundly challenges and subverts authority.

The reclaiming (and making fun) of slurs and discriminatory language is another way comedy can seek to empower. The popular stage show *Wogs Out of Work* (1987), followed by an equally popular television show, *Acropolis Now* (1989–1992), played on Australian stereotypes of Greek culture, while also celebrating that culture. The derogatory word *wog*, as a term for southern Europeans, had increased in use since the late 1950s: *Wogs Out of Work*, written by Nick Giannopolous, Simon Palomares and Maria Portesi, and the television show, written by Giannopolous, Palomares and George Kapiniaris, was an attempt by the children and grandchildren of migrants to reclaim it.

Giannopolous, reflecting on the impact of the show some years later, commented that he believed it empowered every child who had 'ever been called a wog, a nigger, or a slopehead'.[10] Certainly,

Wogs Out of Work proved to be very popular at the time, touring the country for three and a half years.[11] *Acropolis Now* also had enormous appeal, especially with Greek teenagers. A contemporary survey (1990) of 600 Sydney teenagers from migrant backgrounds revealed that they saw nothing offensive in the humour of the show or in its appropriation and use of the word *wog*.[12]

The use of ethnic stereotypes is (and was) not without controversy, however. Some at the time, and certainly since, criticised *Acropolis Now* for its ongoing use of stereotypes. Indeed, Australian humour of the 1980s was notable for its common use of racial and ethnic stereotypes. The appearance of stereotyped migrant characters written and played by Anglo-Australians, such as 'Con the Fruiterer' (played by Mark Mitchell) in *The Comedy Company*, another popular television comedy, underlined that there was still considerable stereotyping going on in 'white' comedy.

Comedian Nazeem Hussain makes the point that comedy that draws on racial (or ethnic) themes and makes use of derogatory slurs only really works when it's the disempowered in society who are doing the comedy. You can make fun of people with more power, he observes, but you must always punch up, never down.[13] His own popular comedy shows, such as *Legally Brown*, play on stereotypes of Muslims (he is a Muslim of Sri Lankan descent) to mock ignorance and prejudices in Australian society. Comedy has long sought to be provocative and make us think about ourselves. It will no doubt continue to do so, although swearing is probably likely to be the least controversial aspect of how it does this.

OUR NEW TABOO LANGUAGE AND THE PC PROBLEM

Slurs, epithets and discriminatory language undoubtedly constitute the bad language of our times. It has become unacceptable to use words that discriminate on the basis of race, sex, gender, sexuality, disability, or other difference from the normative idea of the white, male, heterosexual, able-bodied and middle-class person. Within many workplaces, this kind of language can potentially be a sackable offence. Public utterances of such language can lead to major controversy. This shift has, however, also raised questions about the nature of free speech and has led some to condemn what they regard as 'political correctness'.

The change in what we consider to be taboo language is reflective of the broader changes in society, culture and politics that emerged from the social and political movements of the 1970s and 80s, as well as shifts in Australian migration and demographics that have created a more multicultural and diverse Australia. As various groups, including women and Indigenous people, have drawn attention to the discrimination they face and have begun to achieve concrete policy and political changes, language has been an important site of struggle.

As we saw in the last chapter, sexist and racist language was challenged through the 1970s, and increasingly institutions, such as government and media, responded by introducing language guidelines. There are numerous examples of how our language has been transformed. For example, the change from using the term *disabled person* to *person with a disability* reflects the fact that by doing so a person is not defined solely by their physical or other challenges. Even more so, we have moved away from using terms that were once considered generally acceptable and are now highly offensive, such as *spastic* and *handicapped*. Roly Sussex, a noted commentator on language, calls this new terminology 'dignified language', language that is rooted in the United Nations' Universal Declaration of Human Rights and insists that '[a]ll human beings are born free and equal in dignity and rights'.[14]

Most importantly, perhaps, groups themselves now choose

to lead with naming and labelling practices – whereas in the past names and labels were often imposed with little or no consent from those being named. For example, Aboriginal and Torres Strait Islander people are now sometimes known as *First Nations people*. Such titles claim a different position for Indigenous Australians within the national polity, reflecting claims (as articulated in, for example, the Uluru Statement from the Heart) for a voice in their own governance and a statement of the survival of Indigenous sovereignty. Shifts to acknowledge the names of particular Indigenous peoples, such as Gamilaraay, Wiradjuri, Ngunnawal and Noongar, rather than to use the all-encompassing *Aboriginal people* or *Aborigines*, recognise the diversity and particularity of specific communities and peoples, with their own distinctive languages, Country and culture.

But these shifts have not eliminated the use of slurs and epithets that exist within a broader institutional and structural system that often discriminates, in varying degrees, against various groups in society. Wiradjuri/Wolgalu man Joe Williams (born 1983), a former National Rugby League player, educator and activist, powerfully details his experiences with racism in his book *Defying the Enemy Within* (2018). He describes that when playing sports at his Catholic High School, he was called 'a black c**t', 'a coon' and 'a nigger', 'among many other discriminatory remarks'. His father instructed him to be proud of being black, and not to let 'racially vilifying words stop me from becoming the best person and the best leader for our people that I can be'.[15] His book, which includes advice for how to deal with depression – Williams suffers from bipolar disorder – also encourages young Indigenous people to embrace their own culture and be proud of it, and to 'stare down' racism and discrimination.

The reclamation of slurs and epithets is seen by some as a way that those who experience discrimination can attempt to reclaim power for themselves, as we saw with *wog*. Some women have tried to reclaim insults such as *slut, ho, cunt* and *bitch*.[16] In her book *Wordslut: A Feminist Guide to Taking Back the English Language* (2019), author and linguist Amanda Montell argues that refusing to regard a word such as *slut* as a term of abuse is a 'form of protest against the condemnation of women's sexual independence ... And if enough people rebel, then everyone wins, because a society that's more equal is also one that's more relaxed, more compassionate, and less offended overall.'[17]

But the question of how we as a society deal with discriminatory language – silence it, reclaim it, or just live with it? – is a difficult one. The desire to eliminate discriminatory language has given rise to allegations that such efforts are about 'political correctness' and stifle freedom of speech. 'Political correctness' is a term that has been bandied about since the late 1980s/early 1990s and continues to feature in public debate; it is centrally concerned with the value judgements we as a society place on language.

Until the 1980s 'political correctness' was a term used within the left, usually ironically, as a 'critique of excessive orthodoxy' to communism, and in this sense of adhering to the 'correctness' of communism dates to 1950s discussions of Chinese communism.[18] Use of the term took off in the 1990s, now co-opted by the political right to describe the kind of calls that the left were making for changes in language usage, especially around discriminatory language. Critics claimed 'political correctness' was a form of censorship, and 'enforced civility'.[19] The more extreme critics in the USA, where this backlash first emerged, saw it as 'a leftwing political programme that was seizing control of American universities and cultural institutions'.[20] From the debate over political correctness emerged what is known as the 'culture wars'.

Some scholars otherwise sympathetic with the aims of those who might be labelled politically correct have pointed to what they see as fundamental problems with the approach. For example, linguist Geoffrey Hughes, who has written about swearing and bad language as well as political correctness, notes that these attempts to be more sensitive with respect to language are often liberal in their aims, but illiberal in practice.[21] He also complains that much of the language that results is 'ponderous' and 'dour'.[22]

'Political correctness' is undoubtedly a cultural construction, and one that has served very particular political arguments. Writer Moira Weigel notes that the American right found the term useful because it could be 'used to drum into the public imagination the idea that there was a deep divide between the "ordinary people" and the "liberal elite", who sought to control the speech and thoughts of regular folk'.[23] Debates over political correctness have served similar purposes in Australia, where so-called elites, especially those within universities, have been the target of blanket attacks on 'lefty' efforts to create a more inclusive world.

Linguist Ruth Wajnryb writes that while some people associate inclusive language with priggishness and moral self-righteousness, its influence has been profound, if not on what people think, certainly on what they say in public.[24] Indeed, it is most important to note that what so-called 'political correctness' has most done for us is to alert us to discriminatory language, and to call for us to change the kinds of words we use and to be sensitive to the impact of language that insults and offends. As linguist Deborah Cameron wrote in 1994, there is 'nothing trivial about trying to institutionalise a public norm of respect rather than disrespect'.[25]

Australia continues to argue over inclusive language, however, as the culture wars continue to be fought by some. Kevin Donnelly, an educator and author who has much support from conservative politicians and public figures, including former prime minister Tony Abbott, and right-wing media commentators such as Alan

Jones and Peta Credlin, recently contributed *A Politically Correct Dictionary and Guide* (2019). It lists some 218 terms that range from *bald* to *denier* to *mansplaining* to *woke*.[26] The terms are glossed with a range of comments that either mock some dubious straw example of extreme political correctness or assert a right-wing take on a particular issue such as transgenderism. In her foreword to it, Credlin describes the book as a 'polemic'.[27] That some of it aims to be deliberately provocative is clear. At the launch of the dictionary, Donnelly used the 'n-word' several times in his speech to make a point about the 'censorship' of *Huckleberry Finn*;* the use of such a provocative and offensive word at a public event inevitably gained media exposure for the book.

Concerns about 'political correctness' are not confined to certain conservatives in Australia, but it is likely few people actually agree on and/or understand what it is. A recent survey suggests that more than two-thirds of Australians believe that 'political correctness' has 'gone too far' and that people are too easily offended. Yet, as journalist Annabel Crabb points out, in analysing these results within broader survey results about Australian attitudes, people are in fact more evenly divided in their views on whether they should be able to say what they want, even when it offends others (45 per cent yes, 45 per cent no, 10 per cent undecided).[28] Comments left on an online article about Donnelly's book launch equally reveal these divided views, including over whether language should be modified or changed – but one word repeated in numerous comments is 'respect'.

Few people today would advocate the use of openly racist or sexist language, but many are uncertain about just how far we should punish or censor such language. Some people argue that

---

* Recent editions of the book have variably chosen to replace or disguise the offending word, and/or to provide explanations and context for its use.

they are 'only words'. But language reflects power; it is often those in power who argue for greater freedom to use language in whatever way they feel like. Language can damage and disempower, as we saw with Joe Williams' story. And that is the reason that we should reject blanket condemnations of the 'politically correct' to embrace 'dignified language'. In doing so, however, it is probably also worth reflecting on a recent comment made by gay rights activist and academic Dennis Altman: 'Words matter, but in the contemporary world it is easier to rally people around symbolic hurts rather than structural inequities ... Symbolic issues matter when they draw attention to structural inequalities, but they can too easily become ends in themselves.'[29]

SWEARING IN MULTILINGUAL AUSTRALIA

Many Australians speak more than one language, including having a language other than English as their first. Added to this are the many Indigenous languages spoken by First Nations peoples. A lot of Indigenous languages are endangered or extinct, but many efforts have been made in recent decades to document them, as well as to revitalise and teach them. Indigenous language revitalisation has been important not only because it is a statement of survival but, as Walgett elder and keeper of the Gamilaraay language, Aunty Rose Fernando, argues, 'language is our soul'.[30]

All languages spoken in Australia, as we might expect, include swearing and a variety of taboo terms, and these make up part of the Australian swearing landscape. Indigenous languages, as well as Aboriginal English, include taboo words, insults and obscenities. For example, in Wiradjuri, a penis is *gabinydy* and shit (excrement) is *guna-ng*.[31] In Gamilaraay, a penis is *dhun* and shit is *guna*. A 'wicked' or 'saucy' woman is called a *giwaa-ma-l-dhanny*.[32] In Wik

Mungkan, a Northern Queensland language, taboo words relate to body parts such as the genitals.[33] In Aboriginal English, *gammon* is an equivalent to *bullshit*; words for body parts include *moot* (vagina) and *kwon* (backside); *goona* (faeces) and *doori* (sexual intercourse) are other words that relate to bodily functions.[34] A 2014 guide to Victorian Koori insults compiled by the Victorian Aboriginal Community Controlled Health Organisation records a variety of south-eastern Aboriginal English insults including *coonie head* 'shit head', *coonie moom cheeks* 'shitty bum', *doot head* 'fuck head', and *in your moom* 'in your bum'.[35]

Many different community languages are spoken in Australia, and people who speak these languages swear in them, as well as in English. My parents, who migrated to Australia from Denmark in 1956, spoke English for most of their adult lives. They swore in both English and Danish, but Danish was always the more emotive language to swear in. This is backed up by research that demonstrates that emotive swearing will often be in one's first language. Conversely, though, speakers of more than one language might use their acquired language to swear more freely in non-emotional contexts, because there is less taboo attached to such swear words for them.[36]

A number of vulgar terms and swear words have been borrowed into English from migrant languages, although they are still used predominantly within the next generations of migrant communities rather than more broadly in Australian English. These include *malaka*, a Greek word meaning 'masturbator' and used in Greek as a mild insult; it is used in Australian English for a person who is being stupid or annoying, similar to *wanker*. Another insulting word borrowed from Greek used of a person is *pusti* (from *pousti* 'homosexual'). Borrowed from Italian is *putana*, an insult used of a man (from *puttana* 'prostitute').[37]

Two examples of migrant languages further reveal Australia's diverse swearing vocabulary. Lebanese Australians use numerous Arabic words, including swear words, in their English. Arabic swear words include those that refer to the private parts or that insult the mother or sister of the target.[38] Swearing includes the common use of the exclamation *I swear to God*; and the use of the Arabic insult *jahish* or *hmarr*, meaning 'donkey'.[39] Another word is *sharmut* ('prostitute'), used pejoratively for a girl or woman to imply she is promiscuous, similar to *slut*. Within some male groups in Lebanese-Australian culture, the use of swearing has been identified as an important form of building solidarity.

The Chinese community in Australia includes Chinese Australians whose families have been here since at least the 18th century, recent migrants to Australia and a large international student and transient working population. Compared to Australia, Chinese society frowns more on swearing, as it is perceived to challenge civility. But there are many Chinese swear words and expressions, although they are generally more likely to be used by men and by the younger generation. They include *cào nǐ mā* 'fuck your mother', *tā mā de* literally 'his mother's' and a mild swear word, *jiàn nǚ rén*, 'bitch', and *shǎ bī*, 'stupid cunt'.[40]

SWEARING ON OUR SCREENS

Does anything go on our screens? We've certainly relaxed our attitudes around swearing on television, but with the demise of more formal systems of censorship, there is much less clarity about exactly what's acceptable, and when we can use certain types of language. There is clearly plenty of swearing on television – a 2010 American study showed that '[f]rom 2005 to 2010, the use of profanity on primetime network programming increased by more than 69 percent',[41] and it would likely be a similar statistic in Australia.

But language on television has attracted continuing controversy in all sorts of ways.

The program that is credited with breaking the 'f-word' taboo on Australian television was the 1997 screening of the film *Four Weddings and a Funeral* (1994), in which there is considerable use of the word *fuck*, including by Hugh Grant in the famous opening sequence – ratings for the movie were very high and only 24 people complained to the network.[42] In Australia, all television networks are responsible for their own censorship; complaints go directly to the networks in the first instance, but if the complainant feels that their matter hasn't been dealt with properly, they can take it to the Australian Broadcasting Authority. Formal objections to the use of bad language on (free-to-air) television are generally not large in number, and complaints are far more likely to relate to sex, violence or nudity. The advent of streaming services in Australia has allowed people great choice in what they watch. More importantly, it has given them control over their viewing.

Politicians in Australia have occasionally attempted to take issue with swearing on prime-time television, although this has been relatively unusual. In 2008 Liberal Senator Cory Bernardi called for a Senate inquiry into swearing on television. He cited an episode of a Gordon Ramsay program, *Ramsay's Kitchen Nightmares*, broadcast at 8.30 pm, where the word *fuck* was said over 40 times in a single hour-long show. Ramsay is notorious for his voluminous swearing. Bernardi said in a subsequent interview that while he himself occasionally used the word, he wouldn't use it 'in my public duties, in the Senate or referring to members of my staff or family in that manner. There's a time and a place.' The time and place, he suggested, didn't include television. Social and community standards were important to maintain, he argued.[43] The subsequent inquiry did not lead to a recommendation of any kind of broadcast restrictions but did suggest an improved complaints process.[44]

Ten years later, Bernardi was still complaining about bad language. This time his outrage was directed at a comedy sketch by comedian Tom Ballard in which he called an Australian Conservatives (Bernardi's own party, which he had founded in 2017) candidate a *cunt*. Bernardi objected to this both in terms of defending his candidate – a military veteran who he believed shouldn't be insulted in this way – and in terms of using that sort of language on television, which he argued was not 'an appropriate thing'.[45] Federal Communications Minister Mitch Fifield agreed with Bernardi's concern over the sketch, observing that while candidates for elected office should expect to be criticised and parodied, 'this ABC segment clearly crossed a line, particularly given that it was directed towards an individual who has served his nation in uniform'.[46] The argument that a former soldier should be treated differently from anyone else is perhaps ironic – after all, as we've already seen, those in the services have a reputation for bad language.

Few people really seem to be too fussed about bad language on television, as long as it isn't broadcast at a time or in a context where young children might be exposed to it. Curiously perhaps, we still find that many newspapers, even online news and information sites, continue to censor bad language. Taboo terms in Australian newspapers include *shit, bastard, piss, fuck, arsehole* and *cunt*.[47] If these words appear, they often appear in disguised form, usually with an asterisk – but this hasn't stopped lengthy discussions of swearing and even the satirising of the inability to print the offending words. For example, when the word *cunt* was used on a reality television show, *Married at First Sight* (Australia), numerous articles popped up online. In order to talk about the taboo term, journalist James Weir replaced the word *cunt* with *cantaloupe*, which he then used prolifically, thereby pointing out the silliness of both the show and the censorship applied to it.

Another factor that often complicates any simple discussion of whether bad language should be broadcast (or printed) is that people can have very different views on what words they find offensive, and just how offensive they find them. For example, a recent British study found that half the survey respondents regarded the word *slag* as a 'severe' insult, while the other half saw it as mild.[48] These kinds of results would probably be similar with many swear words, although probably much less so with slurs and epithets, which are now found at or near the top of offensive wordlists. Swear words often continue to be 'bleeped' in a way slurs and epithets do not. However, this may be changing, at least in print media. The 'n-word' is nearly always disguised if not avoided altogether, and very occasionally, and perhaps to an increasing extent, other slurs (for example, *slut*) are being treated similarly.

In recent years, reality television, perhaps more than any other prime-time viewing, is shifting our attitudes towards what is acceptable bad language on television, and reflecting at least to some extent a (relatively) more realistic picture of how people might talk. The Australian versions of two reality television shows have proven to be especially popular: *The Bachelor* and *Married at First Sight* (*MAFS*). Both have presented instances of the word *cunt* being used on television. In doing so, they have generated controversy (or at least media coverage) but also demonstrated the gradual normalisation of the word. The amelioration of *cunt* is well under way, and reality television provides us with an insight into this trend.

MAFS has proven to be a ratings winner in Australia over the past few years. The show involves complete strangers meeting each other for the first time at the altar and then spending a period of time as a 'married' couple (they aren't legally wed) to see how their relationship progresses. In a bid to make it more controversial, badly matched people have been put together, and cheating scandals have ensued. The resulting tensions have led to a lot of conflict on screen – as well as swearing. Swearing in the heat of an argument is perhaps commonplace for many of us. But this hasn't stopped the swearing being controversial in the context of the show.

The first major language-related controversy on the 2019 season of *MAFS* came when one participant, Bronson, called his 'wife' Ines a *cunt*. The word was bleeped and his mouth pixelated, but the episode was heavily promoted in the lead-up to its airing, on the basis of there being a scandal about 'a word' that was going to be uttered on the show. A warning notice was then shown before the relevant segment went to air. The word *cunt* is not specifically banned from being broadcast on Australian television, but considerations of breaches of broadcasting standards are generally based on context and situation of use.[49] *Cunt* has been generally avoided in prime-time slots.

The segment featured the not-so-happy couple enduring a 'therapy' session with the show's resident experts who matched them together, with the pair hurling numerous (bleeped) *fuck*s and *fucking*s at each other. Bronson discussed Ines's changeable personality. At first they had been getting along but then, he claimed, '[t]he next morning, the hulk came out. Straight back to being a cunt.' He was quick to clarify. 'I'm not calling *her* a cunt. I'm saying she acts *like* a cunt.'[50] Bronson was nevertheless reprimanded by one of the show's experts, Mel Schilling, who told him that it was unacceptable to refer to Ines in this way.

Responses in both social media and to online media stories revealed a lot about ordinary Australian viewers' attitudes to swearing, especially the word *cunt*. Many viewers disagreed with Schilling, primarily because of Ines's ongoing verbal abuse of Bronson in the lead-up to the episode and on the episode itself. A typical social media response was 'Bronson just said what everyone was thinking.' Others suggested that producers were irresponsible for airing the whole thing.[51] Some of the online comments on the story echoed social media responses to the show. One contributor made the point that '[o]ften bleeping words out only brings more attention to that it was [sic] said'.[52] Another suggested 'I think we need to hear more of it on tv. People are too uptight as it is … It wasn't violence or sex, just a word.'[53] Overall, few people expressed great outrage about the word itself or in this case even the context in which it was used – by a man of a woman, in an arguably abusive, certainly insulting, manner – perhaps ignored because Ines had been framed as the 'villain' of the show.

Later in the same year, reality dating show *The Bachelor Australia* had its own 'cunt incident'. *The Bachelor*, originally an American show, involves a man, chosen to be 'the Bachelor', dating a bevy of women and asking one of these women at the end of the show to be in a relationship with him. In one episode of the dating show, a contestant named Monique accused the Bachelor, Matt Agnew, of being a *dog cunt* and a 'disrespectful pig' when he kissed another woman, Abbie, at a party. This particular elaboration on *cunt* is an Australianism, and has become more commonly used in recent years, with the *dog* element implying a level of betrayal – it is a derogatory insult, although it can be used in a semi-affectionate way of a friend who might be doing something that annoys you.

Social media found the whole *Bachelor* incident highly amusing. One Twitter user declared: 'I love that the biggest drama of the season is over the use of the term dog cunt. I LOVE IT!'[54] A few commented on the Australianness of the insult: @Retta_Potterfan wrote: 'Australians don't say "I love you" they say "He's a dog cunt" and I think that's really beautiful'; @PastPrainFor tweeted: 'As an Australian, it's hard to decide whether calling Matt a "dog cunt" is mean-spirited or if it's just flirting'[55]; and @babooshka_yaya declared: 'Anyone calling anyone a "dog c*nt" on national telly is an Australian hero the end'.[56] The discussion of *cunt* and its use on popular reality television shows demonstrates that *cunt* has arguably finally made it as a mainstream swear word.

We have also seen shifts in language in advertising in the last few decades. While Australians have on the whole not been particularly offended by swearing in advertising, an exported tourism ad for Australia resides in our popular memory. It was created by the Sydney branch of ad company M&C Saatchi when Scott Morrison was managing director. In 2006, Tourism Australia spent $180 million on a campaign to promote Australia that featured model Lara Bingle asking people 'Where the bloody hell are you?' while promoting the beauty of Australian tourism sites. The ad was subsequently banned in the UK for using *bloody*, in Canada for using *hell* and for depicting the pouring of beer, and in Singapore the ad ran with the *bloody hell* excised. Even as late as 2006, Australians' distinctively relaxed attitude to swearing was not shared by many other countries.

The Australian Association of National Advertisers Code of Ethics currently provides this guidance about swearing in advertising:

> Words and phrases which are innocuous and in widespread and common use in the Australian vernacular are permitted (provided they are used in a manner consistent with their colloquial usage, for example with gentle humour, and not used in a demeaning or aggressive manner). Examples are 'bugger', 'shit', 'pissed-off', 'crap', 'bloody', 'cheap bastard', 'bum', and 'balls'. The 'f' and 'c' words are generally not permitted. Non verbal representations of the 'f' word are also not permitted.

> Words and acronyms that play on the 'f' word, e.g. WTF and LMFAO, but do not use the actual word are normally considered acceptable if used in a light hearted and

humorous way, are in subtitle rather than spoken word and are appropriate to the situation.[57]

The advice proffered here is amusing – why the coyness around spelling out *fuck* in a policy document? The guidelines demonstrate the strange hang-ups we continue to have around swear words: everyone knows what *WTF* means, for example, yet it's fine to use this in an ad but not okay to spell out the word *fuck*.*

Despite these guidelines, numerous advertisers have employed the words *cunt* and *fuck*, but doing so can lead to complaints to Ad Standards (the former Advertising Standards Bureau). A variety of complaints about advertising in recent years relate to language. In 2016, there were complaints about an ad for an SBS Viceland television show called *F*ck, that's delicious*, as well as for social media ads selling merchandise for the unofficial Northern Territory tourism campaign 'C U in the NT'. Both complaints were upheld. SBS defended the *F*ck, that's delicious* ad on several grounds, including that it had used an asterisk, and that the word was used 'in its colloquial sense, as an exclamation of pleasure'. Interestingly, a minority of the board agreed that the colloquial use of *fuck* was 'consistent with common Australian vernacular', but still felt it was considered obscene by 'most' members of the community. The C U in the NT campaign (created by a self-described 'guerilla group, which aims to promote travel awareness in the Northern Territory region') noted in its defence that there was 'no reluctance among any of Australia's mainstream media to reproduce any of our social media posts and our product lines' featuring C U in the NT. They further argued that upholding the complaint would set

---

*   British clothing company French Connection UK has of course long advertised using its initialism FCUK.

a dangerous precedent and 'impose an overly strict moral view on a fine tradition of Australian humour and in particular the great tradition of the Aussie larrikin'.[58]

At the end of 2019, only one of the ads that attracted the most complaints that year even mentioned language (a use of *balls*). Whether this indicates any ongoing shift in tolerance of swearing in advertising is unclear, as complaints wax and wane. But many of the 2019 complaints were related to sexist and, to a lesser extent, racist elements of advertising – while not focused on language specifically, this does once again point to the shift in what we find offensive.

SOCIAL MEDIA

Few things have changed the way we communicate more than digital technology. Social media, texting and the internet have transformed the way we use language, prompting new forms of communication, a surge of informal ways of writing, the development of emojis, and lexical creativity. Swearing is common on social media platforms. Most platforms permit swearing as long as it is not abusive, promoting violence, or used as a form of harassment. The issue of when social media platforms should take action around online abuse is fraught. But in terms of swear words, it is possible to find the full range, sometimes disguised as *f*ck*, *c*nt*, and so on, or in somewhat euphemistic forms, such as *arsehat*. One US study suggested that of 30 000 surveyed Facebook users in 2012, 47 per cent of users had profanity on their Facebook 'walls'.[59]

Social media has encouraged (or at least made visible) a whole range of invented swear words, often compound forms building on words like *shit* and *fuck*. One US writer, Dan Brooks, identified the rise of words such as *fuckbonnet*, *shitsquib* and *fuckstumbling*;

Dictionary.com notes others like *douchenozzle, douchecanoe* and *fucktrumpet*. But Brooks criticises these newly invented words. While acknowledging that they are 'phonetically pleasing', they are little more than faddish and boring because they all follow the same pattern, he argues: 'familiar profanity compounded with a non-profane word of two unaccented syllables'.[60] Interestingly, he observes that these kinds of new swear words tend to function in ways that make them 'safe' – they are usually not gendered, and they do not involve any kind of racial, ethnic, homophobic or other slur.[61] He is critical of their tameness:

> The swear nerds are outraged enough to demand fresh
> profanity but still too comfortable to play for blood ...
> The liberal middle-class is ready to call the president a
> douchecanoe, but it is not yet ready to call him a cunt-lipped
> maidfucker with peasant hips. Things are bad, in other
> words, but they are not serious yet.[62]

Social media, as well as texting and the use of emojis, has also prompted the development of a lexicon of acronyms, initialisms and abbreviations (some first used within the early internet communities, such as bulletin board users). And a number of these relate to swear words, often functioning both as a disguise (because the swear word is not spelled out), and becoming its own expression. *WTF* is one of the most familiar and well established of these (it has now transitioned into everyday writing) – we are probably as likely to say 'W-T-F' as 'What the fuck', whether or not we are squeamish about language. *LMFAO (laughing my fucking arse off)* is also a widely used initialism. Another one that has become popular in recent years is *AF (as fuck)*, not only making an appearance on social media, but also being used in US advertising.[63] Emojis too are used to represent swear words. *Buzzfeed*'s guide to swearing in emoji includes: 💩🏠 *shithouse*; 🤲⚓ *wanker*; 🍑🍩 *arsehole*; and 👶🧑‍🦰👶🚫💩 *bastard*. Many depict the literal rather than figurative sense of the word. They are perhaps not particularly effective profanities – they rely on a certain level of emoji literacy, for one thing.[64]

Social media has raised all sorts of issues around what constitutes free speech and what constitutes hate speech or abusive speech, as well as when it can be punished or censored. According to one prominent journalist on Twitter, Asher Wolf, Twitter will ban you if you get reported for swearing at political parties or at politicians.[65] As one respondent to the thread alerting people to this commented, 'Yep, don't worry about hate speech, neo-Nazis or propaganda, it's swearing where true evil lies'.[66] Social media has been a place where hate and abuse has thrived. It has seen the circulation of slurs and epithets as a form of abuse in a way that would not be acceptable in most other contexts, inflamed by the relative anonymity that social media offers.

Journalist Ginger Gorman, in a recent examination of online trolling, has found that many Australians have experienced internet harassment, and of those who have been harassed, 27 per cent have been the targets of abusive language.[67] Studies have found that men experience more abusive language about religion and ethnicity, but in all other ways women experience more online abuse. Thirty-two per cent of women versus 23 per cent of men who had experienced online harassment had abusive language directed at them.[68] A 2015 study by the United Nations found 73 per cent of women and girls had been exposed to some form of online violence.[69]

It is easy enough to find examples of this online abuse. Founder of the Asylum Seeker Resource Centre Kon Karapanagiotidis writes in his book *The Power of Hope* about the ongoing abuse he experiences on social media, quoting some of the abuse he received on Twitter:

Fuck you Cunt. Hopefully next time your throat gets slashed
… Kon I hope you get terrorist attacked on you and your
family then you'll realise Pauline [Hanson] is a saint … I
hope you get hung up with a rope on a tree by someone, you
have it coming to you … You *cuck*, *mangina*, poofter, faggot
… How dare you come to our already built country you
bludging wog and think you have some voice?[70]

Journalist and playwright Van Badham is another example of someone regularly subjected to misogynistic online abuse and vitriol.
She has received abuse such as: 'Bend over for some diseased anal
before your throat is cut dumbshit, self-loathing hater of your parents.'[71] Women of colour receive racist as well as sexist abuse; as US
journalist Imani Gandy comments, 'They will call white women
a cunt and they'll call me a nigger cunt.'[72] Media scholar Emma
Jane, in her 2016 study of online misogyny and abuse, argues that
gendered cyberhate has become increasingly routine, with little
done to address the profound effects – psychological, social and
even physical – that such abuse has on those who are targeted.
Women report suffering anxiety, depression and panic attacks as
a result of such online abuse, and they can even become targets of
violence in the real world.[73]

   Social media is thus a double-edged sword, bringing both positive and negative changes to our social interactions, communication, and use of bad language. This is also evident when looking at
the role of social media in Indigenous communities. It has transformed Indigenous communities who use social media to maintain ties across distances.[74] But at the same time it has allowed
traditional 'teasing' behaviours to be amplified and fights to be
conducted.[75] For example, anthropologist Petronella Vaarzon-
Morel observes that within the Warlpiri community, mobile
devices can be 'employed to maintain kin relationships, [but] their

use can create and exacerbate conflict'.[76] The social media site Divas Chat has been used within the Warlpiri community for such activities as sexting and cyberbullying, including the use of abusive language. One Warlpiri woman interviewed by Vaarzon-Morel, Napaljarri, also observes, 'Swearing words can hurt people – when some people have passed away. They get really upset *miyalu* and that can make them sick.'[77]

CHALLENGING POWER: BAD LANGUAGE ON STAGE AND IN HIP HOP

A recurring theme in this book has been the way that bad language can challenge existing frameworks of power. This is still the case, even though we now have more relaxed attitudes towards swearing. This section gives two examples of how this has played out in cultural forms: hip hop music and in the stage work of playwright Patricia Cornelius.

Hip hop music, originally an African-American music form, is a genre well known for its use of profanity to express authenticity, creativity and humour. Bad language has been used to make powerful statements about inequalities and racism. Australian hip hop similarly uses bad language and word play. It can use such language to challenge and subvert authority and to make trenchant political statements. This has been particularly true within Indigenous hip hop. A.B. Original, made up of Yorta Yorta man Adam Briggs, who performs as Briggs, and Ngarrindjeri man Daniel Rankine, who performs as Trials, tackle topics in their music such as the rates of Indigenous incarceration and deaths in custody.[78] Swearing here expresses deep anger. On their album *Reclaim Australia* (2016), Briggs and Trials called for a national conversation about the issues Indigenous people face, and also made use of social media to both promote the album and to have a national discussion, including about changing the date of Australia Day (which has run as an ongoing social media campaign #changethedate).[79] Their anger over issues such as the systemic racism of the justice system is expressed in songs such as 'Call 'em out'. In the song, the narrator responds to calls to trust the justice system with expressions like 'what the fuck'.[80]

Another Aboriginal hip hop group, Yuin Soldiers, use their music to comment on the issues, including racism, faced by Indigenous youth in their region (the New South Wales South Coast). Their song 'Subliminal Twist' makes use of abusive language to depict how this language reflects the racism they face on a daily basis. The narrator in this song describes how he is sick of being called a 'little black cunt' and how he experiences 'heartache', 'racism' and 'discrimination'.[81]

Controversy has dogged the broadcasting of hip hop music in Australia, however. In 2003, radio station Triple J was criticised for giving airplay to the word *cunt*, used in The Herd's song '77%'. It criticised John Howard's treatment of boat people and the '77%' of Australians that supported his policies.[82] The country and 'these cunts', argued the song, are in need of a 'fucking shake-up'. Most listeners approved of the song being played in full, but some commentators (especially those who were referred to in the song, notably right-wing media shock jocks) called for government intervention.

Profanity is integral to the art of hip hop, but the popularity of the genre has also helped to make bad language even more public and accepted. Hip hop continues a tradition of bad language being used within a genre to convey social and political criticism, and express defiance and anger. But as in the past, it is also perceived as threatening to established forms of power, and censorship can be used to silence such challenges.

Defiance and anger, as well as bad language, flows strongly

through influential Australian playwright Patricia Cornelius's play *SHIT*. First performed in 2015, the play features three 'hard bit, utterly damaged women … They believe the world is shit, that their lives are shit, that they are shit.'[83] Swearing is an integral part of the women's vernacular, but it is clear that such language has also been used towards them all their lives in order to denigrate them and make them feel worthless. One of the women in the play, Billy, recounts what a man has said to her: 'And he goes, look at you, fuck look at you, what the fuck you done, you fucking done nothing, you never fucking going do something, you fucked-up waste of space, what fucking contribution you made, nothing, nothing at all, you fucked-up nothing, nothing you are, a big fucking nothing, he goes, the biggest fucking nothing, the biggest fucking nothing I know.'[84] The women then talk about their own use of language. Billy says that the word *fuck* is 'like the sharpest blade'. She 'couldn't give them [*fuck* and *cunt*] up if I tried. They're strong … You say fuck or cunt, you watch them run.'[85] They note how many women don't like their language. 'They think we're foul-mouthed sluts', observes Bobby, '[t]hey think we can't string a fucking sentence together without swearing'. But she doesn't care, acidly commenting, '[t]heir life's shit, our life's shit, just different shit'.[86] Language is integral to conveying the anger and frustrations that these women feel.

An interview with Cornelius in September 2019 recounted that '[w]hen the multi-award-winning *SHIT* was staged at the Malthouse, even some wanting to see the play were pre-emptively offended [by the title]'. Some people spelled out the word when asking for tickets. When the play was reviewed in the *New York Times*, it was given glowing reviews, but they couldn't even name it. Says Cornelius: 'They referred to it only as "rhyming with grit". They couldn't even use the asterisks!' The writer of the profile comments: '[Cornelius] at once gives a shit – about representations of class, of political dissent, gender equity – and vehemently *doesn't* give a shit – about offending anyone, speaking her mind, making audiences uncomfortable.' Cornelius argues that she wants to challenge the notion of 'high art'. Swearing is important in this: 'People think if you use swear words, it brings the fineness of the art down, rather than art being something that actually reflects society. And language, in particular, is a source of great information and great knowledge.'[87]

AUSTRALIAN SWEARING: SAME-OLD, SAME-OLD?

Australians continue to be creative in their swearing, with new words entering the Australian offensive language lexicon in recent years. One of these is *shitcunt*, marked as Australian in Urban Dictionary, and used to describe the worst kind of person. *Not here to fuck spiders* is another phrase of fairly recent vintage, used to mean 'not here to waste time'. Words also continue to have their own inflection and meaning in Australia: for example, *wanker* in Australian English is both a milder insult and used to refer to someone considered to be pretentious, rather than used as a strong insult as it is elsewhere. We also continue to see ourselves as more prolific swearers, as do those from other countries: many popular commentaries, for example on internet discussion forums, observe Australians' more relaxed attitude to swearing. One Reddit discussion forum thread is called 'What's up with Australians and swearing?'[88] Yet as we've seen so far in this chapter, there are still various ways in which we seek to circumscribe and police swearing in public, and ways in which we continue to express unease over bad language in certain contexts.

The fraught question of the appropriateness of bad language in different contexts, as well as the question of its Australianness, was highlighted during the controversy around the actions of Victorian union leader John Setka. On 28 June 2019, Setka pleaded guilty to harassing his wife via text messages and breaching a court order. The language he used in the text messages to his wife included: 'you're a [cu]nt just like the rest of your family', 'you've just triggered a hatred … I didn't think existed [fuc]ken dog',[89] and he called her a 'weak f[uck]en piece of shit' and 'a treacherous Aussie f[uck]en c[unt]'.[90] Setka apologised, admitting responsibility.[91]

In September, Setka hit the news again after he commented that federal senators, whom he referred to as 'fucking crossbenchers', would 'wear the consequences' if they voted for a Coalition bill to curb union power. In a subsequent ABC radio interview with journalist Hamish Macdonald, Setka denied that his comments were ever intended to be threatening, saying that senators should 'toughen up'. He then talked about his use of language more generally: 'I might use some bad language, but is that a criminal offence, do we open Alcatraz for that now? … I mean, it is Australia, we've always been told to express ourselves and say what we think. If dropping the f-word or the s-word is now a threat, gee, where is this country going to, really?'[92] He also defended his swearing on the grounds that at most building sites and shop stewards' meetings you'd find lots of swearing: 'Now if we had a swear box at that meeting, I'd probably have a hundred thousand dollars in it by the end of the day,' he argued.[93]

When Macdonald suggested to him that the language used in the texts against his wife was 'just out of touch with the times … do you think you don't get where Australia is at today?' Setka responded by saying that he heard swearing every day of the week: 'Well, are you asking me Hamish if I should just stop swearing, and never swear again? Cause you'd better ask the rest of Australia to do the same. If the rest of Australia do it I'll do it.'[94] Comments written in response to one online news article suggested many people believed him to be a bully. Interestingly, however, few commented on his language specifically or had much of a problem with the words he used.[95]

What the Setka case tells us, perhaps, is not that swearing per se is the problem. Most of us would probably agree with Setka's comments that we all swear sometimes and even that we consider swearing as a particularly 'Australian' way of talking. What many in this case did not agree with was the context in which he used the language and *how* he used it, especially the abusive and threatening language he levelled at his wife.

Running through these stories is the continuing question of gender. Swearing has historically been associated with men. Does this mean swearing is something women should still be protected from? The answer is no – although clearly the link between verbal and physical abuse must be acknowledged. But this shouldn't mean that women should still be regarded as needing to be shielded from bad language more generally, or that they should be stigmatised for using it.

In 2017, an episode of *Court Justice: Sydney*, a television show that filmed cases heard at the Downing Centre Magistrates Court, filmed a defendant appearing before Magistrate Jacqueline Milledge. The defendant was explaining why he had attacked someone and described how the person he had attacked had said to him 'you f[uck]ing c[unt]'. Milledge commented that she had heard this kind of language many times before, to which the defendant said 'sorry darl'. Milledge said, 'but don't call me darl. That's where we fall out with each other.' Later she repeated to the defendant, 'Don't feel worried about using language, but don't call me darl.'[96] Feminists undoubtedly cheered this incident: sexist language had been slapped down, as had the notion that women inherently needed to be apologised to for having swear words uttered in their presence.

Indeed, since the 1980s, women have proven themselves to be prolific swearers, as well as adding some interesting innovations to our bad language lexicon. Author Kathy Lette's books, for example, have contributed much to Australian slang, but also to our stock of swear words and expressions. In *Puberty Blues*, written with Gabrielle Carey and published in 1979, there is use of both slang and swearing to capture the speech of young Sydney girls of the time: girls could be *slack-arsed molls* and *easy roots*; you might be *packin' shit*, and if you didn't like something, you could just *rack off* or *ping off*.[97]

More recently, media personality Sami Lukis published an account of her love life, *Romantically Challenged* (2018). The book is full of colourful language – highly entertaining but perhaps not for the squeamish. Her book includes terms such as *shits and giggles, big fat fucker of a disappointment, fuckwit, slut guts, fuckbucket, shit soda, arsehole, bonk, fucking, douchebag, penis butter, vagina mite, lesbian cunts, WTF, shag, shit, shitload, bullshit artist, a fuckload of, choke and poke, fucking arseholes, shit-motherfucker-fuck-shit situation, fuck-fest* and *holy shitballs*. To my count, there are at least 66 uses of *fuck* on its own or in some kind of combination.[98] But she shows creativity in using bad language to create humour about her dating life and the quest for Mr Right, as well as conveying the occasional sense of Australianness with terms such as *vagina mite* and *bullshit artist*.

Women perhaps feel able to be more fearless in their use of language in recent years, owning it as a kind of feminist action, while also being franker about the realities of life. Amanda Montell argues that swearing can be an act of empowerment for women. But she acknowledges that it is a double-edged sword because women are still condemned for swearing and speaking in ways considered to be 'unladylike'.[99]

Indigenous people are also still punished for swearing. Some

Indigenous writers have continued to challenge these strictures through cultural expression. For example, Vivienne Cleven's novel *Bitin' Back*, winner of the first David Unaipon Award in 2000, makes inventive use of both Aboriginal English and swearing. The novel is a humorous yet cutting story about a young Aboriginal man, Nevil, who decides one morning that he will dress as a woman and asks to be called 'Jean Rhys', to the great consternation of his mother. Words Cleven uses in the novel include: *madfucked*, *fuckin'*, *fucken ratbag*, *fucken mutts*, *who the fuckery*, *fucken pussyboy*, *fucken cunts*, *mad shit*, *grog-fucked* and *crazy prick*.

For all the progress made in the cultural sphere, the reality remains that bad language is still criminalised in some contexts, and Indigenous Australians and the more marginalised in our community remain disproportionately targeted by offensive language laws. Over the past 40 years, legislation changed occasionally, but there has been little or no effort to address the inherent problems and inequities built into these laws. Various laws across the states continue to prohibit the use of insulting, offensive, profane and/or abusive language in public. Nick Greiner's Liberal government's introduction of the *Summary Offences Act 1988* (NSW) was aimed squarely, writes Elyse Methven, at commanding respect for the police, after a 1979 Act had previously narrowed the offensive behaviour provision.[100] In Queensland, the current *Summary Offences Act 2005* (Qld) can lead to a person being charged for behaving in a 'disorderly, offensive, threatening or violent way'.[101] The penalty incurred is a fine or a short term of imprisonment. The most common test of offensiveness of language when considering these charges is what might be considered offensive by a 'reasonable' person.[102] But there are numerous problems with this principle, as Methven points out. What is ultimately considered reasonable? Community standards change over time, context matters, and the definition of a 'public place' is up for debate also.[103]

Little has changed in recent years: between July 2015 and June 2016, New South Wales police issued more than 1836 on-the-spot fines for using offensive language. In that year a further 1167 adults and 145 children appeared before New South Wales courts charged with using offensive language. Of those charged, Indigenous Australians represented 17 per cent of adults and 26 per cent of children, despite only comprising three per cent of the New South Wales population.[104] In that period, Indigenous people were 15 times more likely to be prosecuted for offensive language or conduct than the rest of the state's population.[105]

* & ^ $

As I finish writing this book, Australia has been affected by the global Covid-19 pandemic. But another global movement has also recently found expression in Australia: the Black Lives Matter (BLM) movement. BLM saw worldwide protests take place in response to the death of George Floyd, an African-American man, while being arrested by police. Racial issues also affect Australian society. For Indigenous Australians, deaths in custody and treatment by police are an ongoing problem, and racism remains something many non-white Australians experience. Not long before the Australian BLM protests took place, an Indigenous teenage boy was once again treated violently by the police during an arrest. The boy had used offensive language towards the police officers.

The question of who can use offensive language and whether or not they are punished for it remains an urgent one for us to deal with. Attending to the history of swearing in Australia can provide us with new perspectives on this question, reminding us that the ability to speak or being silenced and censored has been a recurring issue in our history, often reflecting other inequalities in our society. And just because we have moved towards a society that is tolerant of most swearing by most people in most circumstances, it doesn't mean that this will always be the case. Censorship can yet creep back.

Of all the stories I researched for this book, two stand out for me. The first is Vera's story, the women's liberationist who wrote in to *Mejane* to vent her frustrations at being told by a man that feminists would be taken more seriously if they didn't swear. This is a recurring theme in the history of swearing: that across time women have been repeatedly expected to 'behave themselves', including not swearing, and are reprimanded and punished if they don't do so. These attitudes haven't entirely disappeared even today, but they have changed significantly. Women – as well as other marginalised groups in society – have been able to 'claim' bad language as a means of empowerment but too often it has worked, and sometimes still does, as a reason to silence them.

Vera also related in her comments in *Mejane* the story of being arrested for saying *fuck* at an anti–Vietnam War protest, commenting that the real obscenity was not the words that she spoke but the horrors of the war. I think that many of us would likely agree that getting outraged and attempting to suppress and criminalise bad language in a world where much more obscene horrors take place on a daily basis seems highly problematic.

And yet while many of us would probably shake our heads at the various ways in which laws and other social strictures around swearing have been used as a means to stigmatise, oppress and punish people throughout our history – and indeed still are used to target Indigenous and vulnerable people – should we as a society argue for an 'anything goes' approach to swearing? Is there any risk to such an approach? Probably the greatest risk is that we forget that language can be used as a form of abuse. The importance of respect in how we treat each other cannot be overstated.

Respect also seems to be the paramount word to keep in mind when thinking about discriminatory language, especially slurs and epithets. This is a form of bad language we must thoroughly and completely reject as a society. The story of Jimmie Barker, a Murawari man, and his childhood reading of magazines and books full of racist language, followed by a lifetime of experiencing racial discrimination and government intervention, surely reveals the power of language to underpin and reflect the discriminatory structures that have governed, and continue to affect, some people's lives.

The history of bad language has been entwined with what it has meant, and means, to be Australian. But all too often this has been defined along white, masculine lines. This is not to say we should reject our 'swearing' reputation, but if Australians are in fact to be associated with bad language, we might want to think about what that says – and what we want it to say – about our values and identity.

Bad language enjoys a central place in our culture, even when it's been censored or suppressed, and it has become woven into the fabric of our identity. This is unlikely to change any time soon. But a critical reflection on the 'good' and 'bad' of our historical relationship with such language might help us reconsider how we understand our bad language and the way it shapes our society, and, by extension, ourselves.

ACKNOWLEDGMENTS

The process of writing a book about bad language has been enormously interesting, but it has also required attention to some of the darker chapters in Australian history. In working on this book, I have found myself reflecting on significant questions of national character and identity, as well as important issues such as why we continue to criminalise bad language. I hope that this book will help to prompt further debate about these things.

The collections (digital and physical) of the National Library of Australia and the Australian National University were essential to completion of this book; I thank the staff of both for their assistance. I have also built on the work of many fine scholars, and I acknowledge all the authors who I have cited in these pages. As I write this in the midst of the Covid-19 pandemic, when libraries are shut and universities are facing potentially dire financial problems, I hope that they, as well as the publishing and arts sectors, will be properly recognised for their essential role in Australian life.

This book was greatly aided by the research assistance of Phoebe Garrett and the careful copy-editing and advice of Julia Robinson. I owe them both a great deal of thanks. Research led to some interesting discussions over morning teas at the Australian National Dictionary Centre, and I'd like to thank all who participated in these discussions and gave me new perspectives on bad language. Several people read the manuscript or parts of it. They include Michelle Arrow, Frank Bongiorno, Damien Browne and Bruce Moore. I am very grateful for all their ideas and suggestions for improving the manuscript. I also thank Zhengdao Ye and Mark Gwynn for answers to specific research questions, and Jonathon Green for pointing out two small errors in the manuscript.

At NewSouth Publishing, I am grateful to Jocelyn Hungerford for her excellent copy-editing as well as sensitive and thoughtful feedback that has greatly improved the finished product. I thank Phillipa McGuinness for her support and enthusiasm for this project, and Elspeth Menzies for continuing that support and enthusiasm, as well as her valuable comments on the manuscript. I also thank Paul O'Beirne for overseeing this project as it went to publication and for his advice on various aspects of the manuscript.

Damien Browne spent a lot of time discussing various aspects of the book with me, and I am especially grateful to him for all of his advice and feedback, as well as for putting up with me while I was working on it. I thank his parents for their assistance also: Terry Browne for discussing swearing and bodgies, and Kay Browne for permitting me to mention her in the book. I also acknowledge my brother, Niels Laugesen, for his input along the way and for introducing me to a much broader range of swear words over the years than I would otherwise have been exposed to.

I dedicate this book to the memory of my mother, Lotte Laugesen, an inveterate swearer despite my childhood attempts to make her otherwise.

SELECT BIBLIOGRAPHY

All definitions and etymologies for words discussed in this book have been drawn from three sources unless otherwise noted: *The Australian National Dictionary: Australian Words and Their Origins* (second edition, Oxford University Press, 2016); the *Oxford English Dictionary* (online); and *Green's Dictionary of Slang* (online).

Allan, Keith (ed.), *The Oxford Handbook of Taboo Words and Language* (Oxford: Oxford University Press, 2019)

Anon, *Mess Songs and Rhymes of the RAAF 1939–1945* (New Guinea, 1945)

Anon, *The Sydney Slang Dictionary* (Sydney: HJ Franklin, 1882)

Arrow, Michelle, *The Seventies: The Personal, the Political, and the Making of Modern Australia* (Sydney: NewSouth Publishing, 2019)

Arrow, Michelle, and Angela Woollacott (eds), *Everyday Revolutions: Remaking Gender, Sexuality and Culture in 1970s Australia* (Canberra: ANU Press, 2019)

Atkinson, Alan, *The Europeans in Australia: A History Volume 1 – The Beginning* (Melbourne: Oxford University Press, 1997)

Austin, Karen, 'Talkin' Blak: Humour in Indigenous Australian Theatre, 1970–2000', *Philament* 20 (2015), 129–64

Baker, Sidney, *The Australian Language* (Sydney: Angus and Robertson, 1945)

Barker, Jimmie, *The Two Worlds of Jimmie Barker: The Life of an Australian Aboriginal 1900–1972*, as told to Janet Mathews (Canberra: Australian Institute of Aboriginal Studies, 1982)

Barwick, Archie, *In Great Spirits: The World War I Diary of Archie Barwick* (Sydney: HarperCollins, 2013)

Bashford, Alison, and Stuart Macintyre (eds), *The Cambridge History of Australia Volume 1: Indigenous and Colonial Australia* (Melbourne: Cambridge University Press, 2013)

Bellanta, Melissa, *Larrikins: A History* (Brisbane: University of Queensland Press, 2012)

Bergen, Benjamin K, *What the F: What Swearing Reveals about Our Language, Our Brains, and Ourselves* (New York: Basic Books, 2016)

Bongiorno, Frank, *The Sex Lives of Australians: A History* (Melbourne: Black Inc., 2012)

Burgmann, Verity, and Jenny Lee (eds), *Constructing a Culture* (Melbourne: McPhee Gribble, 1988)

Butterss, Philip, *An Unsentimental Bloke: The Life and Work of CJ Dennis* (Adelaide: Wakefield Press, 2014)

Buzo, Alexander, *Norm and Ahmed; Rooted; The Roy Murphy Show* (Sydney: Currency Press, 1979)

Casey, Maryrose, *Creating Frames: Contemporary Indigenous Theatre 1967–1990* (Brisbane: University of Queensland Press, 2004)

Clarke, Marcus, *His Natural Life* (Brisbane: University of Queensland Press, 2001)

Coleman, Peter, *Obscenity, Blasphemy, Sedition: The Rise and Fall of Literary Censorship in Australia* (Sydney: Duffy and Snellgrove, 2000 [1962])

Conor, Liz, 'Classification and Its Discontents', *Interventions* 17, 2 (2015), 155–73

Coombs, Anne, *Sex and Anarchy: The Life and Death of the Sydney Push* (Melbourne: Viking, 1996)

Crowe, Cornelius, *The Australian Slang Dictionary* (Melbourne: Robert Barr, Printer, 1895)

Culotta, Nino, *They're a Weird Mob* (Sydney: Ure Smith, 1974 [1957])

Damousi, Joy, *Colonial Voices: A Cultural History of English in Australia 1840–1940* (Melbourne: Cambridge University Press, 2010)

Damousi, Joy, *Depraved and Disorderly: Female Convicts, Sexuality and Gender in Colonial Australia* (Melbourne: Cambridge University Press, 1997)

Damousi, Joy, *Memory and Migration in the Shadow of War: Australia's Greek Immigrants after World War II and the Greek Civil War* (Cambridge: Cambridge University Press, 2015)

Dening, Greg, *Mr Bligh's Bad Language: Passion, Power and Theatre on the Bounty* (Cambridge: Cambridge University Press, 1992)

Docker, John, *The Nervous Nineties: Australian Cultural Life in the 1890s* (Melbourne: Oxford University Press, 1991)

Downing, WH, *Digger Dialects* (Melbourne: Lothian, 1919)

Duncan, Pearl, 'The Role of Aboriginal Humour in Cultural Survival and Resistance', PhD Thesis, University of Queensland, 2014

Eades, Diana, *Aboriginal Ways of Using English* (Canberra: Aboriginal Studies Press, 2013)

Factor, June, *Kidspeak: A Dictionary of Australian Children's Words, Expressions and Games* (Melbourne: Melbourne University Press, 2000)

Furphy, Joseph, *The Annotated Such Is Life* (Melbourne: Oxford University Press, 1991)

Garde, Murray, 'The Pragmatics of Rude Jokes with Grandad: Joking Relationships in Aboriginal Australia', *Anthropological Forum* 18, 3 (2008), 235–53

Gerster, Robin, and Jan Bassett, *Seizures of Youth: 'The Sixties' and Australia* (Melbourne: Hyland House, 1991)

Gilje, Paul A, *To Swear Like a Sailor: Maritime Culture in America, 1750–1850* (New York: Cambridge University Press, 2016)

Glassop, Lawson, *We Were the Rats* (Sydney: Angus and Robertson, 1944)

Gorman, Ginger, *Troll Hunting* (Melbourne: Hardie Grant, 2019)

Grose, Francis, *1811 Dictionary of the Vulgar Tongue* (Northfield, Illinois: Digest Books, Inc., 1971 [reprint])

Harris, Alexander, *Settlers and Convicts or Recollections of Sixteen Years' Labour in the Australian Backwoods* (Melbourne: Melbourne University Press, 1977 [1847])

Hergenhan, LT (ed.), *A Colonial City: High and Low Life – Selected Journalism of Marcus Clarke* (Brisbane: University of Queensland Press, 1972)

Hogbotel, Sebastian, and Simon Ffuckes, *Snatches and Lays* (Melbourne: Sun Books, 1973)

Hughes, Geoffrey, *Political Correctness: A History of Semantics and Culture* (Chichester: Wiley-Blackwell, 2010)

Hughes, Geoffrey, *Swearing: A Social History of Foul Language, Oaths and Profanity in English* (Oxford: Blackwell, 1991)

Jane, Emma A, *Misogyny Online: A Short (and Brutish) History* (London: SAGE, 2017)

Jay, Timothy, *Cursing in America: A Psycholinguistic Study of Dirty Language in the Courts, in the Movies, in the Schoolyard and on the Streets* (Philadelphia: John Benjamins Publishing Company, 1992)

Jay, Timothy, 'The Utility and Ubiquity of Taboo Words,' *Perspectives on Psychological Science* 4, 2 (2009), 153–61

Jennings, Kate (ed.), *Mother, I'm Rooted: An Anthology of Australian Women Poets* (Melbourne: Outback Press, 1975)

Karskens, Grace, *The Colony: A History of Early Sydney* (Sydney: Allen and Unwin, 2009)

Karskens, Grace, *The Rocks: Life in Early Sydney* (Melbourne: Melbourne University Press, 1997)

Keen, Ian (ed.), *Being Black: Aboriginal Culture in 'Settled' Australia* (Canberra: Aboriginal Studies Press, 1988)

Kent, David, *From Trench and Troopship: The Experience of the Australian Imperial Force 1914–1919* (Sydney: Hale and Iremonger, 1999)

Kimber, Julie, '"A Nuisance to the Community": Policing the Vagrant Woman', *Journal of Australian Studies* 34, 3 (2010), 275–93

Kleinhenz, Elizabeth, *Germaine: The Life of Germaine Greer* (Sydney: Penguin Random House, 2018)

Klugman, Matthew, 'Female Spectators, Agency, and the Politics of Pleasure: An Historical Case Study from Australian Rules Football', *International Journal of the History of Sport* 33, 17 (2016), 2086–2104

Klugman, Matthew, '"*Genus Barracker*": Masculinity, Race, and the Disruptive Pleasures of Rowdy Partisanship in 1880s Melbourne', *Australian Historical Studies* 50, 2 (2019), 171–87

Lennan, Jo, 'The Development of Offensive Language Laws in Nineteenth-Century New South Wales', *Current Issues in Criminal Justice* 18: 3 (March 2007), 449–56

Lothian, Kathy, 'Seizing the Time: Australian Aborigines and the Influence of the Black Panther Party, 1969–1972', *Journal of Black Studies* 35, 4 (March 2005), 179–200

Lyons, Martyn, and Lucy Taksa, *Australian Readers Remember: An Oral History of Reading 1890–1940* (Melbourne: Oxford University Press, 1992)

Marjoribanks, Alexander, *Travels in New South Wales* (London: Smith, Elder, 1847)

Marwil, Jonathan, *Frederic Manning: An Unfinished Life* (Durham: Duke University Press, 1985)

McCalman, Janet, *Struggletown: Public and Private Life in Richmond 1900–1965* (Melbourne: Melbourne University Press, 1984)

McCullough, Megan B, 'The Gender of the Joke: Intimacy and Marginality in Murri Humour', *Ethnos* 79, 5 (2014), 677–98

McGregor, Russell, *Indifferent Inclusion: Aboriginal People and the Australian Nation* (Canberra: Aboriginal Studies Press, 2011)

McLachlan, Noel (ed.), *The Memoirs of James Hardy Vaux Including His Vocabulary of the Flash Language* (London: Heinemann, 1964)

Methven, Elyse, 'Dirty Talk: A Critical Discourse Analysis of Offensive Language Crimes', PhD Thesis, University of Technology, Sydney, March 2017

Mitchell, Tony, 'Wogs Still Out of Work: Australian Television Comedy as Colonial Discourse', *Australasian Drama Studies* 20 (1992), 119–33

Mohr, Melissa, *Holy Shit: A Brief History of Swearing* (New York: Oxford University Press, 2013)

Montagu, Ashley, *The Anatomy of Swearing* (London: Rapp and Whiting, 1967)

Montell, Amanda, *Wordslut: A Feminist Guide to Taking Back the English Language* (New York: HarperCollins, 2019)

Moore, Bruce, *Speaking Our Language: The Story of Australian English* (Melbourne: Oxford University Press, 2008)

Moore, Bruce, *What's Their Story? A History of Australian Words* (Melbourne: Oxford University Press, 2010)

Moore, Nicole, *The Censor's Library* (Brisbane: University of Queensland Press, 2012)

Moore, Tony, *Dancing with Empty Pockets: Australia's Bohemians Since 1860* (Sydney: Pier 9, 2000)

Moore, Tony, *The Barry McKenzie Movies* (Sydney: Currency Press, 2005)

Mudie, James, *The Felonry of New South Wales* (Melbourne: Lansdowne Press, 1964 [1837])

Mullins, Patrick, *The Trials of Portnoy: How Penguin Brought Down Australia's Censorship Regime* (Melbourne: Scribe, 2020)

Neville, Richard, *The Hippie Hippie Shake: The Dreams, the Trips, the Trials, the Love-ins, the Screw-ups, the Sixties* (Melbourne: William Heinemann, 1995)

Piper, Alana Jayne, and Victoria Nagy, 'Versatile Offending: Criminal Careers of Female Prisoners in Australia, 1860–1920', *Journal of Interdisciplinary History* 48, 2 (Autumn 2017), 187–210

Pretty, AG, 'Glossary of Slang and Peculiar Terms in Use in the AIF', unpublished

Rahman, Jacquelyn, 'Missing the Target: Group Practices That Launch and Deflect Slurs', *Language Sciences* 52 (2015), 70–81

Reynolds, Robert, and Shirleene Robinson, *Gay and Lesbian, Then and Now: Australian Stories from a Social Revolution* (Melbourne: Black Inc, 2016)

Ritchie, John (ed.), *The Evidence to the Bigge Reports: New South Wales under Governor Macquarie Volume 1: The Oral Evidence* (Melbourne: Heinemann, 1971)

Robertson, Judith Smyth, *Australian Lexicography 1880–1910: An Evaluation*, PhD Thesis, Australian National University, 2005

Rowse, Tim, *Indigenous and Other Australians Since 1901* (Sydney: UNSW Press, 2017)

Rudd, Steele, *On Our Selection* (Brisbane: University of Queensland Press, 1987 [1903])

Russell, Penny, *Savage or Civilised? Manners in Colonial Australia* (Sydney: UNSW Press, 2010)

Seal, Graham, *The Soldiers' Press: Trench Journals in the First World War* (Basingstoke: Palgrave Macmillan, 2013)

Seymour, Alan, *The One Day of the Year* (Sydney: Angus and Robertson, 1962)

Simes, Gary, *A Dictionary of Australian Underworld Slang* (Melbourne: Oxford University Press, 1993)

Sleight, Simon, *Young People and the Shaping of Public Space in Melbourne 1870–1914* (Farnham: Ashgate, 2013)

Stanley, Peter, *Bad Characters: Sex, Crime, Mutiny, Murder and the Australian Imperial Force* (Sydney: Pier 9, 2010)

Steele, John G, *Brisbane Town in Convict Days 1824–1842* (Brisbane: University of Queensland Press, 1975)

Stewart, Douglas, and Nancy Keesing, *Australian Bush Ballads* (Sydney: Angus and Robertson, 1955)

Straw, Leigh SL, *Drunks, Pests and Harlots: Criminal Women in Perth and Fremantle, 1900–1939* (Kilkerran: Humming Earth, 2013)

Sturma, Michael, *Vice in a Vicious Society: Crime and Convicts in Mid-nineteenth Century New South Wales* (Brisbane: University of Queensland Press, 1983)

Tavan, Gwenda, '"Good Neighbours": Community Organisations, Migrant Assimilation and Australian Society and Culture, 1950–1961', *Australian Historical Studies* 27, 109 (1997), 77–89

Tench, Watkin, *A Complete Account of the Settlement at Port Jackson in New South Wales* (Sydney: University of Sydney Library, 1998 [reprint of 1793 edition])

Thatcher, Charles, *Thatcher's Colonial Songs: Forming a Complete Comic History of the Early Diggings* (Melbourne: Coles Book Arcade, 1864 [Facsimile copy, 1964])

Troy, Jakelin, *Melaleuka: A History and Description of New South Wales Pidgin*, PhD Thesis, Australian National University, Canberra, 1994

Troy, Jakelin, *The Sydney Language* (Canberra: AIATSIS, 1993)

Turner, JW (ed.), *Newcastle as a Convict Settlement: The Evidence Before JT Bigge in 1819–1821* (Newcastle: Newcastle Public Library, 1973)

Vickery, Ann, 'The Rise of "Women's Poetry" in the 1970s', *Australian Feminist Studies* 22, 53 (2007), 265–85

Wajnryb, Ruth, *Language Most Foul* (Sydney: Allen and Unwin, 2004)

Walker, David, *Anxious Nation: Australia and the Rise of Asia 1850–1939* (Brisbane: University of Queensland Press, 1999)

Ward, Russel, *The Australian Legend* (Melbourne: Oxford University Press, 2003 [1958])

White, Isobel, Diane Barwick, and Betty Meehan (eds), *Fighters and Singers: The Lives of Some Australian Aboriginal Women* (Sydney: Allen and Unwin, 1985)

Williams, John F, *The Quarantined Culture: Australian Reactions to Modernism 1913–1939* (Melbourne: Cambridge University Press, 1995)

Williamson, David, *Don's Party* (Sydney: Currency Press, 1980)

Wilson, Patrick (ed.), *So Far from Home: The Remarkable Diaries of Eric Evans, an Australian Soldier During World War I* (Sydney: Kangaroo Press, 2002)

Wood, Sally Percival, *Dissent: The Student Press in 1960s Australia* (Melbourne: Scribe, 2017)

NOTES

Introduction: Australians and their bad language

1   Alexander Marjoribanks, *Travels in New South Wales* (London: Smith, Elder, 1847), 57.

2   Sidney Baker, *The Australian Language* (Sydney: Angus and Robertson, 1945), 256–7.

3   Howard Manns, 'The Lexicon of Australian English', Kate Burridge, 'History of Australian English' in Louisa Willoughby and Howard Manns (eds), *Australian English Reimagined: Structure, Features and Developments* (Milton Park: Routledge, 2020), 87, 188.

4   Chris Rodley, 'One Hundred Rudest Things Australians Say', *Buzzfeed*, 19 May 2016 [online].

5   Timothy Jay, 'The Utility and Ubiquity of Taboo Words', *Perspectives on Psychological Science* 4, 2 (2009), 153.

6   Timothy Jay, *Cursing in America: A Psycholinguistic Study of Dirty Language in the Courts, in the Movies, in the Schoolyard and on the Streets* (Philadelphia: John Benjamins Publishing Company, 1992), 70.

7   Melissa Mohr, *Holy Shit: A Brief History of Swearing* (New York: Oxford University Press, 2013), 5.

8   Emma Byrne, *Swearing Is Good for You: The Amazing Science of Bad Language* (London: Profile Books, 2017), 36, 44. See also Benjamin K Bergen, *What the F: What Swearing Reveals about Our Language, Our Brains, and Ourselves* (New York: Basic Books, 2016), 97.

9   Jay, 'The Utility and Ubiquity of Taboo Words', 155–6.

10 Jay, 'The Utility and Ubiquity of Taboo Words', 156.

11 Ruth Wajnryb, *Language Most Foul* (Sydney: Allen and Unwin, 2004), 58.

12 Jay, *Cursing in America*, 168.

13 Kristin L Jay and Timothy B Jay, 'A Children's Garden of Curses: A Gender, Historical and Age-Related Evaluation of the Taboo Lexicon', *The American Journal of Psychology* 126, 4 (Winter 2013), 463–4.

14 June Factor, *Kidspeak: A Dictionary of Australian Children's Words, Expressions and Games* (Melbourne: Melbourne University Press, 2000), xxii.

15 Bergen, *What the F*, 195–6.

16 Factor, *Kidspeak*, xxii.

17 Jay, *Cursing in America*, 83.

18 Kristin L Jay and Timothy B Jay, 'Taboo Word Fluency and Knowledge of Slurs and General Pejoratives: Deconstructing the Poverty-of-Vocabulary Myth', *Language Sciences* 52 (2015), 257.

19 Geoffrey Hughes, *Swearing: A Social History of Foul Language, Oaths and Profanity in English* (Oxford: Blackwell, 1991), 211. See also Byrne, *Swearing Is Good*

for You, 153; Karyn Stapleton, 'Gender and Swearing: A Community Practice', *Women and Language* 26, 2 (Fall 2003), 22–33.

20 Byrne, *Swearing Is Good for You*, 156.

21 Keith Allan, 'Taboo Words and Language: An Overview', in Keith Allan (ed.), *The Oxford Handbook of Taboo Words and Language* (Oxford: Oxford University Press, 2019), 14.

22 Diana Eades, *Aboriginal Ways of Using English* (Canberra: Aboriginal Studies Press, 2013), 103.

23 Murray Garde, 'The Pragmatics of Rude Jokes with Grandad: Joking Relationships in Aboriginal Australia', *Anthropological Forum* 18, 3 (2008), 237.

24 Marcia Langton, 'Medicine Square', in Ian Keen (ed.) *Being Black: Aboriginal Culture in 'Settled' Australia* (Canberra: Aboriginal Studies Press, 1988), 202, 219.

25 Hughes, *Swearing*, 249.

26 Magnus Ljung, *Swearing: A Cross-Cultural Linguistic Study* (Houndmills: Palgrave Macmillan, 2011), 45.

27 Ashley Montagu, *The Anatomy of Swearing* (London: Rapp and Whiting, 1967), 31–2.

28 Montagu, *Anatomy of Swearing*, 63.

29 Mohr, *Holy Shit*, 155.

30 Hughes, *Swearing*, 103–4.

31 Hughes, *Swearing*, 12.

32 Tony McEnery, *Swearing in English: Bad Language, Purity and Power from 1586 to the Present* (Abingdon: Routledge, 2006), 80.

33 Paul A Gilje, *To Swear Like a Sailor: Maritime Culture in America, 1750–1850* (New York: Cambridge University Press, 2016), 11.

34 Mohr, *Holy Shit*, 176.

35 Hughes, *Swearing*, 152.

36 Hughes, *Swearing*, 127.

37 Wajnryb, *Language Most Foul*, 62.

38 Langton, 'Medicine Square', 218–19.

39 Croom cited in Jacquelyn Rahman, 'Missing the Target: Group Practices That Launch and Deflect Slurs', *Language Sciences* 52 (2015), 70.

40 Rahman, 'Missing the Target', 71, 75.

41 Cassie Herbert, 'Precarious Projects: The Performative Structure of Reclamation', *Language Sciences* 52 (2015), 132, 134.

42 Luke Cooper, 'Sydney Activist Wins Appeal Over Offensive Tony Abbott Sign', *Huffpost*, 29 August 2017.

43 Greg Dening, *Mr Bligh's Bad Language: Passion, Power and Theatre on the Bounty* (Cambridge: Cambridge University Press, 1992), 61.

1   Convicts and bad language

1 Evidence of Robert Cartwright in John Ritchie (ed.), *The Evidence to the Bigge Reports: New South Wales under Governor Macquarie Volume 1: The Oral Evidence* (Melbourne: Heinemann, 1971), 157.

2 Alan Atkinson, *The Europeans in Australia: A History Volume 1 – The Beginning* (Melbourne: Oxford University Press, 1997), 220, 236.

3 Janet Sorenson, *Strange Vernaculars: How Eighteenth-century Slang, Cant, Provincial Languages, and Nautical Jargon Became English* (Princeton: Princeton

University Press, 2017), suggests however that by reading about this language, the upper classes were brought into a common language community with the speakers, and this in turn helped to create a greater 'imagined community' that fed into a sense of Englishness.

4   Henry Hitchings, *The Language Wars: A History of Proper English* (London: John Murray, 2011), 129.

5   Francis Grose, *1811 Dictionary of the Vulgar Tongue* (Northfield, Illinois: Digest Books, Inc., 1971 [reprint]). The 1785 and 1796 editions of Grose are available through Google Books.

6   Noel McLachlan (ed.), *The Memoirs of James Hardy Vaux Including His Vocabulary of the Flash Language* (London: Heinemann, 1964), 223.

7   Julie Coleman, *A History of Cant and Slang Dictionaries, Volume II: 1785–1858* (Oxford: Oxford University Press, 2004), 141–8.

8   Watkin Tench, *A Complete Account of the Settlement at Port Jackson in New South Wales* (Sydney: University of Sydney Library, 1998 [reprint of 1793 edition]), 138–9.

9   Peter Cunningham, *Two Years in New South Wales* (London: Henry Colburn, 1827), 59.

10 *Hobart Town Gazette and Van Diemen's Land Advertiser*, 8 December 1821, 1.

11 *Sydney Herald*, 16 January 1832, 2.

12 Trial of Sophia Lewis, William Cox, October 1786 (t17861025–87), *Old Bailey Proceedings Online* (<www.oldbaileyonline.org>, version 8.0, 16 November 2018).

13 Trial of John Tate (t17840526-115), May 1784, *Old Bailey Proceedings Online* (<www.oldbaileyonline.org>, version 8.0, 16 November 2018).

14 William Falconer's dictionary is available online: <southseas.nla.gov.au/refs/falc/title.html>.

15 Critical Review, 1757, quoted in Peter Linebaugh and Marcus Rediker, *The Many-Headed Hydra: The Hidden History of the Revolutionary Atlantic* (London: Verso, 2000), 152.

16 Gilje, *To Swear Like a Sailor*, 5, 30.

17 Ross Fitzgerald and Mark Hearn, *Bligh, Macarthur and the Rum Rebellion* (Kenthurst: Kangaroo Press, 1988), 11; Stephen Dando-Collins, *Captain Bligh's Other Mutiny* (Sydney: Random House, 2007), 154.

18 Russell Earls Davis, *Bligh in Australia* (Warriewood: Woodslane, 2010), 51; Dando-Collins, *Other Mutiny*, 155.

19 Dando-Collins, *Other Mutiny*, 250–1.

20 Atkinson, *Europeans in Australia*, 95.

21 Atkinson, *Europeans in Australia*, 96.

22 Jo Lennan, 'The Development of Offensive Language Laws in Nineteenth-Century New South Wales', *Current Issues in Criminal Justice* 18, 3 (March 2007), 449.

23 Elyse Methven, 'Dirty Talk: A Critical Discourse Analysis of Offensive Language Crimes', PhD in Law Thesis, University of Technology, Sydney, March 2017, 52.

24 *Trumpeter General* (Hobart), 17 October 1834, 3.

25 Quoted in Methven, 'Dirty Talk', 52.

26 Atkinson, *Europeans in Australia*, 95.

27 Trial transcript available online, UNSW: <www.law.mq.edu.au/research/colonial_case_law/nsw/cases/case_index/1788/r_v_baker_and_others/>.

28 John G Steele, *Brisbane Town in Convict Days 1824–1842* (Brisbane: University of Queensland Press, 1975), 83–4.

29 Letter, John McIntosh to Governor Darling, 2 June 1827, in Steele, *Brisbane Town*, 84.

30 Witness statements in Steele, *Brisbane Town*, 97.

31 Testimony of Morris Landers, Gaoler at Newcastle, January 1820, in JW Turner (ed.), *Newcastle as a Convict Settlement: The Evidence before JT Bigge in 1819–1821* (Newcastle: Newcastle Public Library, 1973), 136.

32 'List of Prisoners Punished at Newcastle 14 July 1818 to 1 January 1821', in Turner, *Newcastle*, 250.

33 Simon Barnard, *Convict Tattoos: Marked Men and Women of Australia* (Melbourne: Text Publishing, 2016), 12.

34 Alison Alexander, *Tasmania's Convicts: How Felons Built a Free Society* (Sydney: Allen and Unwin, 2010), 24.

35 Barnard, *Convict Tattoos*, 6.

36 Quoted in Atkinson, *Europeans in Australia*, 176.

37 Atkinson, *Europeans in Australia*, 178.

38 Richard Johnson, 'An Address to the Inhabitants of the Colonies, Established in New South Wales and Norfolk Island' (London: Matthews, 1794 [reprint, University of Sydney Library, 1998]).

39 Evidence of Samuel Marsden, 1820, in John Ritchie, *The Evidence to the Bigge Reports, New South Wales under Governor Macquarie Volume 2: The Written Evidence* (Melbourne: Heinemann, 1971), 89.

40 Evidence of William Howe, 22 January 1821, in Ritchie, *Bigge Reports Volume 2*, 54.

41 Appendix O, 'A Report on New South Wales to Major General Richard Bourke (by James Backhouse and George Washington Walker), in James Backhouse, *A Narrative of a Visit to the Australian Colonies* (London: Hamilton and Co., 1843), cxxv.

42 James Mudie, *The Felonry of New South Wales* (Melbourne: Lansdowne Press, 1964 [1837]), 114, 113.

43 Grace Karskens, *The Rocks: Life in Early Sydney* (Melbourne: Melbourne University Press, 1997), 45, 44.

44 Grace Karskens, *The Colony: A History of Early Sydney* (Sydney: Allen and Unwin, 2009), 128.

45 Babette Smith, *A Cargo of Women: Susannah Watson and the Convicts of the* Princess Royal (Sydney: NSW University Press, 1988), 36.

46 Joy Damousi, *Depraved and Disorderly: Female Convicts, Sexuality and Gender in Colonial Australia* (Melbourne: Cambridge University Press, 1997), 48.

47 Mudie, *Felonry*, 122.

48 John Hirst, *Convict Society and Its Enemies: A History of Early New South Wales* (Sydney: Allen and Unwin, 1983), 56.

49 Karskens, *The Colony*, 321.

50 Karskens, *The Rocks*, 151.

51 Damousi, *Depraved and Disorderly*, 20.

52 Quoted in Damousi, *Depraved and Disorderly*, 40.

53 Convict Records of Australia, <convictrecords.com.au/convicts/barber/elizabeth/129187>.

54 Damousi, *Depraved and Disorderly*, 61, 73.

55 *Sydney Herald*, 10 March 1834, 2.

56   Damousi, *Depraved and Disorderly*, 40.
57   Anatoly Liberman, 'Beggars, Buggers and Bigots, Part 3', Oxford University Press Blog, <blog.oup.com/2014/03/beggar-bugger-etymology-word-origin/>.
58   Gilje, *To Swear Like a Sailor*, 17.
59   Tracey Banivanua Mar and Penny Edmonds, 'Indigenous and Settler Relations', in Alison Bashford and Stuart Macintyre (eds), *The Cambridge History of Australia Volume 1: Indigenous and Colonial Australia* (Melbourne: Cambridge University Press, 2013), 342.
60   Karskens, *The Colony*, 47.
61   For a close reading of the first interactions between Indigenous Australians and the invaders, see Inga Clendinnen, *Dancing with Strangers: Europeans and Australians at First Contact* (Melbourne: Text Publishing, 2003).
62   For a study of the Sydney Language, see Jakelin Troy, *The Sydney Language* (Canberra: AIATSIS, 1993).
63   Johnson, 'An Address', 25.
64   Robert Dawson, *Present State of Australia* (London: Smith, Elder, 1830), 121.
65   For a full discussion and wordlist of New South Wales Pidgin, see Jakelin Troy, *Melaleuka: A History and Description of New South Wales Pidgin*, PhD Thesis, Australian National University, Canberra, 1994.
66   Cunningham, *Two Years*, 21.
67   Troy, *Melaleuka*, 110, 117.
68   Alexander Harris, *Settlers and Convicts or Recollections of Sixteen Years' Labour in the Australian Backwoods* (Melbourne: Melbourne University Press, 1977 [1847]), 7.
69   Harris, *Settlers and Convicts*, 230.
70   Richard W Bailey, *Nineteenth-century English* (Ann Arbor: University of Michigan Press, 1996), 82.

2   Respectability and its discontents

1   *Ovens and Murray Advertiser* (Beechworth, Victoria), 28 October 1873, 2.
2   Meredith Lake, *The Bible in Australia: A Cultural History* (Sydney: NewSouth Publishing, 2018), 77.
3   Penny Russell, *Savage or Civilised? Manners in Colonial Australia* (Sydney: UNSW Press, 2010), 3.
4   Penny Russell, 'The Brash Colonial Class and Comportment in Nineteenth-Century Australia', *Transactions of the Royal Historical Society* 12 (2002), 437.
5   Russell, 'The Brash Colonial Class', 449. Russell talks about how gentility is fundamentally performative.
6   There are many excellent histories that illuminate this story. See, for example, James Boyce, *1835: the Founding of Melbourne and the Conquest of Australia* (Melbourne: Black Inc., 2013). Boyce makes the point that the terrible outcomes of settler expansion should not be seen as 'inevitable'.
7   Mark Finnane, 'Law and Regulation', in Bashford and Macintyre, *Cambridge History Volume 1*, 399.
8   Michael Sturma, *Vice in a Vicious Society: Crime and Convicts in Mid-nineteenth Century New South Wales* (Brisbane: University of Queensland Press, 1983), argues that newspapers were a 'potent instrument of social control', 124.
9   Sturma, *Vice in a Vicious Society*, 129.
10   Lennan, 'The Development of Offensive Language Laws', 451–2.
11   Methven, 'Dirty Talk', 51, 54.

12   Methven, 'Dirty Talk', 55.
13   Methven, 'Dirty Talk', 57.
14   *Argus* (Melbourne), 8 January 1850, 2.
15   Pat O'Malley, 'The Place of Crime in Popular History', in Verity Burgmann and Jenny Lee (eds), *Constructing a Culture* (Melbourne: McPhee Gribble, 1988), 42.
16   Sturma, *Vice in a Vicious Society*, 129.
17   Mudgee Bench Book, 13 September 1850, NSW SA 4/5591, quoted in Sturma, *Vice in a Vicious Society*, 130.
18   Parramatta Bench Book, 8 August 1853, NSW SA 4/5614, quoted in Sturma, *Vice in a Vicious Society*, 131.
19   Parramatta Bench Book, 20 May 1854, NSW SA 4/5615, quoted in Sturma, *Vice in a Vicious Society*, 131.
20   Parramatta Bench Book, 2 November 1852, NSW SA 4/5614, quoted in Sturma, *Vice in a Vicious Society*, 131.
21   Braidwood Bench Book, 7 February 1856, NSW SA 4/5517, quoted in Sturma, *Vice in a Vicious Society*, 131.
22   *The Australian* (Sydney), 24 February 1834, 3.
23   *Morning Star and Commercial Advertiser* (Hobart), 27 February 1835, 2.
24   *Colonial Times* (Hobart), 1 February 1845, 3.
25   Maitland Bench Book, 7 March 1854, NSW SA 4/5541, quoted in Sturma, *Vice in a Vicious Society*, 132.
26   *Maitland Mercury and Hunter River General Advertiser*, 10 March 1859, 2.
27   For example, see list of charges in *North Australian, Ipswich and General Advertiser*, 1 March 1859, 3; *Queensland Times, Ipswich Herald and General Advertiser*, 2 March 1865, 3.
28   *Melbourne Daily News*, 13 December 1850, 2.
29   Sturma, *Vice in a Vicious Society*, 131, 135.
30   Parramatta Bench Book, 31 January 1852, NSW SA 4/5613, quoted in Sturma, *Vice in a Vicious Society*, 131.
31   *Hobarton Guardian, or, The True Friend of Tasmania*, 12 January 1850, 2.
32   *Hobarton Guardian, or, The True Friend of Tasmania*, 12 January 1850, 2.
33   Parramatta Bench Book, 20 October 1854, NSW SA 4/5614, quoted in Sturma, *Vice in a Vicious Society*, 134.
34   See Edmund Campion, *Rockchoppers: Growing up Catholic in Australia* (Melbourne: Penguin, 1982); Elizabeth Malcolm and Dianne Hall, *A New History of the Irish in Australia* (Sydney: NewSouth Publishing, 2018).
35   *Colonial Times* (Hobart), 11 April 1837, 7.
36   *Colonial Times* (Hobart), 21 April 1835, 8.
37   *The Empire* (Sydney), 4 February 1853, 2.
38   For example, *South Australian Register*, 11 October 1859, 3.
39   *Hobart Town Courier*, 30 March 1838, 4.
40   *Ovens and Murray Advertiser* (Beechworth, Vic.), 16 April 1857, 2.
41   *The Empire* (Sydney), 5 February 1852, 2.
42   *Sydney Morning Herald*, 7 January 1853, 2.
43   *The Argus* (Melbourne), 2 January 1850, 2.
44   Methven, 'Dirty Talk', 61.
45   Methven, 'Dirty Talk', 59–60.
46   *Sydney Morning Herald*, 28 May 1859, 8.

47   Peter Coleman, *Obscenity, Blasphemy, Sedition: The Rise and Fall of Literary Censorship in Australia* (Sydney: Duffy and Snellgrove, 2000 [1962]), 104.

48   *Australian Town and Country Journal* (Sydney), 4 February 1871, 18.

49   *The Argus* (Melbourne), 24 February 1871, 6.

50   *Brisbane Courier*, 21 February 1871, 4; *Sydney Mail and New South Wales Advertiser*,
      11 March 1871, 521; Coleman, *Obscenity, Blasphemy, Sedition*, 103.

51   See Melissa Bellanta, 'A Hard Culture? Religion and Politics in Turn-of-the Century Australian History', *Australian Journal of Politics and History* 56, 1 (2010), 55–65.

52   *Brisbane Courier*, 1 March 1871, 3.

53   *Ovens and Murray Advertiser* (Beechworth, Vic.), 11 March 1871, 1.

54   *Maitland Mercury and Hunter River General Advertiser*, 27 December 1873, 2.

55   Harris, *Settlers and Convicts*, 7, 184.

56   *The Colonist* (Sydney), 2 March 1837, 6.

57   *The Monitor* (Sydney), 2 June 1826, 4.

58   *The Argus*, 19 September 1868, 7.

59   *Sydney Morning Herald*, 6 February 1850, 3.

60   *Sydney Morning Herald*, 7 February 1850, 2.

61   *Geelong Advertiser*, 11 May 1850, 2.

62   *Portland Guardian and Normanby General Advertiser*, 26 October 1857, 2.

63   *Sydney Gazette and New South Wales Advertiser*, 15 November 1826, 3.

64   *Hobart Town Daily Mercury*, 3 February 1859, 3.

65   Penny Russell, 'A Wish of Distinction': Colonial Gentility and Femininity (Melbourne: Melbourne University Press), 1994, 189.

66   *Moreton Bay Courier*, 11 May 1850, 2.

67   *Sydney Monitor and Commercial Advertiser*, 25 March 1840, 2.

68   *Cornwall Chronicle* (Launceston), 24 February 1849, 394.

69   *Sydney Herald*, 3 February 1840, 2.

70   *Geelong Advertiser*, 29 August 1850, 2.

71   *Hobarton Mercury*, 20 August 1856, 2.

72   *Sydney Morning Herald*, 6 March 1848, 3.

73   *Sydney Morning Herald*, 4 September 1850, p. 3.

74   See the Colonial Frontier Massacres Map, University of Newcastle website, <c21ch.newcastle.edu.au/colonialmassacres/map.php>.

75   Tracey Banivanua Mar and Penny Edmonds, 'Indigenous and Settler Relations', in Bashford and Macintyre, *Cambridge History Vol. 1*, 351.

76   Anne Scrimgeour, 'Notions of Civilisation and the Project to "Civilise" Aborigines in South Australia in the 1840s', *History of Education Review*, 35, 1 (2006), 37.

77   Cunningham, *Two Years*, 21.

78   Lancelot Threlkeld, Eighth Annual Report, 31 December 1838, in Niel Gunson (ed.), *Australian Reminiscences of LE Threlkeld, Missionary to the Aborigines 1824– 59, Volume 1* (Canberra: Australian Institute of Aboriginal Studies, 1974), 144.

79   Johann Handt, Journal entry, 7 September 1834, The Papers of Reverend Johann Christian Simon Handt (digitised), The Wellington Valley Project, University of Newcastle website, <downloads.newcastle.edu.au/library/cultural%20collections/ the-wellington-valley-project/handt/handt-journals/vii-april-sept-1834.html>.

80   James Günther, Journal entry, 8 November 1837, The Papers of Reverend James Günther (digitised), Wellington Valley Project, <downloads.newcastle.edu.au/

library/cultural%20collections/the-wellington-valley-project/gunther/gunther-journals/i-aug-dec-1837.html>.

81 Ian D Clark, *The Journals of George Augustus Robinson, Chief Protector, Port Phillip Aboriginal Protectorate, Volume Two: 1 October 1840 – 31 August 1841* (Melbourne: Heritage Matters, 1998), 238.

82 Frank Bongiorno also cites a bushman's song from around this time with the line 'I can ride a hack and fuck a black' in *The Sex Lives of Australians: A History* (Melbourne: Black Inc., 2012), 25.

83 *Maryborough Chronicle, Wide Bay and Burnett Advertiser*, 5 November 1863, 2.

84 Threlkeld, Ninth Annual Report, 31 December 1839, in Gunson, *Australian Reminiscences*, 159.

85 William Watson, Journal, 10 May 1833, The Papers of Reverend William Watson (digitised), Wellington Valley Project, <downloads.newcastle.edu.au/library/cultural%20collections/the-wellington-valley-project/watson/watson-journals/iv-april-july-1833.html>.

86 Watson, Journal, 26 February 1834, <downloads.newcastle.edu.au/library/cultural%20collections/the-wellington-valley-project/watson/watson-journals/vii-jan-march-1834.html>.

87 Christina Twomey, 'Vagrancy, Indolence and Ignorance: Race, Class and the Idea of Civilization in the Era of Aboriginal "Protection" 1835–49', in Tracey Banivanua Mar and Julie Evans (eds), *Writing Colonial Histories: Comparative Perspectives* (Melbourne: University of Melbourne, 2002), 97. See also Jessie Mitchell, *In Good Faith? Governing Indigenous Australia through God, Charity, and Empire, 1825–1855* (Canberra: ANU ePress, 2011), 104.

88 *Melbourne Daily News*, 25 January 1850, 4.

89 *Gundagai Times and Tumut, Adelong and Murrumbidgee District Advertiser*, 23 March 1877, 3.

90 Mohr, *Holy Shit*, 210, 212.

91 George Augustus Robinson quoted in *Australian National Dictionary* (second edition).

92 Marjoribanks, *Travels in New South Wales*, 57–8.

93 *Evening News* (Sydney), 7 March 1870, 2.

94 *Bendigo Advertiser*, 13 August 1858, 3.

95 For example, *Maryborough Chronicle, Wide Bay and Burnett Advertiser*, 22 December 1874, 2; *Maryborough Chronicle, Wide Bay and Burnett Advertiser*, 22 May 1875, 2.

96 *Cornwall Chronicle* (Launceston), 28 January 1852, 60.

97 David Goodman, *Gold Seeking: Victoria and California in the 1850s* (Sydney: Allen and Unwin, 1994), xx, 61.

98 Catharine Coleborne, 'Regulating "Mobility" and Masculinity through Institutions in Colonial Victoria, 1870s–1890s', *Law Text Culture* 15 (2011), 52.

99 *The Empire* (Sydney), 18 September 1851, 3.

100 *Geelong Advertiser and Intelligencer*, 2 January 1852, 2.

101 For example, see *Goulburn Herald and County of Argyle Advertiser*, 6 March 1852, 3.

102 *South Australian Gazette and Mining Journal* (Adelaide), 4 March 1852, 3.

103 Louisa Anne Meredith, *Travels and Stories in Our Gold Colonies* (London: Charles Griffith and Company), 248.

104 James Bonwick, *Notes of a Gold Digger and Gold Diggers' Guide* (Melbourne: The Hawthorn Press, 1852), 29–30.

105 *Sydney Morning Herald*, 16 April 1853, 2.
106 *West Australian* (Perth), 11 November 1893, 14.
107 Raffaello Carboni, *The Eureka Stockade* (Melbourne: State Library of Victoria, 1962 [1855]), 11.
108 Carboni, *Eureka Stockade*, 67.
109 Clare Wright, *The Forgotten Rebels of Eureka* (Melbourne: Text Publishing, 2013), 218.
110 Philip Butterss, *Australian Ballads: The Social Function of British and Irish Transportation Broadsides, Popular Convict Verse and Goldfield Songs*, PhD Thesis, University of Sydney, 1989, 222. Emphasis mine.
111 Anthony Trollope, *John Caldigate* (London: The Trollope Society, 1995 [1877]), 63.
112 Finnane, 'Law and Regulation', 409.
113 O'Malley, 'The Place of Crime in Popular History', 37.
114 *Riverine Herald* (Echuca, Vic.), 31 March 1869, 3.
115 *Mount Alexander Mail*, 27 June 1864, 3.
116 *Brisbane Courier*, 3 October 1868, 6.
117 Transcription of the Jerilderie Letter, written by Ned Kelly, 1879, National Museum of Australia website <www.nma.gov.au/explore/features/ned-kelly-jerilderie-letter/transcription>.

3   Bullocky and the bush

1   WT Goodge, 'The Great Australian Adjective' in *The Bulletin Reciter: Collections of Verses for Recitation* (Sydney: NSW Bookstall Company, 1933), 242–3.
2   Russel Ward, *The Australian Legend* (Melbourne: Oxford University Press, 2003 [1958]), 2.
3   *Morning Bulletin* (Rockhampton), 31 December 1885, 4.
4   Extracts from *Melbourne Punch* reprinted in the *South Australian Register*, 17 January 1856, 3.
5   *The Age* (Melbourne), 14 January 1864, 4.
6   *Horsham Times*, 22 December 1885, 2.
7   'The Lady and the Bullock Driver', *Thatcher's Colonial Songs: Forming a Complete Comic History of the Early Diggings* (Melbourne: Coles Book Arcade, 1864 [Facsimile copy, 1964]), 14.
8   *Bendigo Independent*, 6 January 1894, 2.
9   'Getting Colonized', *Thatcher's Colonial Songs*, 35.
10 *Gippsland Guardian*, 14 June 1861, 1.
11 John Barnes and Lois Hoffmann, *Bushman and Bookworm: Letters of Joseph Furphy* (Melbourne: Oxford University Press, 1995), 1.
12 Joseph Furphy, *The Annotated Such Is Life* (Melbourne: Oxford University Press, 1991), 20.
13 Russell, *Savage or Civilised*, 361.
14 For an exploration of this, see Deryck M Schreuder and Stuart Ward (eds), *Australia's Empire* (New York: Oxford University Press, 2008).
15 Nick Dyrenfurth, *Mateship: A Very Australian History* (Melbourne: Scribe, 2015), 59.
16 Tony Moore, *Dancing with Empty Pockets: Australia's Bohemians Since 1860* (Sydney: Pier 9, 2000), 49.
17 *Geraldton Express*, 26 February 1912, 4.

18   Vance Palmer, *The Legend of the Nineties* (Melbourne: Melbourne University Press, 1963 [1954]), 88.
19   Chris McConville, 'Conflicting Loyalties', in Verity Burgmann and Jenny Lee (eds), *Staining the Wattle* (Melbourne: McPhee Gribble, 1988), 21.
20   John Docker, *The Nervous Nineties: Australian Cultural Life in the 1890s* (Melbourne: Oxford University Press, 1991), 122.
21   Quoted in the *Australian National Dictionary* (second edition).
22   Francis Adams, *The Australians: A Social Sketch* (London: T Fisher Unwin, 1893), 165.
23   *Border Watch* (Mount Gambier, SA), 18 February 1882, 2.
24   Harry Morant, 'Beyond His Jurisdiction', in Douglas Stewart and Nancy Keesing, *Australian Bush Ballads* (Sydney: Angus and Robertson, 1955), 233.
25   *Barrier Miner* (Broken Hill), 2 September 1891, 4.
26   *Manning River Times and Advocate for the Northern Coast Districts of New South Wales* (Taree, NSW), 18 June 1898, 2.
27   *The Mercury* (Hobart), 22 June 1898, 3.
28   *Western Champion and General Advertiser for the Central-Western Districts* (Barcaldine, Qld), 22 August 1899, 12.
29   Paul Eggert, *Biography of a Book: Henry Lawson's* While the Billy Boils (Sydney: Sydney University Press, 2013), 29.
30   *Melbourne Punch*, 13 June 1889, 2.
31   *Goulburn Evening Penny Post*, 11 August 1894, 5.
32   Letter, Furphy to William Cathels, 10 August 1897, in Barnes and Hoffmann, *Bushman and Bookworm*, 37. Furphy was also concerned with making distinctions between, for example, *begog*, which he described as 'a mere conversational washer, to fill up space', and *by gog*, 'an oath'. See letter, Furphy to AG Stephens, 8 January 1902, 81.
33   Quoted in *Green's Dictionary of Slang* [online].
34   A copy of the poem can be found online, Australian Poetry Library, <www.poetrylibrary.edu.au/poets/lawson-henry/poems/the-captain-of-the-push-0022049>.
35   For example, Marcus Clarke, *His Natural Life* (Brisbane: University of Queensland Press, 2001), 34.
36   Clarke, *His Natural Life*, 332.
37   Clarke, *His Natural Life*, 252.
38   Richard Fotheringham, *Australian Plays for the Colonial Stage 1834–1899* (Brisbane: University of Queensland Press, 2006), 520, 542. Interestingly, the first instance cited here is disguised, the other spelled out. Fotheringham suggests that the actual lines spoken in colonial plays could vary considerably from the script.
39   Steele Rudd, *On Our Selection* (Brisbane: University of Queensland Press, 1987 [1903]), 24, 106.
40   Rudd, *On Our Selection*, 64, 343, 418, 487.
41   Price Warung, *Half-crown Bob and Tales of the Riverine* (Melbourne: George Robertson, 1898).
42   Warung, *Half-crown Bob*, 116.
43   Martyn Lyons and Lucy Taksa, *Australian Readers Remember: An Oral History of Reading 1890–1940* (Melbourne: Oxford University Press, 1992), 52.
44   Lyons and Taksa, *Australian Readers Remember*, 44–5.

45 *Australian Star*, 8 February 1890, 5.
46 *The Sun* (Sydney), 7 December 1913, 2.
47 Ashley Montagu, *The Anatomy of Swearing* (London: Rapp and Whiting, 1967), 256–7.
48 *Australian Etiquette or the Rules and Usages of the Best Society in the Australasian Colonies* (Melbourne: People's Publishing Company, 1885), 102–3.
49 Anna Wierzbicka, 'Australian Cultural Scripts – Bloody Revisited', *Journal of Pragmatics* 34 (2002), 1178.
50 RW Thompson, quoted in the *Australian National Dictionary* (second edition).
51 *South Australian Chronicle and Weekly Mail*, 6 January 1872, 14.
52 For a full version of the poem, see <www.australianculture.org/the-bastard-from-the-bush/>.
53 *Wellington Times*, 2 May 1907, 3.
54 *The Sun* (Kalgoorlie), 26 July 1903, 4
55 *Windsor and Richmond Gazette*, 25 August 1984, 12.
56 *Express and Telegraph* (Adelaide), 27 July 1901, 5.
57 *The Queenslander* (Brisbane), 8 August 1903, 9.
58 *Sunday Sun* (Sydney), 2 October 1910, 12.
59 *The Truth* (Sydney), 7 December 1913, 11.
60 *The Sun* (Sydney), 7 December 1913, 2.
61 *The Argus* (Melbourne), 28 July 1885, 6.

4   The perils and profanity of the city

1   REN Twopeny, *Town Life in Australia* (Sydney: Sydney University Press, 1973 [1883]), 124, 111.
2   Simon Sleight, *Young People and the Shaping of Public Space in Melbourne 1870–1914* (Farnham: Ashgate, 2013), 132.
3   Melissa Bellanta, *Larrikins: A History* (Brisbane: University of Queensland Press, 2012), 10.
4   Bellanta, *Larrikins*, 87.
5   Sleight, *Young People and the Shaping of Public Space*, 144.
6   *Launceston Examiner*, 23 May 1872, 2.
7   *Express and Telegraph* (Adelaide), 2 March 1875, 3.
8   *Rockhampton Bulletin*, 19 July 1877, 3.
9   *Sydney Morning Herald*, 14 April 1881, 3.
10   *Queanbeyan Age*, 23 September 1886, 1.
11   *The Argus* (Melbourne), 4 March 1873, 4.
12   *Sydney Daily Telegraph*, 24 June 1882, 6.
13   Bellanta, *Larrikins*, 49.
14   Leigh SL Straw, *Drunks, Pests and Harlots: Criminal Women in Perth and Fremantle, 1900–1939* (Kilkerran: Humming Earth, 2013), 135.
15   Melissa Bellanta, 'The Larrikin Girl', *Journal of Australian Studies* 34, 4 (2010), 508.
16   *Wellington Times* (NSW), 2 May 1907, 3.
17   Louis Stone, *Jonah* (London: Methuen and Company, 1911 [reprinted by University of Sydney Library, Sydney, 1997]).
18   *Sydney Daily Telegraph*, 24 June 1882, 6.
19   Paul Schoff, 'Hunting of the Larrikin: Law, Larrikinism, and the Flight of Respectability in Nineteenth-century South Australia', *Australian Journal of Legal History* 1 (1995), 101.

20 Penelope Hetherington, *Settlers, Servants and Slaves: Aboriginal and European Children in Nineteenth-century Western Australia* (Perth: UWA Publishing, 2002), 75.

21 Schoff, 'Hunting of the Larrikin', 103.

22 Andrew Brown-May, *Melbourne Street Life: The Itinerary of Our Days* (Melbourne: Australian Scholarly Publishing, 1998), 56, 62.

23 *National Advocate* (Brisbane), 8 December 1900, 3.

24 *Sunday Times*, 10 November 1907, 5.

25 See, for example, Julie Kimber, '"A Nuisance to the Community": Policing the Vagrant Woman', *Journal of Australian Studies* 34, 3 (2010), 275–93.

26 Straw, *Drunks, Pests and Harlots*, 3.

27 Susanne Davies, '"Ragged, Dirty … Infamous and Obscene": The "Vagrant" in Late Nineteenth Century Melbourne', in David Philips and Susanne Davies (eds), *A Nation of Rogues? Crime, Law and Punishment in Colonial Australia* (Melbourne: Oxford University Press, 1994), 142.

28 Alana Jayne Piper and Victoria Nagy, 'Versatile Offending: Criminal Careers of Female Prisoners in Australia, 1860–1920', *Journal of Interdisciplinary History* 48, 2 (Autumn 2017), 192, 196. See also Judith A Allen, *Sex and Secrets: Crimes Involving Australian Women Since 1880* (Melbourne: Oxford University Press, 1990), 20, 24.

29 Straw, *Drunks, Pests and Harlots*, 10.

30 *Daily News* (Perth), 5 June 1886, 3.

31 Alana Piper, '"A Growing Vice": The *Truth* about Brisbane Girls and Drunkenness in the Early Twentieth Century', *Journal of Australian Studies* 34, 4 (2010), 492.

32 *Burra Record*, 28 April 1882, 3.

33 *Bega Gazette and Eden District or Southern Coast Advertiser*, 24 October 1883, 2.

34 *Geelong Advertiser*, 8 February 1896, 4.

35 Straw, *Drunks, Pests and Harlots*, 68.

36 Janet McCalman, *Struggletown: Public and Private Life in Richmond 1900–1965* (Melbourne: Melbourne University Press, 1984), 28.

37 McCalman, *Struggletown*, 136.

38 *Bendigo Independent*, 12 January 1893, 2.

39 *Barrier Miner*, 24 November 1896, 2.

40 *Williamstown Chronicle*, 12 August 1911, 3.

41 *The Telegraph* (Brisbane), 27 April 1885, 5.

42 *The Mercury* (Hobart), 8 February 1917, 7.

43 *Darling Downs Gazette*, 24 September 1909, 1.

44 *The Advocate* (Melbourne), 24 February 1912, 27.

45 *The Pioneer* (Yorketown, SA), 31 August 1912, 3.

46 Ian Tyrrell, *Woman's World, Woman's Empire: The Woman's Christian Temperance Union in International Perspective, 1880–1930* (Chapel Hill: University of North Carolina Press, 1991).

47 Sara Cousins, 'Drunken, Selfish "Boors?": Images of Masculinity in *The Dawn*', *Hecate* 25, 2 (1999), 88.

48 Maggie Brady, *Teaching "Proper" Drinking? Clubs and Pubs in Indigenous Australia* (Canberra: ANU Press, 2017), 4–5. See also Jocelyn Pixley, 'Wowser and Pro-woman Politics: Temperance against Australian Patriarchy', *Australian and New Zealand Journal of Sociology* 27, 3 (November 1991), 293–314.

49 Straw, *Drunks, Pests and Harlots*, 56.
50 Docker, *The Nervous Nineties*, 52.
51 Bruce Moore, *What's Their Story? A History of Australian Words* (Melbourne: Oxford University Press, 2010), 192–3.
52 Moore, *What's Their Story?*, 192.
53 Marcus Clarke, 'The Language of Bohemia', *Australasian*, 17 July 1869, reproduced in LT Hergenhan (ed.), *A Colonial City: High and Low Life – Selected Journalism of Marcus Clarke* (Brisbane: University of Queensland Press, 1972), 154.
54 Clarke, 'The Language of Bohemia', 155.
55 Clarke, 'The Language of Bohemia', 161.
56 Fergus Hume, *The Mystery of a Hansom Cab* (London: The Leisure Library, 1886).
57 I haven't been able to verify this story, but see Montagu, *Anatomy of Swearing*, 260.
58 Bruce Moore, *Speaking Our Language: The Story of Australian English* (Melbourne: Oxford University Press, 2008), 120; Judith Smyth Robertson, *Australian Lexicography 1880–1910: An Evaluation*, PhD Thesis, Australian National University, 2005, 12. Moore notes that of 558 entries, only 51 were uniquely Australian; of 2574 entries in Crowe, 117 are uniquely Australian.
59 Robertson, *Australian Lexicography*, 39.
60 Cornelius Crowe, *The Australian Slang Dictionary* (Melbourne: Robert Barr, Printer, 1895), n.p.
61 Robertson, *Australian Lexicography*, 165–6.
62 Robertson, *Australian Lexicography*, 166. Stephens asked Joseph Furphy to assist in the compilation of the dictionary but it is unclear if he in fact contributed anything. Letter, Furphy to AG Stephens, 12 March 1902, Barnes and Hoffman, *Bushman and Bookworm*, 96.
63 Robertson, *Australian Lexicography*, 181.
64 Liz Conor, 'Classification and Its Discontents', *Interventions* 17, 2 (2015), 158.
65 Liz Conor, *Skin Deep: Settler Impressions of Aboriginal Women* (Perth: UWA Publishing, 2016), 7.
66 David Walker, *Anxious Nation: Australia and the Rise of Asia 1850–1939* (Brisbane: University of Queensland Press, 1999), 229.
67 For a discussion of the system of protection after 1901, see Tim Rowse, *Indigenous and Other Australians Since 1901* (Sydney: UNSW Press, 2017).
68 Jimmie Barker, *The Two Worlds of Jimmie Barker: The Life of an Australian Aboriginal 1900–1972*, as told to Janet Mathews (Canberra: Australian Institute of Aboriginal Studies, 1982), 59.
69 Walker, *Anxious Nation*, 36.
70 Deposition of George Gossip, Victoria, quoted in the *Australian National Dictionary* (second edition).
71 Bongiorno discusses this case in *Sex Lives*, 116.
72 WH Downing, *Digger Dialects* (Melbourne: Lothian, 1919). See chapter 5.
73 Brian Stoddart, *Saturday Afternoon Fever: Sport in the Australian Culture* (North Ryde NSW: Angus and Robertson, 1986), 48.
74 Richard Waterhouse, *The Vision Splendid: A Social and Cultural History of Rural Australia* (Fremantle: Fremantle Arts Centre Press, 2005), 137.
75 *Sydney Sportsman* (Surry Hills), 21 October 1914, 1.
76 *The Independent* (Footscray), 10 November 1894, 2.
77 *The Bulletin*, 5 January 1922, 40.
78 *The Bulletin*, 8 August 1891, 19.

79   *Bendigo Independent*, 8 August 1894, 4.
80   *Broadford Courier and Reedy Creek Times*, 22 June 1894, 3.
81   *The Herald* (Melbourne), 28 August 1907, 2.
82   Matthew Klugman, '"*Genus Barracker*": Masculinity, Race, and the Disruptive Pleasures of Rowdy Partisanship in 1880s Melbourne', *Australian Historical Studies* 50, 2 (2019), 183.
83   *The Sun* (Kalgoorlie), 2 April 1899, p. 4.
84   Matthew Klugman, 'Female Spectators, Agency, and the Politics of Pleasure: An Historical Case Study from Australian Rules Football', *International Journal of the History of Sport* 33, 17 (2016), 2091.
85   *The Bulletin*, 28 July 1910, 28.
86   *Daily News*, 26 May 1905, 2.

5   The First World War digger and his bad language

1   Joseph Lievesley Beeston, *Five Months at Anzac* (Sydney: Angus and Robertson, 1916), 21.
2   *All Abaht It* (February 1919), 33.
3   George Cuttriss, *'Over the Top' with the Third Australian Division* (London: Charles H Kelly, 1918), 29.
4   Peter Stanley, *Bad Characters: Sex, Crime, Mutiny, Murder and the Australian Imperial Force* (Sydney: Pier 9, 2010), 23.
5   Stanley McDowell, November 1914, quoted in Stanley, *Bad Characters*, 20.
6   Diary entry, 22 February 1915, *The Burford Sampson Great War Diary* (Richard G Sampson, 1997), 47.
7   Diary entry, 23 December 1915, Jean Kelshaw and Bruce Thornton (eds), *Born to Be a Soldier: War Diary of Lieutenant John G Ridley MC* (Baptist Society of New South Wales, 2010), 28.
8   Diary entry, 27 March 1919, *Born to Be a Soldier*, 130.
9   Diary entry, 31 October 1918, *World War I Diary of William James Birch* (Windsor, Vic.: B. Birch, 2006), 40.
10   Diary entry, 21 March 1917, Patrick Wilson (ed.), *So Far from Home: The Remarkable Diaries of Eric Evans, an Australian Soldier During World War I* (Sydney: Kangaroo Press, 2002), 33.
11   Diary entries, 8 July 1917 and 13 August 1918, *So Far from Home*, 84, 192.
12   Diary entry, 21 October 1916, Archie Barwick, *In Great Spirits: The World War I Diary of Archie Barwick* (Sydney: HarperCollins, 2013), 187.
13   Diary entry, 28 January 1917, Barwick, *In Great Spirits*, 233.
14   William Naughton, NAA B2455, quoted in Stanley, *Bad Characters*, 68.
15   *Kerang New Times*, 14 December 1917, 4.
16   Diary entry, Douglas Bruce Searle, 21 September 1915, in James McA Woolley, *We Fought the Battles* (Self-published, June 2000), 24.
17   Letter, Captain Ted Fethers, 6 May 1915, in Woolley, *We Fought the Battles*, 7.
18   Letter, Sapper Gilbert Douglas Perry, 23 February 1917, in Woolley, *We Fought the Battles*, 53.
19   Private Eion Campbell, undated account, in Woolley, *We Fought the Battles*, 30.
20   Diary entry, 22 July 1915, Sir Ronald East (ed.) *The Gallipoli Diary of Sergeant Lawrence of the Australian Engineers – 1st AIF 1915* (Melbourne: Melbourne University Press, 1981), 50.

21 Graham Seal, *The Soldiers' Press: Trench Journals in the First World War* (Houndmills: Palgrave Macmillan, 2013), 17.

22 David Kent, *From Trench and Troopship: The Experience of the Australian Imperial Force 1914–1919* (Sydney: Hale and Iremonger, 1999), 13, 19, 21.

23 Kent, *From Trench and Troopship*, 58. See also Graham Seal, '"Written in the Trenches …": Trench Newspapers of the First World War', *Journal of the Australian War Memorial* 16 (1990), 34.

24 Seal, *Soldiers' Press*, 49.

25 Seal, *Soldiers' Press*, 76, 43.

26 *Aussie* 3 (March 1918), 11.

27 Koolawarra, 'Going Home', *Kia Ora Coo-ee*, April 1918, 20.

28 Reproduced in Kent, *From Trench and Troopship*, 26.

29 Clémentine Tholas-Disset and Karen A Ritzenhoff, 'Introduction: Humour, Entertainment, and Popular Culture During World War I', in Tholas-Disset and Ritzenhoff (eds), *Humor, Entertainment, and Popular Culture During World War I* (New York: Palgrave Macmillan, 2015), 7.

30 Reproduced in Kent, *From Trench and Troopship*, 50.

31 Reproduced in Kent, *From Trench and Troopship*, 65.

32 *Aussie* 1 (January 1918), 2.

33 *Aussie* 3 (March 1918), 11.

34 Julian Walker, *Words and the First World War: Language, Memory, Vocabulary* (London: Bloomsbury, 2017), 107.

35 Graham Seal, *Inventing Anzac: The Digger and National Mythology* (Brisbane: University of Queensland Press, 2004), 61.

36 John Brophy and Eric Partridge, *Songs and Slang of the British Soldier: 1914–1918* (Second edition) (London: Scholartis Press, 1930), 49.

37 Brophy and Partridge, *Songs and Slang*, 49.

38 Letter, 12 May 1916, Daphne Elliott (ed.), *Arthur James Russell Davison: From Private to Captain in the 17th Battalion 1915–1918* (Adelaide: DPA Publishing, 2013), 94.

39 Robin Gerster, *Big-Noting: The Heroic Theme in Australian War Writing* (Melbourne: Melbourne University Press, 1992), 29.

40 DA Kent, 'The Anzac Book and the Anzac Legend: CEW Bean as Editor and Image-Maker', *Historical Studies* 21, 84 (April 1985), 390.

41 Oliver Hogue, *Trooper Bluegum at the Dardanelles* (London: Andrew Melrose, 1916), 175.

42 Schoff, 'Hunting of the Larrikin', 94.

43 Philip Butterss, *An Unsentimental Bloke: The Life and Work of CJ Dennis* (Adelaide: Wakefield Press, 2014), 37.

44 Butterss, *An Unsentimental Bloke*, 82.

45 Butterss, *An Unsentimental Bloke*, 85, 87–8.

46 Lyons and Taksa, *Australian Readers Remember*, 67.

47 Butterss, *An Unsentimental Bloke*, 113.

48 *The Queenslander*, 2 September 1916, 3.

49 *Graphic of Australia* (Melbourne), 17 November 1916, 11.

50 *The Critic* (Adelaide), 30 January 1918, 3.

51 Michael Gladwin, *Captains of the Soul: A History of Australian Army Chaplains* (Sydney: Big Sky Publishing, 2013), 52.

52 *Albury Banner and Wodonga Express*, 26 March 1915, 46.

53   *Port Pirie Recorder and North Western Mail*, 14 June 1915, 1.

54   Brophy and Partridge, *Songs and Slang*, 15–16.

55   *The Methodist* (Sydney), 9 June 1917, 5.

56   *Port Pirie Recorder and North Western Mail*, 6 November 1916, 4.

57   Downing, *Digger Dialects*; AG Pretty, 'Glossary of Slang and Peculiar Terms in Use in the AIF', unpublished. For a version of the original manuscript, as well as an annotated edition, see Australian National Dictionary Centre website, <slll.cass.anu.edu.au/centres/andc/glossary-slang-and-peculiar-terms-use-aif-1921-1924>.

58   Publisher's circular, Box 9, Folder 6B, Lothian Publishing Company Archives, MS6026, State Library of Victoria.

59   Review clipping from the *Sydney Morning Herald*, 27 December 1919, Box 9, Folder 6B, Lothian Archives.

60   Review clipping from *The Bayonet* (Melbourne), Box 9, Folder 6B, Lothian Archives.

61   For a discussion of the glossary, see Amanda Laugesen, 'Australian First World War "Slanguage"', *Journal of the Australian War Memorial* 38 (2003), available online, <www.awm.gov.au/articles/journal/j38/slanguage>.

62   *Sunday Times*, 9 March 1919, 7.

63   *Daily News (Perth)*, 16 October 1922, 4.

64   *Shepparton Advertiser*, 3 February 1936, 4.

65   Jonathan Marwil, *Frederic Manning: An Unfinished Life* (Durham: Duke University Press, 1985), 156–67.

66   Marwil, *Frederic Manning*, 254.

67   Marwil, *Frederic Manning*, 255.

68   Marwil, *Frederic Manning*, 273.

69   For a detailed discussion of its reception, see Christina Spittel, 'A Portable Monument?: Leonard Mann's *Flesh in Armour* and Australia's Memory of the First World War', *Book History* 14 (2011), 187–220.

70   Leonard Mann, *Flesh in Armour* (Melbourne: Robertson and Mullens, 1944), 49, 57, 102.

71   *The Telegraph* (Brisbane), 14 February 1930, 15.

72   *Midlands Advertiser* (Moora, WA), 7 March 1930, 2.

6   Censorship, control, and bad language

1   *Southern Cross* (Adelaide), 14 May 1948, 6.

2   See John F Williams, *The Quarantined Culture: Australian Reactions to Modernism 1913–1939* (Melbourne: Cambridge University Press, 1995).

3   *Sydney Morning Herald*, 14 February 1964, 3.

4   Brian Hubber, 'The Victorian Customs Department and Respectable Limits of Taste: Émile Zola and Colonial Censorship', *The French Australian Review* 9 (December 1990), 3–16.

5   Coleman, *Obscenity, Blasphemy, Sedition*, 3.

6   Bongiorno, *Sex Lives*, 82.

7   Nicole Moore, 'Secrets of the Censors: Obscenity in the Archives', paper delivered 2 May 2005, available at National Archives of Australia [online], 2.

8   Nicole Moore, *The Censor's Library* (Brisbane: University of Queensland Press, 2012), 18, 33.

9   Deana Heath, *Purifying Empire: Obscenity and the Politics of Moral Regulation in*

Britain, India and Australia (Cambridge: Cambridge University Press, 2010), 106, 120.

10 Coleman, *Obscenity, Blasphemy, Sedition*, 20.

11 Moore, *Censor's Library*, 19.

12 Moore, *Censor's Library*, 22.

13 Coleman, *Obscenity, Blasphemy, Sedition*, 26.

14 Chris Forster, *Filthy Material: Modernism and the Media of Obscenity* (New York: Oxford University Press, 2019), 93.

15 Moore, *Censor's Library*, 102.

16 *World's News* (Sydney), 17 May 1941, 24.

17 *Daily Telegraph* (Sydney), 9 May 1943, 5.

18 *Evening Advocate* (Innisfail, Queensland), 2 November 1943, 2.

19 The wordlists are unpublished but can be accessed at the Australian War Memorial archives, Gavin Long Papers, PR88/072.

20 *Mess Songs and Rhymes of the RAAF 1939–1945* (New Guinea, 1945), 47.

21 See Moore's discussion of this in *Censor's Library*, 157–75.

22 Lawson Glassop, *We Were the Rats* (Sydney: Angus and Robertson, 1944), 70–1.

23 Glassop, *We Were the Rats*, 255.

24 Moore, *Censor's Library*, 169.

25 Coleman, *Obscenity, Blasphemy, Sedition*, 58.

26 Moore, *Censor's Library*, 172, 181.

27 Moore, *Censor's Library*, 181.

28 Moore, *Censor's Library*, 186.

29 *The Mercury* (Hobart), 27 October 1948, 5.

30 *Khaki, Bush and Bigotry: Three Australian Plays* (Brisbane: University of Queensland Press, 1968), 27.

31 Sydney figures are noted in the Wikipedia entry for the play; Melbourne figures in Geoffrey Serle, *From Deserts the Prophets Come: The Creative Spirit in Australia, 1788–1972* (Melbourne: Heinemann, 1973), 197.

32 Rowse, *Indigenous and Other Australians*, 93.

33 Russell McGregor, *Indifferent Inclusion: Aboriginal People and the Australian Nation* (Canberra: Aboriginal Studies Press, 2011), 14.

34 Barker, *Two Worlds*, 21.

35 Barker, *Two Worlds*, 56.

36 Barker, *Two Worlds*, 123.

37 Janet Mathews, 'Lorna Dixon', in Isobel White, Diane Barwick and Betty Meehan (eds), *Fighters and Singers: The Lives of Some Australian Aboriginal Women* (Sydney: Allen and Unwin, 1985), 101. For more on Lorna Dixon, see Heather Goodall, 'Dixon, Lorna Rose (1917–1976), *Australian Dictionary of Biography*.

38 Arthur Malcolm in Judy Thompson (ed.), *Reaching Back: Queensland Aboriginal People Recall Early Days at Yarrabah Mission* (Canberra: Aboriginal Studies Press, 1989), 53.

39 Rowse, *Indigenous and Other Australians*, 246.

40 Suzanne Nurra, 'My Own Experiences in Education', *Ngoonjook* 7 (September 1992), 18.

41 Therese Forde, '"Confinement and Control": A History of Woorabinda Aboriginal Community 1927–1990', BA Hons Thesis, University of Queensland, 1990, 30.

42 Agnes Page, 'My Own Experiences in Education', *Ngoonjook* 7 (September 1992), 13.

43 David S Trigger, *Whitefella Comin': Aboriginal Responses to Colonialism in Northern Australia* (Cambridge: Cambridge University Press, 1992), 98. Ellipses and additions by Trigger.

44 Mathews, 'Lorna Dixon', 99.

45 *The Mirror* (Perth), 10 July 1948, 10.

46 Catherine Berndt, 'Mondalmi: One of the Saltwater People', in White, *Fighters and Singers*, 31–2.

47 Piers Kelly, 'Does Moomba Really Mean "Up Your Bum"?' *Crikey* blog, <blogs.crikey.com.au/fullysic/2011/03/14/does-moomba-really-mean-up-your-bum/>.

48 Gwenda Tavan, '"Good Neighbours": Community Organisations, Migrant Assimilation and Australian Society and Culture, 1950–1961', *Australian Historical Studies* 27, 109 (1997), 83.

49 Tavan, '"Good Neighbours"', 78.

50 Jennifer Jones, 'Voluntary Organisations and the Assimilation of Non-British Migrant Women in Rural Australia: the Efforts of the Country Women's Association of New South Wales, 1952–66', *Journal of Australian Studies* 48, 3 (2017), 392.

51 Joy Damousi, *Memory and Migration in the Shadow of War: Australia's Greek Immigrants after World War II and the Greek Civil War* (Cambridge: Cambridge University Press, 2015), 61.

52 Damousi, *Memory and Migration*, 96, 101.

53 Gillian Bottomley, *From Another Place: Migration and the Politics of Culture* (Cambridge: Cambridge University Press, 1992), 125.

54 Jayne Persian, *Beautiful Balts: From Displaced Persons to New Australians* (Sydney: NewSouth Publishing, 2017), 118–19.

55 Damousi, *Memory and Migration*, 136, 238.

56 David Carter, 'Case Study: *They're a Weird Mob* and Ure Smith', in Craig Munro and Robyn Sheahan-Bright (eds), *Paper Empires: A History of the Book in Australia, 1946–2005* (Brisbane: University of Queensland Press, 2006), 25–6.

57 Nino Culotta, *They're a Weird Mob* (Sydney: Ure Smith, 1974 [1957]), 13.

58 Culotta, *Weird Mob*, 58.

59 Culotta, *Weird Mob*, 52.

60 Culotta, *Weird Mob*, 200.

61 Culotta, *Weird Mob*, 204.

62 *Canberra Times*, 3 November 1966, 3.

63 John O'Grady, *Aussie English* (Sydney: Ure Smith, 1968 [1966]), vii.

64 *World's News* (Sydney), 13 January 1937, 6.

65 Catherine Horne Fisher, 'Let's Talk it Over: Colloquial Language and Women's Print Media Cultures in Australia, 1950–1966', *Outskirts*, 36 (2017), 7.

66 *South Eastern Times* (Millicent, SA), 9 September 1952, 3.

67 *Warwick Daily News*, 3 November 1954, 5.

68 *Truth* (Brisbane), 14 December 1952, 40.

69 *Pix* 26, 10 (10 March 1951), 23.

70 Leigh Straw, *The Worst Woman in Sydney: The Life and Crimes of Kate Leigh* (Sydney: NewSouth Publishing, 2016), 157.

71 Michael Duffy and Nick Hordern, *Sydney Noir: The Golden Years* (Sydney: NewSouth Publishing, 2017), 65.

72 Gary Simes, *A Dictionary of Australian Underworld Slang* (Melbourne: Oxford University Press, 1993), xi.
73 Drew Cottle, 'A Bowyang Historian in the Cold War Antipodes: Russel Ward and the Making of *The Australian Legend*', *Journal of Australian and Colonial History* 10, 2 (2008), 179; Sean Scalmer, 'Imagining Class: Intellectuals in the 1950s and Insights into the Present', *Overland* 146 (1997), 23.
74 WS Ramson, 'Baker, Sidney John (Sid) (1912–1976)', *Australian Dictionary of Biography* [online].
75 Baker, *Australian Language*, 251, 256.
76 Baker, *Australian Language*, 258.
77 Anne Coombs, *Sex and Anarchy: The Life and Death of the Sydney Push* (Melbourne: Viking, 1996), 8.
78 Tim Burstall, diary entry, 21 November 1954, in Hilary McPhee (ed.), *Memoirs of a Young Bastard: The Diaries of Tim Burstall* (Melbourne: Miegunyah Press, 2012), 283.
79 Editors' Foreword to 1973 edition, Sebastian Hogbotel and Simon Ffuckes, *Snatches and Lays* (Melbourne: Sun Books, 1973), 4.
80 Editors' Foreword, *Snatches and Lays*, 4.
81 Introduction to 1962 edition, *Snatches and Lays*, 5–6.
82 Coombs, *Sex and Anarchy*, 156.
83 Hogbotel and Ffuckes, *Snatches and Lays*, 31.
84 Hogbotel and Ffuckes, *Snatches and Lays*, 101.

7   Liberating bad language
1 Robin Gerster and Jan Bassett, *Seizures of Youth: 'The Sixties' and Australia* (Melbourne: Hyland House, 1991), 58.
2 Moore, *Censor's Library*, 251.
3 For a full account of Penguin Australia's efforts to challenge the censorship regime and the trials that took place, see Patrick Mullins, *The Trials of Portnoy: How Penguin Brought Down Australia's Censorship System* (Melbourne: Scribe, 2020).
4 Gerster and Bassett, *Seizures of Youth*, 43.
5 Sally Percival Wood, *Dissent: The Student Press in 1960s Australia* (Melbourne: Scribe, 2017), 8.
6 Moore, *Dancing with Empty Pockets*, 231.
7 Richard Neville, *The Hippie Hippie Shake: The Dreams, the Trips, the Trials, the Love-ins, the Screw-ups, the Sixties* (Melbourne: William Heinemann, 1995), 30.
8 *Oz* 18 (April 1965), 19, 16.
9 Moore, *Dancing with Empty Pockets*, 233.
10 *High Times* 1, 5 (December 1971).
11 See for example, *High Times* 3, 1 (January 1972), 5; *Mejane* 9 (November 1971), 8.
12 Michelle Arrow and Angela Woollacott, 'Revolutionising the Everyday: The Transformative Impact of the Sexual and Feminist Movements on Australian Society' in Arrow and Woollacott (eds), *Everyday Revolutions: Remaking Gender, Sexuality and Culture in 1970s Australia* (Canberra: ANU Press, 2019), 5.
13 *Kings Cross Whisper: The Way It Was*, 1988, n.p.
14 *Kings Cross Whisper*, 120.
15 *Tharunka*, 23 June 1970, 11.
16 Wood, *Dissent*, 83.
17 Neville, *Hippie Hippie Shake*, 295.

18   'Author's Note', Alan Seymour, *The One Day of the Year* (Sydney: Angus and Robertson, 1962), 5.
19   Seymour, *One Day of the Year*, 12.
20   Seymour, *One Day of the Year*, 81, 82.
21   Alexander Buzo, *Norm and Ahmed*; *Rooted*; *The Roy Murphy Show* (Sydney: Currency Press, 1979).
22   Gerster and Bassett, *Seizures of Youth*, 58–60.
23   Mullins, *Trials of Portnoy*, 32.
24   Gerster and Bassett, *Seizures of Youth*, 58.
25   Gerster and Bassett, *Seizures of Youth*, 58.
26   *Canberra Times*, 21 June 1969, 1.
27   *Canberra Times*, 10 October 1969, 3.
28   Buzo, *Norm and Ahmed*; *Rooted*; *The Roy Murphy Show*.
29   David Williamson, *The Removalists* (Sydney: Currency Press, 1973).
30   *Sydney Morning Herald*, 25 September 1973, 13.
31   Tony Moore, *The Barry McKenzie Movies* (Sydney: Currency Press, 2005), 2.
32   Sandra Hall, *Critical Business: the New Australian Cinema in Review* (Adelaide: Rigby, 1985), 20–1.
33   Moore, *McKenzie Movies*, 24.
34   Moore, *McKenzie Movies*, 7.
35   Moore, *McKenzie Movies*, 26.
36   John McCallum, 'Cringe and Strut: Comedy and National Identity in Post-war Australia', in Stephen Wagg (ed.), *Because I Tell a Joke or Two: Comedy, Politics and Social Difference* (London: Routledge, 1998), 218.
37   Quoted in Bongiorno, *Sex Lives*, 261.
38   Hall, *Critical Business*, 9–10.
39   James Curran and Stuart Ward, *The Unknown Nation: Australia after Empire* (Carlton: Melbourne University Press, 2010), 122.
40   Quoted in the *Australian National Dictionary* (second edition).
41   Quoted in the *Australian National Dictionary* (second edition).
42   Jim Davidson, 'Interview with David Williamson', *Meanjin* 38, 2 (July 1979), 180.
43   This line is in both the play and the movie. See David Williamson, *Don's Party* (Sydney: Currency Press, 1980), and *Don's Party* (dir. Bruce Beresford, 1976).
44   Lisa Jacobson, 'The Ocker in Australian Drama', *Meanjin* 49, 1 (Autumn 1990), 142.
45   Jacobson, 'The Ocker', 144.
46   Hughes, *Swearing*, 195.
47   Neville, *Hippie Hippie Shake*, 50.
48   Mike McColl Jones, *Graham Kennedy Treasures: Friends Remember the King* (Melbourne: Miegunyah Press, 2008), 42.
49   Jones, *Graham Kennedy Treasures*, 51.
50   Susan Bye, 'Pretending to be himself: Graham Kennedy, Television, Film, and Authenticity', *Film and History Conference Papers* 41, November 2006 [online].
51   This segment can be seen on YouTube: <www.youtube.com/watch?v=_MHKCmmi_QU>.
52   Anne Pender, *Seven Big Australians: Adventures with Comic Actors* (Melbourne: Monash University Publishing, 2019), 94.
53   *Canberra Times*, 28 June 1969, 2.
54   *Canberra Times*, 23 February 1971, 8.

55   *Sydney Morning Herald*, 19 January 1972, 14.

56   House of Representatives, 27th Parliament, 2nd Session, 22 February 1971.

57   Senate, 27th Parliament, 2nd Session, 21 September 1972.

58   *Sydney Morning Herald*, 22 September 1975, 9.

59   See Factor, *Kidspeak*.

60   Michelle Arrow, *The Seventies: The Personal, the Political, and the Making of Modern Australia* (Sydney: NewSouth Publishing, 2019), 8.

61   Coombs, *Sex and Anarchy*, 265.

62   Anne Pauwels, 'Women and Language in Australian and New Zealand Society', in Pauwels (ed.), *Women and Language in Australian and New Zealand Society* (Sydney: Australian Professional Publications, 1987), 21.

63   For a fuller discussion of the attempts to change sexist language, see Amanda Laugesen, 'Changing "Man Made Language": Sexist Language and Feminist Linguistic Activism in Australia', in Arrow and Woollacott, *Everyday Revolutions*, 241–60.

64   Nancy Keesing, *Lily on the Dustbin: Slang of Australian Women and Families* (Melbourne: Penguin, 1982), 24.

65   Quoted in Elizabeth Kleinhenz, *Germaine: The Life of Germaine Greer* (Sydney: Penguin Random House, 2018), 57.

66   Kleinhenz, *Germaine*, 110.

67   Kleinhenz, *Germaine*, 113.

68   Kleinhenz, *Germaine*, 121.

69   Neville, *Hippie Hippie Shake*, 215.

70   Kleinhenz, *Germaine*, 202.

71   *Sydney Morning Herald*, 10 March 1972, 1.

72   Kleinhenz, *Germaine*, 203.

73   *Australian Women's Weekly*, 2 February 1972, 4.

74   Arrow, *The Seventies*, 118–19.

75   Ann Vickery, 'The Rise of "Women's Poetry" in the 1970s', *Australian Feminist Studies* 22, 53 (2007), 274.

76   Kate Jennings (ed.), *Mother, I'm Rooted: An Anthology of Australian Women Poets* (Melbourne: Outback Press, 1975), iii.

77   Vickery, 'Rise of "Women's Poetry"', 273, 279.

78   Colleen Allen, unnamed poem, in Jennings (ed.) *Mother, I'm Rooted*, n.p.

79   Vickery, 'Rise of "Women's Poetry"', 271.

80   *Mejane* 2 (May 1971), 2.

81   McGregor, *Indifferent Inclusion*, 141.

82   Larissa Behrendt, 'The 1967 Referendum: 40 Years On', *Australian Indigenous Law Review* 11 (2007), 14.

83   Gary Foley, 'Teaching Whites a Lesson', in Burgmann and Lee, *Staining the Wattle*, 203.

84   Kevin Gilbert, *Living Black: Blacks Talk to Kevin Gilbert* (Melbourne: Penguin Books, 1977), 3.

85   Rowse, *Indigenous and Other Australians*, 266, 268.

86   McGregor, *Indifferent Inclusion*, 169–70.

87   Laura Rademaker, *Found in Translation: Many Meanings on a North Australian Mission* (Honolulu: University of Hawaii Press, 2018), 117.

88   Steve Mam, interviewed by Gilbert, *Living Black*, 232.

89   McGregor, *Indifferent Inclusion*, 122.
90   McGregor, *Indifferent Inclusion*, 122.
91   McGregor, *Indifferent Inclusion*, 123.
92   This date for first usage in an Australian context is suggested by Karen Austin, 'Talkin' Blak: Humour in Indigenous Australian Theatre, 1970–2000', *Philament* 20 (2015), 136.
93   Kathy Lothian, 'Moving Blackwards: Black Power and the Aboriginal Embassy', in Ingereth McFarlane and Mark Hannah (eds), *Transgressions: Critical Australian Indigenous Histories* (Canberra: ANU Press, 2007), 20.
94   Kathy Lothian, 'Seizing the Time: Australian Aborigines and the Influence of the Black Panther Party, 1969–1972', *Journal of Black Studies* 35, 4 (March 2005), 183–4.
95   Lothian, 'Seizing the Time', 189.
96   Lothian, 'Seizing the Time', 190, 192.
97   Lothian, 'Moving Blackwards', 23.
98   *Sydney Morning Herald*, 15 July 1972, 3.
99   Pearl Duncan, 'The Role of Aboriginal Humour in Cultural Survival and Resistance', PhD Thesis, University of Queensland, 2014, 79.
100 Lothian, 'Moving Blackwards', 24.
101 Bob Maza, quoted in 'Redfern Oral History: Community Stories from Redfern and Surrounds', <redfernoralhistory.com.au>.
102 Maryrose Casey, *Creating Frames: Contemporary Indigenous Theatre 1967–1990* (Brisbane: University of Queensland Press, 2004), 13.
103 Duncan, 'The Role of Aboriginal Humour', 169.
104 Austin, 'Talkin' Blak', 134–5.
105 Maryrose Casey, 'Nindethana and the National Black Theatre: Interrogating the Mythology of the New Wave', *Australasian Drama Studies* 36 (April 2000), 26.
106 Casey, *Creating Frames*, 56.
107 Casey, *Creating Frames*, 61.
108 Austin, 'Talkin' Blak', 137.
109 Alan McKee, '"Superboong! ..." The Ambivalence of Comedy and Differing Histories of Race', *Continuum: Journal of Media and Cultural Studies* 10, 2 (1996), 49.
110 Austin, 'Talkin' Blak', 139.
111 The episode is available to watch online: <vimeo.com/201243373>.
112 Casey, *Creating Frames*, xxi.
113 Casey, *Creating Frames*, 76, 84.
114 Casey, *Creating Frames*, 80.
115 Casey, *Creating Frames*, 79.
116 See Robert Reynolds and Shirleene Robinson, *Gay and Lesbian, Then and Now: Australian Stories from a Social Revolution* (Melbourne: Black Inc, 2016).
117 Graham Willett, 'The Darkest Decade: Homophobia in 1950s Australia', in John Murphy and Judith Smart (eds), *The Forgotten Fifties: Aspects of Australian Society and Culture in the 1950s* (Melbourne: Melbourne University Press, 1997), 127, 132.
118 Gerster and Bassett, *Seizures of Youth*, 66.
119 Arrow, *The Seventies*, 56.
120 Arrow, *The Seventies*, 104.
121 Reynolds and Robinson, *Gay and Lesbian, Then and Now*, 7, 63.

8 C U in the NT: Bad language in modern Australia

1 Australian Broadcasting Corporation, *Stop Laughing … This Is Serious*, Series 1, Episode 1 'Faark, Faark'.

2 *Stop Laughing*, Series 1, Episode 1. See also Rodney Rude, *The Sit Down Comedy Club* <www.standup.com.au/comedian/rodney-rude>.

3 *Stop Laughing*, Series 1, Episode 2, 'Look at Moi, Look at Moi'.

4 You can listen to some of this on YouTube. See <www.youtube.com/watch?v=TC0A9dOBQQY>.

5 *Stop Laughing*, Series 1, Episode 1. For the lyrics, see <genius.com/Tim-minchin-the-pope-song-lyrics>.

6 This scene is available on YouTube: </www.youtube.com/watch?v=iQfiDFq2PtQ>.

7 Megan B McCullough, 'The Gender of the Joke: Intimacy and Marginality in Murri Humour', *Ethnos* 79, 5 (2014), 678.

8 McCullough, 'Gender of the Joke', 680.

9 McCullough, 'Gender of the Joke', 691.

10 *Stop Laughing*, Series 1, Episode 2.

11 Tony Mitchell, 'Wogs Still Out of Work: Australian Television Comedy as Colonial Discourse', *Australasian Drama Studies* 20 (1992), 1.

12 Mitchell, 'Wogs Still Out of Work', 8.

13 *Stop Laughing*, Series 1, Episode 2.

14 Roly Sussex, 'From "Demented" to "Person with Dementia": How and Why the Language of Disability Changed', *The Conversation*, 7 December 2017 [online].

15 Joe Williams, *Defying the Enemy Within* (Sydney: ABC Books, 2018), 35, 37.

16 Amanda Montell, *Wordslut: A Feminist Guide to Taking Back the English Language* (New York: Harper Collins, 2019), 39.

17 Montell, *Wordslut*, 48.

18 Moira Weigel, 'Political Correctness: How the Right Invented a Phantom Enemy', the *Guardian*, 30 November 2016 [online]. See also Geoffrey Hughes, *Political Correctness: A History of Semantics and Culture* (Chichester: Wiley-Blackwell, 2010), 63. The *Oxford English Dictionary* records earlier examples of *political correctness*, all from the USA, but not specifically with reference to communism.

19 Edwin L Battistella, *Bad Language: Are Some Words Better than Others?* (New York: Oxford University Press, 2005), 94.

20 Moira Weigel, 'Political Correctness: How the Right Invented a Phantom Enemy', the *Guardian* 30 November 2016 [online].

21 Hughes, *Political Correctness*, 4.

22 Hughes, *Political Correctness*, 111.

23 Weigel, 'Political Correctness'.

24 Wajnryb, *Language Most Foul*, 209–10.

25 Deborah Cameron, '"Words, Words, Words": The Power of Language', in Sarah Dunant (ed.), *The War of the Words: The Political Correctness Debate* (London: Virago Press, 1994), 26.

26 Kevin Donnelly, *A Politically Correct Dictionary and Guide* (Redland Bay, Queensland: Connor Court Publishing, 2019).

27 Peta Credlin, 'Foreword', in Donnelly, *Politically Correct Dictionary*, 1.

28 Annabel Crabb, 'Australians Say "Political Correctness Has Gone Too Far" – But It's Complicated', ABC News Online, 28 November 2019.

29   Dennis Altman, *Unrequited Love: Diary of an Accidental Activist* (Melbourne: Monash University Press, 2019), 133.

30   Peter K Austin, 'Going, Going, Gone? The Ideologies and Politics of Gamilaraay-Yuwaalaraay Endangerment and Revitalization', *Proceedings of the British Academy* 199 (2014), 115.

31   Stan Grant and John Rudder, *A New Wiradjuri Dictionary* (Wagga Wagga: Restoration House, 2010).

32   Anna Ash, John Giacon and Amanda Lissarag_ue (eds), *Gamilaraay, Yuwaalaraay, and Yuwaalayaay Dictionary* (Alice Springs: IAD Press, 2003).

33   Donald Thomson (1935) quoted in Langton, 'Medicine Square', 206.

34   See JM Arthur, *Aboriginal English* (Melbourne: Oxford University Press, 1996).

35   Victorian Aboriginal Community Controlled Health Organisation, *Koorified: Aboriginal Communication and Well-being* (Melbourne, 2014), 19.

36   Jean-Marc Dewaele, '"Christ Fucking Shit Merde!" Language Preferences for Swearing among Maximally Proficient Multilinguals', *Sociolinguistic Studies* 4, 3 (2010), 599–600. See also Dewaele 'The Emotional Force of Swearwords and Taboo Words in the Speech of Multilinguals', *Journal of Multilingual and Multicultural Development* 25, 2–3 (2004), 209, 213–14.

37   Factor, *Kidspeak*.

38   Fouad Abi-Esber, Ping Yang, Hiromi Muranaka and Mohamed Moustakim, 'Linguistic Taboos: A Case Study of Australian Lebanese Speakers', *Asian Culture and History* 10, 1 (2018), 90.

39   Paul Tabar, '"Habiibs" in Australia: Language, Identity, and Masculinity', *Journal of Intercultural Studies* 28, 2 (2007), 167.

40   There are a number of websites and blogs that list Chinese swear words. See for example the Chinese Language blog, <blogs.transparent.com/chinese/swear-words-in-chinese/>. Thanks to Zhengdao Ye at the ANU for discussing these with me.

41   Timothy Bella, 'The "7 Dirty Words" Turn 40, But They're Still Dirty', the *Atlantic*, 24 May 2012 [online].

42   Liam Bartlett, 'Much Ado about that (Bleep) Word', *Sunday Times* (Perth), 24 August 2003 [online].

43   Roy Eccleston, 'Warning: Contains Coarse Language', the *Australian*, 7 June 2008 [online].

44   Chris Middendorp, 'We Do Solemnly *!?&@!', the *Age*, 7 February 2009 [online].

45   Matthew Doran, 'Sketch on Tom Ballard Show *Tonightly* Cops Criticism, Cory Bernardi Says "Someone Needs to Lose their Job"', ABC Online, 22 March 2018 [online].

46   Doran, 'Sketch'.

47   Gabriele Azzaro, 'Taboo Language in Books, Film, and the Media,' in Allan (ed.), *Oxford Handbook of Taboo Words*, 303.

48   Bergen, *What the F*, 13.

49   David Knox, 'Actually Yes You Can Say the C-Word on TV', *TV Tonight*, 11 February 2019 [online].

50   James Weir, 'MAFS 2019 Episode 9 Recap', News.com.au, 11 February 2019.

51   'Married at First Sight's Ines and Bronson Spiral into Brutal Fight', News.com.au, 11 February 2019 [online].

52   Comment by robertrhenry, 'Actually Yes You Can Say the C-word on TV'.

53   Comment by joely, 'Actually Yes You Can Cay the C-word on TV'.

54   Screenshot of tweet, James Hennessy, 'You All Had a Series of Fascinating Thoughts about the Phrase "Dog C*nt" After Tonight's "Bachie"', *Pedestrian Daily*, 14 August 2019 [online].

55   Screenshot of tweet, Hennessy, 'You All Had a Series'.

56   Screenshot of tweet, Hennessy, 'You All Had a Series'.

57   Australian Association of National Advertisers, Code of Ethics Practice Note, November 2018 Section 2.5, 7.

58   Elle Hunt, 'Advertising Standards Ruling Threatens "Great Tradition of Aussie Larrikin"', Guardian.com, 29 December 2016 [online].

59   Bella, '"7 Dirty Words" Turn 40'.

60   Dan Brooks, 'The Rise of the Swear Nerds', the *Outline*, 29 January 2019 [online].

61   Brooks, 'Rise of the Swear Nerds'.

62   Brooks, 'Rise of the Swear Nerds'.

63   Nancy Friedman, 'Mainstream AF', *Strong Language* (blog), 8 July 2019.

64   Philip Seargeant, 'The Whimsical World of Emoji Swearing', *Strong Language*, 14 March 2017.

65   @Asher_Wolf, Twitter, 10 December 2019.

66   @cycleunionkp, Twitter, 11 December 2019.

67   Ginger Gorman, *Troll Hunting* (Melbourne: Hardie Grant, 2019), 66.

68   Gorman, *Troll Hunting*, 66.

69   Emma A Jane, *Misogyny Online: A Short (and Brutish) History* (London: SAGE, 2017), 16.

70   Kon Karapanagiotidis, *The Power of Hope* (Sydney: HarperCollins, 2018), 145.

71   Quoted in Gorman, *Troll Hunting*, 69.

72   Quoted in Gorman, *Troll Hunting*, 207.

73   Jane, *Misogyny Online*, 63.

74   Ellie Rennie, Tyson Yunkaparta and Indigo Holcombe-Jones, 'Privacy versus Relatedness: Managing Device Use in Australia's Remote Aboriginal Communities', *International Journal of Communication* 12 (2018), 1298.

75   Rennie, 'Privacy versus Relatedness', 1302, 1304.

76   Petronella Vaarzon-Morel, 'Pointing the Phone: Transforming Technologies and Social Relations among Warlpiri', *Australian Journal of Anthropology*, 25 (2014), 249.

77   Vaarzon-Morel, 'Pointing the Phone', 250, 252.

78   Elyse Methven, 'How Pop Culture Can (and Should) Change Legal Views on Swearing', *The Conversation*, 12 April 2017 [online].

79   Suzi Hutchings and Dianne Rodger, 'Reclaiming Australia: Indigenous Hip-Hop group A.B. Original's Use of Twitter', *Media International Australia* 169, 1 (2018), 88.

80   Lyrics available online: <genius.com/Ab-original-call-em-out-lyrics>.

81   Quoted in Andrew Warren and Rob Evitt, 'Indigenous Hip-hop: Overcoming Marginality, Encountering Constraints', *Australian Geographer* 41, 1 (2010), 153.

82   'Taboo or Not Taboo', *Sydney Morning Herald*, 3 June 2003 [online].

83   Patricia Cornelius, *Shit* (Sydney: Currency Press, 2017), 113.

84   Cornelius, *Shit*, 113.

85   Cornelius, *Shit*, 115.

86   Cornelius, *Shit*, 117, 118

87   Kylie Northover, 'Theatre, mostly, is very bourgeois: Lunch with Patricia
      Cornelius', *Sydney Morning Herald*, 20 September 2019 [online].
88   Reddit, 'Ask an Australian: what's up with Australians and
      swearing?' <www.reddit.com/r/AskAnAustralian/comments/8vpuhy/
      whats_up_with_australians_and_swearing/>.
89   James Hancock and Staff, 'Victorian CFMEU Boss John Setka Gets Good
      Behaviour Bond for Harassment', ABC News Online, 28 June 2019.
90   Dana McCauley, '"I am Not a Bully": Controversial Union Boss John Setka
      Denies Threatening Senators, Refuses to Step Down', *Sydney Morning Herald*,
      18 September 2019 [online].
91   Hancock, 'Victorian CFMEU boss'.
92   RN Breakfast, 'Union Construction Boss John Setka's Comments Being
      Examined by AFP, Senator Rex Patrick Says', ABC News Online, 18 September
      2019.
93   Interview on Radio National, ABC, John Setka interviewed by Hamish
      Macdonald,
      18 September 2019.
94   Interview, 18 September 2019.
95   McCauley, '"I am Not a Bully"'.
96   Jane Caro, 'Swear in Front of Me, But Don't Call Me "Darl": A Lesson in
      Respect', *Sydney Morning Herald*, 12 July 2017 [online].
97   Gabrielle Carey and Kathy Lette, *Puberty Blues* (Melbourne: Vintage Books,
      1979).
98   Sami Lukis, *Romantically Challenged* (Melbourne: Penguin, 2018).
99   Montell, *Wordslut*, 207.
100   Methven, 'Dirty Talk', 73–4.
101   Methven, 'Dirty Talk', 78.
102   Methven, 'Dirty Talk', 90.
103   Methven, 'Dirty Talk', 91–5.
104   Methven, 'How pop culture can'.
105   Methven, 'Dirty Talk', 9.

INDEX

This index includes a word index. All words and expressions mentioned in the text are included here in italic font.